Living Islam
TREADING THE PATH OF THE IDEAL

Presented to ....

....

From ....

Date ....

Also by Ruqaiyyah Waris Maqsood

Living Islam : Treading the Prophet of Ideal

The Beautiful Commands of Allah

The Muslim Prayer Encyclopaedia

The Beautiful Promises of Allah

The Muslim Marriage Guide

A Basic Dictionary of Islam

Muslim Travel Guide

After Death, Life!

Living Islam
TREADING THE PATH OF THE IDEAL

RUQAIYYAH WARIS MAQSOOD

Goodword
B·O·O·K·S

First published 1998
© Goodword Books 2006
Reprinted 2000, 2006

Goodword Books Pvt. Ltd.
1, Nizamuddin West Market
New Delhi 110 013
e-mail: info@goodwordbooks.com
Printed in India

www.goodwordbooks.com

Contents

Introduction

Muslims are people who have committed themselves to submission to God's will as expressed in the Holy Qur'an, the revelations given to the Blessed Prophet Muhammad, and by studying his way of life. They are people who are aware of the reality of the existence of God, and this awareness (or ihsan) leads to a deepened consciousness of the importance and meaningfulness of the gift of human life and the responsibilities that go with it.

In this book, Ruqaiyyah Waris Maqsood examines the social view of Islam, taking each important issue and aspect of Islamic life and conduct, and giving a comprehensive outline of the aims and duties of every Muslim in respect of that particular topic. Each chapter gives reference to the relevant verses in the Qur'an and hadith that deal with that topic. The subjects include human rights, the sanctity of life, women's rights, the duties of the Muslim in the workplace, the family, sexual relationships, alcohol, drugs, crime and punishment, 'green' issues, and the true meaning of Jihad.

Belief is the key to the Muslim way of life. That moment when true belief dawns in a Muslim's consciousness and takes hold of the Muslim heart is only the beginning of a long spiritual journey. The effort to live in accordance with God's will is known as the Greater Jihad. There are two aspects to it—firstly, a person's developing religious devotion and the ritual practice of the five pillars of the faith of Islam, and secondly, the practical everyday manner in which one strives to put the principles of faith into practice. Belief in God makes a person aim high, and try to live in the best possible way with the best possible character.

The road of life is known in Islam as the Shari'ah. One must search for it and follow it, through all life's tests and temptations, difficulties and tragedies, consciously considering in every situation what the will of God would be for any individual at any given moment.

The aim of the book is to show how Muslims strive to bring God-consciousness (*taqwa*) into every area of their daily lives, from the important and profound to the mundane and simple tasks; and in this devotion and urge to serve, striving for the greater pleasure of their Lord, they find their own fulfilment and happiness.

The Social View of Islam

THE AWARENESS

'Who is it that sustains you? Or Who is it that has power over everything you see and hear? And Who is it that brings the living from the dead, and the dead from the living? Who is it whose Law governs all the universe of matter?' They will soon say: 'God!' Will you not then show piety towards Him?' (10:31)

When considering any social issue from the Islamic point of view, the starting point must always come from the definition of Islam, and what a Muslim is. 'Muslim' does not mean people from around the world who happen to have been born to a Muslim family. Some members of Muslim families are decidedly un-Islamic. It does not mean being an Arab (or an Asian, or Iranian, or any other nationality). For those in the West, it needs to be made clear that it certainly does not mean 'someone with brown skin'!

Being a Muslim is a matter of deep personal conviction. Becoming Muslim is not something that any person can do at 'second hand.' It has to be experienced in each individual heart, because it is a total commitment of submission of one's life to the belief that there is no God but One, and the Blessed Muhammad was His genuine Messenger.

Muslims are people who have become genuinely aware at some point in their lives of the reality of the existence of

God, and have committed themselves to submission to God's will as it was expressed in the particular revelations given to the Arabian Prophet Muhammad ﷺ, those revelations now collected into a book known as the Holy Qur'an, or Umm al-Kitab (Mother of Books). These were not the first messages sent to humanity from the One, for He sent messengers to every generation before the historical life of the Prophet Muhammad ﷺ. There were other holy writings, in particular those of the Jews and Christians, whose faith is in the same One True God. However, these texts were not preserved so accurately or carefully, and the direct revelation of the Qur'an over 23 years was intended to bring those who had deviated from the True Faith back to its Straight Path.

> 'It is He who sent down to you in truth the Book, confirming what went before it; and He sent down the Law and the Gospel before this as a guide to humanity; and He sent down a Criterion (of judgement between right and wrong).' (3:3)

The awareness of the Reality of God (known as *ihsan* or 'realisation') leads to a deepened consciousness of the importance and meaningfulness of the gift of human life, and the responsibility that goes with it. Like a dry and curled up desert plant suddenly being given the drop of moisture that will make it spread out its leaves and sink its roots, and flourish—the human being suddenly becomes aware of the great thirst, the great dependence, and the great joy in being at one with the Creator.

> 'It is a guide and a healing to those who believe; and for those who do not believe, there is deafness in their ears and blindness in their eyes.' (41:44)

To call God 'He' has become traditional—but this is for the convenience of the restrictions of our language. God only describes Himself using the male gender, but God does not have human sexuality and cannot be compared with the human race. Muslims therefore prefer to use the name Allah (meaning 'the Almighty') in place of the word 'god' which can be made plural or female.

EXPERIENCE OF GOD

Once this realisation that God is Real has dawned in a person, life is never the same again. It cannot be. It is like the experience of being in love. Once you have known this powerful awakening, you cannot put the clock back and un-know it. Life is seen from a totally different perspective. Before realisation, life is just life, the daily grind, the gradual progress from birth to death. After realisation, every aspect of life is seen as having a spiritual dimension; there is a reason, an aim and a goal to it all, a sense of justice and fulfilment, and a sense of relationship with a Good Power that is not only Supreme and above all, but also cares very much for humanity and is deeply involved with every action and thought of our lives.

> 'It is God who gives life and death, and God sees well all that you do.' (3:156)
>
> 'Truly, my Lord casts the (mantle of) Truth (over His servants), He that has full knowledge of (all) that is hidden... If I am astray, I only stray to the loss of my own soul: but if I receive guidance, it is because of the inspiration of my Lord to me; it is He Who hears all things, and is ever near.' (34:48, 50)

The Muslim word for this God-consciousness is taqwa. People who have no awareness of God cannot understand the joy, the devotion, the urge to serve, that goes along with it. The concept of slavery through love is meaningless to them. It cannot be adequately explained in human words to someone who has no awareness of it, any more than an adult can explain what sexual ecstasy is like to a child who has no knowledge of it.

Belief is the key to the way of life. There are two aspects of this belief—firstly, a person's developing religious devotion and practice of the five pillars of Islam, and secondly, the everyday manner in which one strives to please God by putting the principles of faith into practice. Belief in God makes a person aim high, and try to live in the best possible way with the best possible character. This personal effort is what is known as the Greater Jihad.

Just belief in God on its own is not enough—a person's life must show evidence of transformation because of that belief. Many people might pray and bow down and fast and go without personal pleasures because they claim to believe in God, but still remain selfish and cruel in their lives. They believe, but their Islam is only skin-deep. They fast and pray, but if their hearts are not changed all they gain from this is hunger and sleeplessness, coupled with a self-deceiving pride.

Belief in God on its own does not make a person Muslim. No one had greater belief in God than Shaytan— but he used his free will to oppose God's will and not to submit. Maybe he even thought he 'knew better' than God. Some religious people can and do remain totally untouched by Islam. Allah never forces them—He leaves it to them to start the change in themselves.

> 'Truly, Allah does not change the condition of a people until they change what is in themselves.' (13:11)

One of 'Aishah's hadiths put the matter into a perspective the 'ritual prayer' might find disturbing. She recorded: I heard the Blessed Prophet of Allah say: 'By his *good character* a believer can attain the degree of one who prays during the night, and fasts during the day.' (Abu Dawud, 4780)

However, simply being a good person and living in a pleasant and kindly manner is not sufficient either.

Abu Hurayrah reported the Blessed Muhammad as pointing out that 'there is no person whose deeds alone can secure salvation for him (or her). They said: 'Allah's Messenger, not even you?' Whereupon he said: 'Not even I, but that the mercy of Allah takes hold of me.' (Muslim, 6763)

There is no such thing as the perfect human person. We are all limited, and have numerous shortcomings. We are sometimes blind as to our faults and sins, and sometimes we give in to selfishness and temptation and quite deliberately do things that we know are wrong. All of us, as we have journeyed from childhood into adult life, have committed so many sins, or omitted doing so many things we ought to have done, that it can seem an almost hopeless situation and far too late to claim that we now wish to be believers in God. How can we possibly put right all the things we have done wrong?

Thanks be to God for His great mercy. When a person finds belief and takes the decision to become Muslim, one of the greatest benefits and mercies of Allah is the knowledge that all the wrongdoings of the past, the sins, misdeeds or omissions, are completely wiped out, and one can put down the heavy burden of guilt and regret and make a completely fresh start.

Ibn Shamasa Mahri recorded that the Blessed Muhammad said: 'Are you not aware of the fact that Islam wipes out all previous misdeeds?' (Muslim 220)

The mercy of Allah deals with believers in the most gentle and gracious of ways. Allah, our dear Lord, is the Compassionate One, the Most Merciful, and everything is known to Him. Nothing escapes Him—no action, no thought, no motive, no background circumstance, no genetic or programmed factor. Whenever a person does something wrong it is certainly recorded in detail — the Holy Qur'an mentions the two guardian angels for each human, who take note of everything.

'Behold, two (guardian angels) appointed to learn (his doings), learn and note them, one sitting on the right and one on the left; not a word does he utter but there is a sentinel by him ready (to note it).' (50:17-18)

However, thanks to God's grace and mercy, the record of a person's sins and failings only lasts until that person repents. The moment a person is truly sorry, then the record is wiped clean again. On the other hand, if a person does good, or even if they only intend to do good without actually doing it, it always counts to their credit. This is expressed many times in the hadith—those sayings and teachings of the Blessed Prophet Muhammad.

Abu Hurayrah recorded: 'The one who intended to do good, but did not do it, has one good recorded for him; for the one who intended to do good and actually did it, ten to seven hundred good deeds are recorded for him. And he who intended to do evil but did not do it, no entry was made against his name; only if he did it, was it recorded.' (Muslim 236)

'Whenever My bondsman intends to commit an evil, do not record it against him; but if he actually commits it then write it as one evil. And when he intends to do good but does not do it, take it as one act of goodness; but if he does it, then write ten good deeds.' (Muslim 233)

THE JOURNEY

The moment of belief may be one climax in a person's life, but it is only the beginning of a long journey. The

Muslim suddenly sees that everything in life, every ambition, every object, every possession, is not quite what it had seemed before. There is no human, and no part of the planet on which they live, which is permanent. Every part of it is a gift, a contingent matter—something which might not ever have existed, but which only does because God wills it so; and likewise, when its time comes, every part of it will cease to be because God wills it so. The real meaningful life is not this one in which we are at present involved, but that which is to come, the Hereafter—for which our human life here is but a training and a test.

> 'The life of the world is but a past-time and a game. Lo! Real life is the Home of the Hereafter, if you but knew it.' (29:64)

Once this belief sinks deep into the soul, there is no longer any meaning to fear, or ambition, or ownership, or pride. The human role in the universe is not to own or to have, but simply to be—and to be a traveller at that.

Abdullah ibn Umar reported: The Messenger of Allah took me by the shoulder and said: 'Be in the world like a stranger or like a traveller on the road.' (Bukhari)

HUMANS, THE KHALIFAHS

> 'It is He who has created for you all the things that are on earth; His design formed the heavens, and He gave order and perfection to the completeness of space; of everything that exists He has perfect knowledge. Behold, He said to the angels 'I will create a vicegerent on earth.' They said: 'Will You place there one who will make trouble, and shed blood?'... He said: 'I know things that you do not.' And He taught Adam the nature of all things.' (2:29-31)

Muslims believe that angels are a different kind of being from humans. Angels are holy and pure and granted power by Allah, but they are apparently without passion or emotion. They do not love, or hate. When humans were created, these already existing life-forms were quick to realise that if humans were to be given emotions, the power of freewill would also go along with them, leading to the possibility of humans reaching the greatest of heights, or the most desperate of depths.

This gift of human freewill in a way brings humanity closer to Allah than the angels, in the sense that they have to some extent a mastery over their own fortunes, and over nature, and so are 'like' Allah who has supreme mastery and will. For the Muslim, the perfect vicegerent is the one who has the power of initiative, but whose independent action always perfectly reflects the will of Allah.

THE TRUE AMBITION OF A MUSLIM

There is only one aim or ambition which continues to make any sense—and that is to accept, or submit (the meaning of the word 'Muslim'); to live out of the will of God so far as is humanly possible, in whatever circumstances you pass along your way of life. The road of life is known in Islam as *Shari'ah*—the way. One must search for it, and follow it, through all life's tests and temptations, difficulties and tragedies, consciously considering in every situation what the will of God would be for any individual at any given moment.

> 'Show us the Straight Way, and the way of those on whom You have bestowed Your grace, whose (portion) is not wrath, and who do not go astray.' (1:6-7)

That is why Islam is not just a matter of ritual—prayers or fasting or feasts; it is the conscious bringing of every moment of the day, every decision, every detail of one's thoughts and actions, into deliberate line with what one accepts as being the will of Allah.

THE REVELATION

How is this will to be known? The Muslim bases all decisions on the revealed words of the Holy Qur'an, the messages that were delivered over a period of some 23 years to the inspired Prophet Muhammad—may peace be upon him. Not one word in the Qur'an is believed by Muslims to be thought or teaching created by Muhammad ﷺ himself— although he is revered above all humanity as one of the most perfect of God's messengers. Other messengers were Abraham ﷺ, Moses ﷺ, Jesus ﷺ, and in fact at least 24,000 prophets.

Many Christians are surprised to discover that Muslims concede and respect the greatness of Jesus ﷺ; they accept his virgin-birth (without drawing the inference that this made him in any way a 'divine' person), and honour him as a great teacher and miracle-worker; Muhammad's ﷺ ministry was not based on any miracles other than the receiving of the Qur'an—but that in itself is regarded as the greatest of miracles. Muhammad ﷺ is so important to Muslims because he was the *last* prophet, the seal of all that was revealed to the prophets before him.

'Muhammad is... the Messenger of God and the Seal of the prophets.' (33:40)

He is the completion of all the revelation of God that came to humanity before him, the 'missing brick in the wall'.

Abu Hurayrah reported that the Blessed Prophet said: 'The parable of myself and the messengers before me is like that of a person who constructed a building, and built it fine and well, and made it complete except for one brick in one of its corners. People began to walk round it, and the building pleased them, and they said: 'But for this one brick, your building would have been perfect.' Muhammad said: 'I am that final brick.' (Muslim 5674)

Muslims believe that if the pure teachings of the earlier prophets had not been altered and changed by those who later wrote about them, it would be easily seen that the revealed message was the same!

> 'To those who believe in God and His apostles, and make no distinction between any of the messengers, We shall soon give their due rewards. (4:152)

FREEWILL AND WORTH

Islam teaches that every human being is no more nor less than a creation of Allah, and all are born equal. Sadly, the worth of individuals as they grow into adults becomes spoiled by the extent to which they fall away from the standards set for humanity by the Creator. Natural reason enables any person whose mind is not damaged to 'see' the evidence for the existence of Allah, but no person is forced to accept it or act upon it. It is purely a matter of choice.

This does not mean that Allah loves the deliberate wrongdoer any less. Many human parents know only too well just how much one can love a child that is making terrible mistakes in life; they never cease to love them, but they can see that they are building up for themselves a pattern of inevitable consequences. However, Muslims believe that the universe is based on justice, and the hope that God's justice is always tempered with mercy.

'A'ishah recorded: 'When a person acknowledges sin and repents, Allah forgives him.' (Bukhari, Muslim)

Ibn Abbas recorded: 'If anyone continually asks pardon, Allah will appoint a way out of every distress and a relief from every anxiety, and will provide for him in a way he did not expect.' (Ahmad, Abu Dawud and Ibn Majah)

Allah's mercy is far beyond what any humans have the right to expect, or indeed, what they would show to each other!

> 'O My servants, who have transgressed against their souls! Do not despair of the mercy of God; for Allah forgives all sins; He is Oft-Forgiving, Most Merciful.' (39:53)

> 'It is part of the mercy of Allah that you should deal gently with those (who have offended you, or who have sinned). If you were severe with them, or harsh-hearted, they would have broken away from about you. So pass over (their faults), and ask for forgiveness for them.' (3:159)

> 'Not for you (but for God) is the decision whether He turn in mercy to them or punish them, for they are indeed wrongdoers. To God belongs everything that is in the heavens and on earth, and He forgives whom He pleases and punishes whom He pleases; but God is Oft-Forgivng and Most Merciful.' (3:128-129)

There are many, many passages that show Allah's kindness and mercy. The same teaching is clearly represented in the hadith.

Abu Sa'id reported that: 'Truly, the devil said: By my honour, O Lord, I shall never stop misguiding Your servants so long as life remains in their bodies. The Almighty, the Glorious Lord said: By My honour, I shall never cease forgiving them so long they ask forgiveness of Me.' (Ahmad)

Abu Dharr recorded: 'He who does a good deed will receive ten times that amount of blessing... but he who does an evil deed will receive just the equivalent amount of evil. Or, 'I shall grant him forgiveness. If anyone draws the length of a hand's span near to Me, I shall draw the length of a cubit near to him... If anyone comes to Me walking, I shall come to him at the run; and if anyone meets Me with sins the size of earth, but has not associated anything with Me, I shall forgive him.' (Muslim)

What wonderful mercy of God! How gracious, and how undeserved.

Anas ibn Malik recorded: 'O son of Adam—so long as you call upon Me and ask of Me, I shall forgive you for what you have done, and I shall not mind. O son of Adam, were your sins to reach the clouds of the sky and were you then to ask forgiveness of Me, I would forgive you. O son of Adam, were you to come to Me with sins nearly as great as the earth itself, and were you then to face Me ascribing no partner to Me, I would bring you forgiveness in equal measure.' (Tirmidhi, Ahmad)

However, it has to be said that just as some humans refuse to stop their crazy path to their own doom despite the desperate love of those who love them—in the same way the future state of existence for some people will be extinction, because of their absolute refusal to accept the love and mercy of God, or to live in a way acceptable to Him.

THE TRIALS

Everybody faces suffering, fears and disappointments. No-one should expect to get through the years of their earthly life without tests and trials, for these will come to all people. They do not mean that God has abandoned you, or forgotten you. It does not (necessarily) mean He is angry with you, or is punishing you. The most saintly people sometimes have to endure the most appalling sufferings. They are part and parcel of our existence.

> 'We shall most certainly try you with fear and hunger and with the loss of goods or lives or the fruits of your toil. But give encouragement to those who patiently persevere, and, when calamity befalls them, say: 'Behold, to Allah we

belong, and to Him do we return.' (2:155-156)

'Or do you think that you shall enter the garden without such trials as came to those who passed away before you? (2:214)

It is Allah who grants the conditions of your birth, whether you are born wealthy or poor, intelligent or stupid, beautiful or ugly, and so on. It has nothing to do with the will of the parent.

Muslims have a duty to consider their circumstances, and make the best they can of every situation and talent.

It is pointless to complain to Allah about one's lot—the Muslim who has faith knows that all situations can be reversed in the twinkling of an eye, and disaster or good fortune can come upon people whenever Allah wills it.

'Nobody knows what they will earn tomorrow, nor does anyone know is what land they are to die. Only Allah has full knowledge, and is acquainted with all things.' (31:34)

The *Shari'ah*

'The basis of Shari'ah is wisdom, and the welfare of people in this world as well as the Hereafter. This welfare lies in the pursuance of justice, mercy, care and wisdom. Anything that departs from justice to oppression, from mercy to harshness, from caring to misery, and from wisdom to folly, has nothing to do with the Shari'ah.' (Saying of the Muslim scholar Ibn Qayyim)

Every aspect of true Muslim life is governed by submission to Allah, and this means not only carrying out religious practices and devotions such as the five daily prayers, the month-long fast of Ramadan, and the giving of regular

charity, but also considering the will of Allah in all the business of daily living, whether at home, at work or at school.

It applies as much to affairs of state as to the humble routine of the bathroom, and affects all matters relating to everyday exchanges and routines-what one might call 'manners'. The Qur'an is not just to be read or listened to, but to be lived:

Abu Wayl recorded: 'Truly there are people who recite Qur'an, but it does not go down below their collar bones. It is of benefit only when it settles in the heart and is rooted deeply in it.' (Muslim 1791)

Abu Hurayrah recorded: The most perfect believer in respect of faith is he (or she) who is best of them in manners.' (Abu Dawud 4665)

The Blessed Prophet ﷺ was a perfect example in his own lifetime, and did all he could to encourage high moral living in others:

Masruq reported of the Prophet ﷺ that 'he was never immoderate in his talk and he never reviled others.' He also said: 'The best amongst you are those who are best in morals.' (Muslim 5740)

Islam is a complete way of life because it permeates every waking moment. It gives a criterion for judging all behaviour and conduct, determines relationships with other individuals, with society as a whole, and with one's own self.

Reverence and morality is seen as the basis of self-confidence and strength, the fundamental ideals of which are the all-consuming love of Allah, and the absolute unshakable conviction that one is loved by Allah in return.

'My God and my Lord,
Eyes are at rest, stars are setting,

Hushed are the movements of birds in their nests,
Of monsters in the deep...
The doors are locked, watched by their bodyguards.
But Thy door is open to him who calls on Thee.
My Lord, each lover is now alone with his beloved.
Thou for me art the Beloved One.'
                (a poem by the Sufi mystic Rabi'a al-'Adawiyya)

When a person loves Allah, and feels loved in return, that person does not want to leave in his or her character any trait of personality that would cause the Beloved to be sad, or ashamed, or disappointed. This is not to suggest that Allah the Almighty has feelings in any way like those of a human being—but the believer who loves Allah understands what qualities they themselves admire and cherish in other human beings, and they desire Allah to see them in the best possible way.

The ideals to be aimed at are those that will form the perfect Muslim character—humility, modesty, naturalness and unselfishness. Pride and arrogance are neither attractive qualities nor acceptable ones for the Muslim, for Islam teaches that no individual is superior to another except in the amount of faith and performance of good deeds. The essentials are kindness, modesty, gentleness, courage, steadfastness, consideration for others, and the general desire for the promotion of the happiness and welfare of society.

These are the very qualities it is natural for a human being to love and respect in others, and it is these qualities in us that make others love, admire and trust us.

Umar heard the Messenger of Allah say: 'He who is humble for the sake of Allah will be exalted by Allah, for though he considers himself lowly he is great in the eyes of men; but he who is proud will be abased by Allah, for though he considers himself great he is lowly in the eyes of men to

such an extent that he is of less value than a pig or a sheep.'
(Bayhaqi)

Ibn Umar also reported: 'A Muslim is a Muslim's
brother; he does not wrong him or abandon him. If anyone
cares for his brother's anxiety, Allah will remove from him
one of the anxieties on the Day of Resurrection.' (Bukhari
and Muslim)

'A'ishah was once asked about the moral greatness of
Muhammad ﷺ, and she said: 'His morals are the Qur'an.'

He was sweet and kind and always used polite language.
He was most indulgent to his servants and companions, and
would never let his young servants be scolded.

Anas b. Malik, the son of Umm Sulaym who lived in
the Prophet's household, reported: 'Ten years was I about the
Prophet, and he never said as much as 'uff!' to me. He was
very affectionate towards his family... He was very fond of
children. He would stop them in the streets and pat their little
heads... When asked to curse someone, he replied: 'I have
not been sent to curse, but to be a mercy to all mankind.'
(Muslim 5773; 5350 n. 2535)

AWARENESS

Shari'ah, which means 'the straight path', is the code
of behaviour for the Islamic way of life, the law that
determines the rightness (halal) or wrongness (haram) of any
particular action.

The moment people become aware of Allah, it alters
their entire motivation for doing things, makes them do
certain things they would not otherwise have dreamt of
attempting, and stops them from doing many things that
would have given a great deal of selfish pleasure. It even alters
the way they think—because they know that Allah is close

to them, and is aware of everything, even their innermost secret thoughts.

> 'We created Man, and We know what his soul whispers to him. We are nearer to him than the vein in his neck.' (50:16)

Abu Hurayrah recorded: 'Allah does not look upon your bodies and faces; He looks upon your hearts and your deeds.' (Muslim)

THE PRINCIPLES BEHIND *SHARI'AH*

The first principle accepted by any Muslim is that Allah really does exist, and so does *Akhirah* or life after death, with all that implies. The choice to believe in God or not believe is the first and fundamental choice for every rational human being—there is no other alternative. There is no third possibility. It is really that simple—either there *is* a God or there is not. However, Allah's existence cannot be proved like a fact of science—it always remains a matter of faith and commitment. The choice has to be made—but once it is made and the rational mind has become aware that it accepts the existence of God, all the rest follows on.

> 'He is with your wheresoever you may be, and He sees clearly all that you do.' (57:4)

The second principle is that Muslims believe that there *will* definitely come a time of judgment, and that Allah is aware of everything you have ever done or thought, and all the motives for your actions. He alone is the Judge. Other people may have opinions, and may act in certain judge-mental ways, but it is Allah alone who knows the full picture and who can judge with equity.

> 'They say: What! When we are reduced to bones and dust, shall we really be raised up, a new creation?' (17:49)

'Man says: What! When I am dead, shall I be raised up alive? But does not Man call to mind that We created him before, out of nothing?' (19:66-67)

'Allah is never unjust in the least degree; if there is any good done, He doubles it, and gives from His own presence a great reward.' (4:40)

The third principle is that the world is full of hardships and evils that should be tackled and not just ignored. There is a constant battle with 'evil' in all its shapes and forms, and the sin of omitting to do something that should have been done is just as great as the sin of doing something wrong. All of life is a test, a school of faith, a preparation leading up to the real life which is to come.

'But he (Satan) has no power over them—except that We might test the person who believes in the Hereafter from the one who is in doubt concerning it.' (34:71)

'Or do you think that you will enter the Garden without such trials as came to those who passed away before you? They encountered suffering and adversity, and were so shaken in spirit that even the Messenger and those of faith who were with him cried: When will come the help of God?' (7:714)

Abdallah b. Umar recorded: 'Every one of you is a shepherd, and will be questioned about the well-being of his flock. A man is a shepherd over the members of his family, and shall be questioned about them; a woman is a shepherdess over the household of her husband and his children, and shall be questioned about them. A slave is a shepherd over the property of his master, and shall be questioned about it. Beware, every one of you is a guardian and shall be questioned with regard to his trust.' (Muslim 4496, Abu Dawud 7977)

The fourth principle is that all humans belong to the family of Allah, and are equal—whatever sex, colour, class or country they happen to be born in. Their worth comes from the quality of their lives, and not from any aspect such as mental ability, wealth, particular talent, and so forth—all of which were given to them at birth and over which they had no choice or control.

'All people are equal, as the teeth of a comb. There is no claim of merit of an Arab over a non-Arab, or a white over a black person, or of a male over a female. All God-fearing people merit a preference with God.' (Al-Bukhari)

'O Humanity! Lo! I am the messenger of God to you all.' (7:158)

Sahl b.Sa'd recorded: 'The Book of Allah is one, and among you are the red, and among you are the white, and among you are the black.' (Abu Dawud 830)

Abu Musa al-Ashari recorded: 'Allah created Adam from a handful of dust which He took from the whole of the earth: some red, some white, some black, some a mixture, also smooth and rough, bad and good.' (Abu Dawud 4676)

In his final sermon, the Blessed Messenger ﷺ said:

'No Arab is superior to a non-Arab, nor a non-Arab superior to an Arab, except by having a greater degree of God-consciousness.'

Another saying of the Prophet ﷺ was:

'O people! All of us belong to One God, one father and one religion. Arabic is only a language, and he who speaks Arabic is an Arab.'

To follow the Shari'ah means living a morally responsible life. If you recognise all people as one family, are aware of their rights, grieve when they get hurt, are determined to bring about their good and not their harm, then you have already started living according to the Shari'ah.

Abu Hurayrah recorded: 'Those who relieve the suffering of others from the sufferings of the world, Allah will alleviate their sufferings on the Day of Resurrection.' (Muslim 6518)

Abu Hayyan recorded: 'The Book of Allah contains right guidance, the light, and whoever adheres to it and holds it fast, is upon right guidance; and whoever deviates from it goes astray.' (Muslim 5977)

FREEDOM TO CHOOSE

Muslims submit to Allah, and that means they must not pick and choose which of the revealed laws they will or will not keep. It is no good trying to work out which ones are more important than others—only Allah knows the full reasoning behind them. It is the Muslim's duty not to question Allah's will, but simply to try to obey it.

Yet submission to Allah is the highest freedom, for it implies that a person has the utmost choice of all—the choice to disobey Allah, if they wish. Many do.

WORKING OUT THE RULES

The Qur'an is the basis of Shari'ah, and gives all the principles and commands to be accepted by Muslims without question.

Further guidance comes from the Sunnah, the example of the Blessed Muhammad ﷺ, who spent his entire life after the Night of Power in guiding and directing the people in God's way. Whatever he said, did, or approved, provided an example.

'We have truly sent you as a witness, as a bringer of good news, and as a warner—in order that people may believe in Allah and His apostle... truly, those who promise their loyalty to you do no less than promise it to Allah; the hand of Allah is over their hands.' (48:8-10)

'You have indeed in the Messenger of God a beautiful pattern of conduct for anyone whose hope is in Allah and the final Day.' (33:71).

The Prophet ﷺ said: 'All my people will enter Paradise except those who refuse.' On being asked who refused, he replied: 'Those who obey me will enter Paradise, and those who disobey me have refused.' (Bukhari)

'Those who love my Sunnah have loved me, and those who love me will be with me in Paradise.' (Tirmidhi)

So we must follow the Sunnah. The problem for us, as we enter the twenty-first century, is that we can no longer be certain that all recorded hadiths really present the true Sunnah. The hadith collections make the Prophet's personal authority quite clear. Here is an example showing how the principle could stem from a simple case of judgement that took place during the Prophet's lifetime, concerning the vanity of ladies adding false hair to their own. The Blessed Prophet ﷺ did not approve of artificial beauty aids, and said so, which annoyed a great many ladies with whom they were popular. One such lady was Umm Yaqub of the Banu Asad, who happened to be a good scholar. She stated:

'I have read it (Allah's Book) from cover to cover and have not found in it (any mention of forbidding beauty aids). He said: 'I swear by Allah, if you had read it, you would have found it.' He then read: 'What the Apostle has brought you, accept, and what he has forbidden you, refrain from it.' (59:7) (Abu Dawud 4157—the version of Uthman)

The two most authentic collections of hadith are known as Bukhari and Muslim. Other respected collections include Abu Dawud, Ahmad, Tirmidhi, Ibn Majah and

Bayhaqi. The problem of taking guidance from the hadith is that there is no cast-iron guarantee that all of the sayings are genuine (there were certainly cases of 'pious fraud' in the early centuries of Islam!), and it has to be admitted that each collection is subject to the selection of human authors, with their own motives and interests. It has been pointed out, for example, that the Prophet's beloved wife 'A'ishah recorded over two thousand hadiths, but less than two hundred of them appear in Bukhari's collection.

IJTIHAD AND IJMA

In any case, how can a law laid down fourteen centuries ago in the Middle East meet all the complex demands and pressures of modern technological civilisation? How can anyone know whether it is right or wrong to play transistors, or go to discos, etc.?

Working out Muslim principles is called *ijtihad*. This means using modern reason and judgement to decide on the course of action most in keeping with the spirit of Qur'an and hadith. Decisions made in this manner are called *ijma*, but they are not regarded as totally binding (like a Qur'anic command) since they are based on human opinions. The only ijma accepted as binding are those ones made by the first caliphs, who had been Muhammad's 鏃 closest companions.

'Some companions of Mu'adh b. Jabal said: When the Apostle of Allah 鏃 intended to send Mu'adh to the Yemen, he asked: 'How will you judge when the occasion of deciding a case arises?' He replied: 'I shall judge in accordance with Allah's Book.' He asked: 'What will you do if you do not find guidance in Allah's Book?' He replied: 'I will act in accordance with the Sunnah of the Apostle of Allah 鏃.' He asked: 'And if you do not find guidance in the Sunnah or

Allah's Book?' He replied: 'I shall do my best to form an opinion and spare no pains.' The Apostle of Allah ﷺ then patted him on the breast and said: 'Praise be to Allah who helped the messenger of Allah's Messenger to find a thing which pleases Allah's Messenger.' (Abu Dawud 3585)

In making decisions, account must always be taken of the opinions of respected people (present and past); previous decisions and the reasons for them; the general sense of justice; concern for the public good; and one most practical one that is sometimes overlooked by the ambitious—the acceptance of the masses.

The technique for working out Shari'ah Law is called *fiqh* from the word for 'intelligence' or 'knowledge'.

All Shari'ah principles are based on the insistence of the Blessed Prophet ﷺ that 'He who believes in Allah and the Last Day should either utter good words or keep silent, should treat his neighbours with kindness, and should share hospitality to his guest.' (Abu Hurayrah in Muslim 75)

The deeds which draw people to Paradise are to 'worship Allah and never associate anything with Him, establish prayer and pay zakah, and do good to your kin.' (Muslim 13—Abu Ayyub)

Abu Hurayrah recorded: 'There is none whose deeds alone can secure salvation for him. They said: Allah's Messenger, not even you? He said: Not even I, but that Allah wraps me in His forgiveness and mercy.' (Muslim 6762)

In other words, Allah does not accept your belief if it is not expressed in deeds; and He does not accept your deeds if they do not conform to your beliefs.

Abdullah b. Amr b al-Aus recorded: 'None of you is a true believer unless he makes his passions follow what I have been commissioned with.' (Miskat al-Masabih)

BE CAREFUL WITH GOD'S WORD

It is absolutely vital that Muslims follow Allah's guidance before any professed opinion of a fallible human being, no matter how eminent that human.

> 'If the whole of humanity and jinns were to combine together to produce the like of this Qur'an, they could not produce the like thereof, even if they helped one another.' (17:88)

Some Muslim have a tendency to follow the rulings of particular imams, or their madhhabs, with great devotion, but almost a blind zeal—unaware, apparently, of the great humility and honesty of the historical leaders. The five great madhhabs—Hanafi, Shafi'i, Maliki, Hanbali and Ja'afari—do not always agree with each other; and a Muslim is free to disagree with any or all of them.

The imams of these schools were great people, and highly to be respected for their nobility and erudition. Nevertheless, they were *human* and therefore fallible. Every saying, every ruling purporting to be theirs must be judged on the touchstone of the Holy Qur'an alone (4:59). Abu Hanifa is himself reported to have said: 'Give up my word for the Word of Allah; give up my word for the word of the Messenger of Allah.'

A true Islamic scholar should never compromise Qur'anic principles, and never place Divine Guidance on the sacrificial altar of man-made, questionable, defective, dubitable, juristic entanglements, and wrong fatwas that throw the Ummah of our Nabi into utter confusion and unsightly disarray.

> 'And the Messenger will say: "My Lord! Surely my people treat this Qur'an as a discarded thing."' (25:30)
> 'Surely this is My way, leading straight, so follow it, and

do not follow other ways, lest they cause you to deviate from His way. All this He has enjoined upon you, so that you may remain conscious of Him.' (6:154)

Every matter that purports to be Shari'ah, or a ruling taken from the hadith, must be tested scrupulously against the principles taught in the Qur'an. None should fear this scrutiny and judgement.

True knowledge is absolutely vital. We most heed the warning given by the Prophet ﷺ (recorded by Ali) that a very dangerous time would come 'when Islam will remain in name only, and the words of the Holy Qur'an will remain on pages only. At that time, you may find the mosques full of worshippers, seemingly inhabited, but there will be no trace of guidance coming from them, and from that point of view they (the mosques) will be deserted. Their *ulama* will be the worst propagators of *fitnah* and evil from among the dwellers (of earth) below the skies, and they will be the ones from whom the fitnah and evil will rise, spread, and come back to them.' (Baihaqi, Mishkat)

It is easy to forgive a child who is afraid of the dark. The real tragedy is when intelligent adults are afraid of the *light*.

So, for example, if a hadith scholar rules that a Muslim male may be forgiven every possible sin, but will never attain Paradise if he does not grow a beard—an example claimed to be a genuine hadith—one must take care to test such statements against the final and inexorable teachings of the Qur'an.

'And they say: If only we had listened, or used our intelligence, we would not have been among the inmates of the Blazing fire.' (67:10).

33

Halal and Haram

Halal means that which is allowed and wholesome for humanity; haram is that which is forbidden, and harmful. Before the coming of Islam, there were numerous opinions as to what things or sorts of behaviour were haram or halal. Some religious people were highly fanatical and extremist in their outlook, forbidding all sorts of foods, normal sexual behaviour in marriage, and so forth. On the other hand, others considered certain barbaric and uncouth behaviour to be perfectly permissible—things like cruelty to women and slaves, sexual licence, drunkenness. Islam established certain legal principles which were to become the determining criteria on which all future decisions as to what was haram or halal could be based. The Ummah was to follow a Middle Path. Muslims should constitute:

> 'The middle Ummah, the best Ummah that has ever been brought forth for humanity, enjoining what is right and forbidding what is wrong, and believing in God.' (3:110).

As the first principle, humans should consider all the things that Allah has created and bestowed for the benefit of humanity.

> 'Do you not see that Allah has subjected to your use all things in the heavens and on earth, and has made His bounties flow to you in exceeding measure, both seen and unseen?' (31:20)

Humanity was given control over the earth and was expected to utilise the vastness of all its resources wisely and well. Only a very few things are prohibited, and the prohibition is always for specific reasons.

The second principle of the Shari'ah is that anything that has not specifically been forbidden falls under the general principle of the permissibility of things, and is *allowed* by Allah.

Al-Bazzar recorded: 'What Allah has made lawful in His Book is halal, and what He has forbidden is haram, and that concerning which He is silent is allowed as His favour. So accept from Allah His favour, for Allah is not forgetful of anything. He then recited 'And thy Lord is not forgetful' (19:64).' (Al-Hakim. A similar hadith was recorded by Salman al-Farsi in Tirmidhi and Ibn Majah)

This principle is very important to counteract unnecessary extremism and zealotry. The early Companions never applied the word 'haram' to anything unless they knew it to be definitely prohibited. If there was the slightest doubt, they would only say 'We disapprove of it,' or 'We do not like it.' It is very important that religious fervour does not lead believers into taking a fixed position on something which is not fixed, without weighing their opinions against the opinions and arguments of others, after comparison and critical evaluation. The leading scholars never claimed that they were infallible, but merely researchers who tried to find out the truth.

The Blessed Prophet ﷺ said: 'Allah has prescribed certain obligations for you, so do not neglect them; He has defined certain limits, so do not transgress them; He has prohibited certain things, so do not do them; and He has kept silent concerning other things out of mercy for you, and not because He forgot about them, so do not ask questions concerning them.' (Al-Darqutni)

If any Muslim reads that any particular thing is forbidden in Islam, and is surprised by this or has doubts, then he or she has the right to check the reference to that command either in Qur'an or hadith, or to trace the similar case from which the principle might be deduced. If there is no such evidence to be found, then the writer or teacher who forbade it has wrongly usurped the prerogative of Allah, and has committed the sin of making haram what Allah had allowed. It can and does happen, and the Blessed Prophet specifically warned against it. Obviously, with the passage of centuries, and the changing of civilisation with the spread of Islam to many different cultures, there is even more scope nowadays for the same error to be committed, and every Muslim should be alert to it.

The specific obligations are mainly the religious acts of worship. Nothing should be legislated concerning worship except what Allah Himself legislated. The Blessed Prophet ﷺ said:

'Any innovation in our matter (worship) which is not a part of it must be rejected.' (Bukhari and Muslim)

As far as living habits are concerned, the principle is of freedom and conscience—nothing is prohibited except what Allah Himself prohibited. No human authority, no matter how learned or exalted, has the right to prohibit anything allowed by Allah, or stand in judgement over people who act according to their consciences. Those who do this are indeed usurpers, and are in danger of setting themselves up as partners or associates with God. The tendency to set up prohibitions results in hardship for human beings, and is not justified.

'Do you see what Allah has sent down to you for

sustenance? Yet *you* have made some part of it halal and some part haram.' (10:59)

'Do not say... 'This is halal and that is haram' in order to fabricate a lie against Allah; assuredly those who fabricate lies against Allah will not prosper.' (16:116)

The Blessed Prophet ﷺ fought hard against pseudo-pietism and zealotry, regarding these believers as 'trouble-makers' and warning them 'the zealots will perish' three times (reported by Muslim, Ahmad and Abu Dawud). Such people may be very devout, but their attitude towards religion actually makes people feel uncomfortable and drives them away, rather than drawing them closer to Allah in brother-hood. By comparison to their stern, unbending attitude, the Prophet's ﷺ message was always loving, compassionate, gracious and straightforward.

For example, certain Muslims in Madinah began to show zealot tendencies, trying to make themselves 'better' than others by denying themselves all sorts of permissible aspects of life, and looking down on other believers who did not wish to follow their ways. The Blessed Prophet ﷺ received the revelation:

> 'O believers! Do not make haram the good things which Allah has made halal for you, and do not transgress; indeed, Allah does not like the transgressors. Eat of what Allah has provided for you, lawful and good, and fear Allah, in Whom you are believers.' (5:90-91)

It is not correct Islam to deprive oneself of any halal thing in order to try to become more pious, or to eradicate some sin. Allah, in His graciousness, has laid down numerous other ways by which sins can be wiped out—in example, good deeds as compensation for evil ones, spending in charity, enduring trials and sufferings. In Islam, things are only prohibited if they really are impure or harmful. If a thing is entirely harmful it is haram, and if it is entirely beneficial it is halal.

The third principle of Shari'ah follows from this—if a thing is prohibited, then anything which leads to it is also prohibited. For example, as sex outside marriage is haram, so also is seductive clothing, private meetings between people who might be tempted, pornography, obscene songs, and so on. In other words, that which leads to the haram is also haram.

The Blessed Prophet ﷺ said:

'The halal is clear and the haram is clear. Between the two there are doubtful matters concerning which people do not know whether they are halal or haram. Those who avoid them in order to safeguard their religion and their honour are safe, while if someone engages in a part of them he (or she) may be doing something haram, like one who grazes animals near the hima (grounds reserved for the animals of the King)... Truly, every king has a hima, and the hima of Allah is what He has prohibited.' (Bukhari, Muslim, Tirmidhi and others)

The final principle of the Shari'ah is that necessity removes the restrictions, and the person who does or eats the haram thing out of necessity is not held to blame for it. Four times in the Qur'an, after mentioning prohibited foods, Allah stated:

'But if one is compelled by necessity, neither craving nor transgressing, there is no sin in him; indeed, Allah is Forgiving, Merciful.' (2:173, 5:4, 6:119, 6:145)

However, even though compelled by necessity, a person must not do the haram thing or eat the haram food eagerly, or become accustomed to it, or use this principle as an excuse to enjoy it under the pretext of necessity.

In these ways the Shari'ah intends to remove from humanity all harmful, burdensome customs and superstitions, and it aims to simplify and ease the business of day-to-day living in a way that protects humans from evil and benefits them in all aspects of their lives.

> 'My mercy extends to all things. Thus shall I ordain it for those who do right, and practise regular charity, and those who believe in Our signs—those who follow the Apostle, the Unlettered Prophet... for he commands them what is just and forbids them what is evil; he allows them as lawful what is pure and prohibits them from what is bad; he releases them from their heavy burdens and from the yokes that are upon them. So it is those who believe in him, honour him, help him, and follow the Light which is sent down with him; it is they who will prosper.' (7:156-7)

RULES OF BEHAVIOUR

These are divided into five major categories:-

Fard or Wajib—things which are compulsory for Muslims and *must* be done, for example, the daily prayers, the fast of Ramadan.

Haram—things which are forbidden and must *never* be done, for example worshipping another besides Allah, or cruel and selfish behaviour.

Mandub—recommended actions, for example the giving of unselfish hospitality, generous compassion, truthfulness and justice.

Makruh—actions not forbidden, but disapproved of—like divorce, slavery, vengeance, extremism.

Mubah—actions to be decided by conscience, because there is no clear guidance—matters such as white lies to protect someone's feelings, or reporting or not reporting someone's failings.

Whatever is not actually forbidden is permitted in Islam, under the guidance of one's conscience. However, if an action is harmful to oneself or anyone else, it cannot be recommended by a Muslim.

'We send down in the Qur'an that which is a healing and a mercy to those who believe; to the unjust it causes nothing but loss after loss.' (17:82)

MISREPRESENTING ISLAM

We can see how these principles answer the question of how a person calling himself or herself Muslim can possibly become involved in acts of terrorism. Someone may be an 'extremely devout' Muslim, and belong to an organisation deeply concerned with promoting belief in Allah, and yet be completely astray in what they are doing. This situation has arisen over and over again in circumstances where Muslims have been involved in politics and nationalism.

One has only to go back to the principles, and the sunnah of the Prophet ﷺ, to see the tragedy of their misrepresentation of the faith they claim to love. The Prophet ﷺ never slaughtered indiscriminately villagers, tourists, opposing political figures—even if they disagreed openly with him. He certanly did not seek to hijack or imprison people; the hadith shows clearly his nobility, his efforts to help captive prisoners of war and arrange their honourable release, and so on.

Any Muslim, no matter how oppressed and persecuted, should consider the principles and spirit of Islam very carefully, and not throw away their hope of Paradise by becoming a persecutor or a murderer. It is not possible to be a real Muslim, and then blow up a busload of passersby, (they may well include other Muslims anyway!), or destroy an entire home and household on the possiblity that one person in it was a genuine enemy, or hijack an aircraft full of individuals and subject them to mental and physical sufferings, or kidnap and keep hostage those who are wayfarers or even sympathetic helpers in their territory, or slaughter groups or villages in reprisals (especially for things they have not done)—even if that one claims to be doing it for the sake of Allah. (See the chapter on Jihad).

EXCLUSIVENESS

Some leading scholars in Islam have claimed—particularly in Shi'ite Iran—that only their intellectual equals have the talents and abilities necessary to determine if any other such scholar has the ability to the same degree—therefore only a mujtahid is qualified to appoint another one safely (an important point behind the Iranian 1908 Constitution).

Did God intend this exclusiveness? Should the exercise of ijtihad be limited to none but qualified jurists? Or should the consensus of saintly laymen in the community also be allowed, and if not, why not? Are not jurists, although experts, actually out of touch with the real needs and feelings of ordinary people? Should the 'gate of ijtihad' be locked or open?

DOUBT

When a Muslim is more occupied with over-fastidious concern with ritual precision rather than paying attention to the great principles of honour, compassion and a 'clean and noble heart', it can have the effect of making these devout believers suffer from pharisaism, or 'waswas'—agonising about the validity of personal purity and the desire to carry out the will of God correctly, an agony so destructive that it can actually prevent devout people from achieving their objective. 'Waswas' implies hesitation, or doubt, and some mujtahids have taught that this is nothing less than the plotting of the Devil, since we should always place our trust in God's loving kindness and mercy.

Allah desires heaven for us, not difficulties beyond our scope. Islam is not intended to be a heavy, restrictive, burdensome faith, only really appreciated by hair-splitting Islamic intellectuals and those who have time to spare for the endless chanting of pious phrases, selfishly expecting this to earn them merit. It is a simple matter of loving God, and serving Him as best we can.

The Qur'an teaches that Allah will never place upon us a burden greater than we can bear—and therefore we should never despair but live in an attitude of trust and hope, and the certain knowledge that we are forgiven our shortcomings if we are sorry for them.

> 'On no soul do We place a burden greater than it can bear; before Us is a record which clearly shows the truth; they will never be wronged.' (23:62)

One of the most beautiful passages in the Qur'an is the moving prayer at end of surah 2, that takes up this theme:

> 'On no soul does God place a burden greater than it can bear. It gets every good that it earns, and it suffers every ill that it earns. Pray: Our Lord! Do not condemn us if we forget or fall into error; our Lord! Do not lay on us a burden like that You laid on those who came before us; our Lord! Do not lay on us a burden greater than we have the strength to bear. Blot out our sins and grant us forgiveness. Have mercy on us. You are our Protector; help us against those who stand against faith.' (2:286)

GOING BACKWARDS

Shaykh Murtaza Ansari once observed one of his students making the same round at the pool, over and over again. He asked what on earth he was doing. The youth said that his intention was to pray with full intention (niyyah), but he was not sure at what stage this intention had come into force, and since he doubted at every step, he was literally going backwards! Murtaza asked angrily who his teacher was, and when told it was himself, declared curtly—'I do not hold niyyah to be mandatory (wajib); get on with it, get it done!'

GOD WILLING, IT WAS THE GOAT

There is one famous Iranian story that certainly 'opens the gates' involving a dog and a goat, and makes gentle fun of the attitude of mind that is so over-devout it can never 'get on with it.'

Supposing a person had become ritually clean by performing wudu, but was then splashed by water from an unseen source above? Looking up, one can see a wet dog shaking itself on the roof of the house. If the water has come from this dog, the person has been defiled, since the dog is a contaminating animal. It seems obvious that the water did come from the dog, but who knows? Only Allah knows the full story.

Don't making assumptions based on ignorance. Maybe there is also a wet goat on the roof, which, being a clean animal, would not render the person ritually unclean. The fact that no-one has seen such a goat is irrelevant. The continuity of the known condition (the person's cleanliness) takes a merciful legal precedence over an assumption based on an uncertain point (that the water came from the dog)—therefore one could say 'Insha'Allah, buz bud'—'God willing, it was the goat.'

To cynics, however, the expression soon became the saying for all occasions when someone did not want to face reality! It is important for Muslims to face situations of uncertainty honestly and boldly, and to do the best that they can in all circumstances.

Human Rights

'O Believers! If you fear Allah He will grant you a standard (by which you may judge between right and wrong), to remove from you all the evil that may afflict you, and forgive you. For Allah is the Lord of unbounded grace.' (8:29)

Muslims believe that whether they are aware of it or not, all human beings are the creations of God, and loved by Him. Therefore there are certain basic rights which should be shared by the whole of humanity, and which should be observed in any society, whether the people are Muslims or not.

For example, all human beings have the right to be fed, clothed, educated and cared for by the society which governs their existence. No society could possibly be called civilised that did not tend its sick, or take care of its orphans and old people, and bury (or otherwise courteously dispose of) its dead.

Every society contains people whose disabilities prevent them from working, or who are too sick or too weak to earn sufficient wages to secure a decent life. There are children who have lost parents, wives who have lost husbands, old people who have passed the age of being able to work. Any society with the least respect for human dignity would not allow such people to be left neglected and uncared for.

Islam makes it obligatory for the wealthy and able-bodied to support those less fortunate. Partly this is done through the zakah system payable on all tangible assets; partly it is done through charity; but mainly it is done through responsible and honest hard work of those who are able, who support themselves and those for whom they are responsible.

No society should victimise or terrorise its weak members, or deprive people of liberty for no reason. No society should try to 'brainwash' the conscious awareness of its members, or attempt to force people to believe certain things against their natural will, ability or awareness.

These human rights have been granted by Allah, and not by any ruler or government, and it is the duty of Muslims to protect them actively. Failure to do so results in the loss of these rights, and this can lead to tyranny.

'Those who do not make their decisions in accordance with that revealed by Allah are the deniers of Truth.' (5:44)

Abu Ishaq reported: 'As you are, so will you have rulers over you.' (Bayhaqi)

People have the right not to be disturbed or hurt or victimised by others—and since so many people are selfish and cruel this often involves taking defensive or protective action.

Abu Hurayrah reported: 'He will not enter Paradise whose neighbour is not secure from his wrongful conduct.' (Muslim)

Abdullah ibn Amr reported: 'The (true) Muslim is the one from whose tongue and hand the Muslim is safe.' (Bukhari)

Jabir ibn Abdullah reported: 'A person should help his brother whether he is an oppressor or an oppressed. If he is the oppressor, he should be prevented from doing it, for that is his help; and if he is oppressed he should be helped (against oppression).' (Muslim 6254)

Anas b. Malik recorded: 'None of you truly believes until you wish for your fellows what you wish for yourself.' (Bukhari and Muslim)

1. THE RIGHT TO LIFE

Life is sacred, and is considered by the Muslim to be a divine gift which we are meant to preserve, enjoy and put to its fullest use. Life should never be ended without justification, and no true Muslim should ever consider attempting suicide or exposing himself or herself foolishly to unnecessary danger. Life is not a human's personal property, to be disposed of as an individual might wish, but a precious gift.

The Muslim therefore has the duty to protect all forms of life and treat them with respect. No person, no matter how great or powerful, has the right to usurp another's right to life.

> 'We decreed for the children of Israel that whoever kills a human being for murder or for spreading corruption in the earth, it would be as if he killed all mankind; and whosoever saves the life of one, it is as if he had saved the life of all mankind.' (5:35)

Even if someone wished to kill you, a Muslim should not consider it his or her right to kill that person.

> 'If you stretch your hand against me to slay me, it is not for me to stretch my hand against you to slay you; for I do fear Allah, the Cherisher of the Worlds.' (5:31)

Every time a Muslim kills an animal for food, it should be done by the halal method, with prayer. As regards the killing of humans, this is always thought to be wrong—with certain very limited exceptions. Contraception which prevents the sperm reaching the egg is allowed by most madhhabs, but abortion is not, unless the mother's life is

47

genuinely in danger. 'Mercy' killing is not allowed, and neither is the convenient disposal of sick or old people.

Killing on the battlefield of war can only be condoned under certain conditions, the chief of which is that the war is defensive—to protect the honour of Allah, or His people (in the widest sense and in whatever country they happen to be born). Killing as legal execution is also only condoned under certain very stringent conditions. These matters are discussed in a separate chapter of their own (see pp. 74-82, 197-199, 216-217, 256-270).

2. THE RIGHT TO PROTECT ONE'S HONOUR

Honour is a very important matter to a Muslim. It is the most precious thing a person possesses. Rather than lose one's honour, a Muslim should be prepared to lose anything else—for once lost, honour is not easily replaced!

During his Farewell Pilgrimage, the Blessed Prophet ﷺ told his followers:

'Your lives, your honour, and your property are as sacred to each other as the sacredness of this your day, in this your month, and in this your city.' (Muslim)

The honour of a man involves the protection of those in his care. No Muslim man should oppress the women, children, old people, the sick or the wounded, or indeed, any people that are in his care or under his protection.

Abu Hurayrah recorded: 'Everything of a Muslim is sacred to a Muslim; his property, honour and blood. It is enough evil for any person to despise his (or her) fellow Muslim.' (Abu Dawud 4864)

'If anyone defends his brother's honour in this world, Allah will shield his face from the fire on the Day of Resurrection.' (Tirmidhi)

The honour and chastity of all women is to be respected. Every woman has the right to be an innocent virgin, a cherished bride, a loved and respected wife, a responsible mother, and a beloved grandmother. Muslims believe that every child should be born wanted, within the security of a family; and that every child has the right to know who its father is.

Muslims also believe that every woman has the right to be unmolested by predatory males. No man has the right to harass a woman, or to abuse her in any way sexually. Muslim families usually take enormous pains to protect their daughters from the sexual advances of amorous males, and seek to settle them in happy and rewarding marriages as soon as this seems the best course of action.

However, it is vitally important that Muslim men grasp the point that they are not *responsible* or *accountable* for the failings of those in their care. It is a fundamental teaching of Islam that each individual is judged on his or her account alone, and not for the sins of others (6:164). Therefore, although the feeling of purging a family's stained honour is very strong in many Islamic societies, it does not give any individual the right to 'execute' or murder any other individual. This is really a subtle form of *shirk,* the avenging person taking on God's role of Judge and Purifier.

In practice, this includes the meanings that no father, uncle or brother (or anyone else) has the right to destroy a family member who has sinned—particularly if it is a raped or seduced woman, who is the victim and not the criminal; and no Muslim father has the right to force a daughter to marry a man she has not seen, or does not feel she could form a successful relationship with (see pp. 189-191).

3. THE RIGHT TO THE BASIC NECESSITIES OF LIFE

The earth is a wealthy place, and there is enough for all. No human being should go in need, while others are able to waste what they have. The fact that many people are rich and live in luxury while others starve is abhorrent to a Muslim.

Ibn Abbas reported: 'He is not a believer who lives in luxury while his neighbour goes hungry.' (Bayhaqi)

The needs of any suffering person should be attended to—the hungry fed, the naked clothed, and the wounded or diseased treated whether they are Muslim or not, friend or enemy. Any person who refused to help a wounded or needy 'enemy' could not be called Muslim. Muslims believe that it is by showing an example of compassion and generosity that many non-believers will be drawn to Allah.

'A'ishah reported that: 'Gabriel kept on commending the neighbour so much that I thought he would make him an heir!' (Bukhari and Muslim)

4. THE RIGHT TO PRIVACY, AND SECURITY OF PRIVATE LIFE

To any Muslim, the home is a private refuge. No person should enter another's home, or spy on it, without consent. It should be a safe haven for all who live in it.

> 'O believers! Do not enter houses other than your own until you have received permission, and greeted those within; this is the best politeness. If you find no-one in the house, do not enter it without permission; and then, if you are invited back, go back.' (24:27-28)

The conventions of propriety and privacy are essential to the Muslim life. No person has the right to 'catch another out' by surprise, or enter their home against their wishes. It is sometimes the case that when a visitor knocks there is no answer because the people within do not wish at that time to be disturbed, or are not in the required modest and presentable state. The fact that the visitor did not receive a reply to his knock does not give him the right to poke his head in, or go inside. The polite thing is to knock a few times, and if no reply is given, to withdraw for the time being. A Muslim should be trustworthy, and is not expected to go into someone's house unasked.

Abu Sa'id Khudri recorded: 'Permission should be sought three times, and if permission is granted to you (then go in), otherwise go away.' (Muslim)

The Blessed Prophet commented robustly on the subject of peeping in and prying, trying to see into someone's private area:

Sahl b. Sa'd as-Saydi reported that a person peeped through the hole of the Blessed Prophet's ﷺ door, while he had a pointed thing in his hand with which he had been adjusting his hair. He said: 'If I had known you were peeping I would have thrust it into your eyes!' (Muslim 5367)

Abu Hurayrah recorded: 'Those who peep into the houses of people without their consent, it is permissible to poke out their eyes!' (Muslim 5370; Abu Dawud 1428)

The atmosphere of the home should be private and loving, and should reflect the compassion and generosity of Allah. It should be a place in which every child or old person feels secure, created and sustained by the hard work and self-sacrifice of the parents.

It should be place of welcome, able to give refuge and protection, consolation, and encouragement. If a stranger comes, or any visitor, they should feel welcomed, in the name of Allah.

Many Muslim homes keep a place ready to receive guests at any time, and regard it as basic hospitality to refresh them and offer them food and drink.

5. THE RIGHT NOT TO BE ABUSED OR RIDICULED

No-one has the right to abuse, or defame, or insult, or threaten.

Ridicule is never fun, especially when there is arrogance or selfishness or malice behind it. We may laugh with people, to share in the happiness of life; we must never laugh *at* people, or cause them distress.

> 'O believers! Do not laugh at one another; it may be that the (latter) are better (than the former)... Do not defame one another, nor be sarcastic to each other, nor call each other by offensive names... Avoid suspicion, and spy not on each other, nor speak ill of others behind their backs.' (49:11-12)

Abu Hurayrah recorded: 'Woe to the one who lies in conversation just to create laughter. There is woe for that person!' (Tirmidhi)

The hadiths record an incident when Abu Dharr al-Ghifari, who later became one of the greatest Muslims and recorders of the Prophet's ﷺ sayings, scorned and abused a man simply because he happened to be black and a slave.

The Prophet ﷺ said: 'How dare you revile him because of his mother's colour? You still have traces of pre-Islamic attitudes. You have gone too far. A white woman's son has no superiority over a black woman's son, except due to greater piety and righteousness.' Upon hearing this, Abu Dharr put his face on the ground and said to the slave: 'Come and step over my face.' (Bukhari, Muslim and Abu Dawud)

Whispering and sniggering together are also condemned in Islam. The Prophet ﷺ said:

'If you are three people, two of you should not speak in a confidential manner in the presence of a third until you mix with other people, because that brings sadness to the heart of the third person (who has been left out) and would alienate him.' (Ahmad, Bukhari and Muslim)

6. THE RIGHT TO PERSONAL FREEDOM

Muslims believe that no people accused of crime should ever be sentenced to imprisonment unless they are *proved* guilty in an open and unbiased court. No person should be deprived of liberty on the basis of suspicion only, or not given reasonable opportunity to provide a defence. No individual should ever be arrested or imprisoned for the offences of others.

'No bearer of burdens shall be made to bear the burden of another.' (6:164)

Abu Malik reported: 'A ruler who having gained control over the Muslims does not strive for their betterment, does not serve them sincerely, shall not enter Paradise with them.' (Muslim 4502)

No Muslim person in authority should ever be guilty of incarcerating innocent people, keeping people locked away awaiting a judgement on their fate for years before they come to trial, kidnapping or hijacking people, not allowing condemned people the right to appeal properly, torturing or abusing prisoners, or raping prisoners—male or female.

(This even includes the wretched business of a Muslim father imprisoning or ill-treating a daughter because she refuses to marry the man of *his* choice).

7. THE RIGHT TO PROTEST AGAINST TYRANNY

The power of any human is only given as a trust from Allah. It is therefore the duty of every Muslim to speak out against tyranny, and protect the weak from tyrants.

> 'Why should you not fight in the cause of Allah and of those who being weak, are ill-treated and oppressed? Men, women and children, whose cry is: Our Lord, rescue us from this town whose people are oppressors, and raise for us from you one who will protect and help us.' (4:75)

Umar ibn al-Khattab reported: 'Truly the best of the servants of Allah... on Resurrection Day will be a ruler, just and kind; and the worst of men in rank in the sight of Allah... will be a ruler tyrannical and hard-hearted.' (Bayhaqi).

A tyrant is a ruler who attempts to assert his own will upon the people in his charge, rather than seek to do for them the will of Allah—which will always be kind and just. If such a person takes power, it is the Muslim's right to point out the errors, and turn the tyrant back to the right way—even by force if this becomes necessary. This is because it is the Muslim's duty to protect the weak and oppressed, and not hang back out of cowardice or thought for themselves.

Aus ibn Shurajil reported: 'If anyone walks with an oppressor to strengthen him, knowing that he is an oppressor, he has gone forth from Islam.' (Bayhaqi)

Hadrat Anas reported: 'How are rights neglected? He (the Prophet ﷺ) answered: When sins are committed openly, and he does not prevent the sinners from wrongdoing.' (Targhib)

If a thing should be disapproved of, the Muslim has the right to disapprove of it, and even though he or she may not be able to do anything about it, they should try.

Abu Sa'id al-Khudri recorded: 'Those among you who see something abominable should try to alter it with the help of the hand; if you have not strength enough to do it, then you should do it with your tongue; and if you have not the strength enough for that, then you should at least (abhor it) from your heart.' (Muslim)

Islam also encouraged people who were being oppressed to emigrate from their country or place of origin if it was possible for them to move elsewhere to a place where they could live in freedom and dignity.

> When the angels take the soul of those who died in sin against their souls, they say: 'In what plight were you?' They reply: 'Weak and oppressed in the earth.' They say: 'Was not Allah's earth spacious enough for you to move yourselves away (from evil)?' Such people will find their abode in Hell—except those who are (truly) weak and oppressed, men, women and children who have no means in their power, nor a (guide-post) to direct their way. (4:97-98)

8. THE RIGHT TO FREEDOM OF EXPRESSION

This is granted to every Muslim, provided it is used in accordance with the will of Allah. Unfortunately the concept of freedom of expression frequently becomes confused with debased and inferior notions, and has come to be associated with anarchic disorderliness and immorality in values—the pursuit of one's passions and desires along with an escape from social restrictions. People who advocate this kind of 'freedom' have no hesitation about violating the liberty, rights and privacy of others.

True freedom of expression does not mean that people can say whatever they like, but there are social implications that demand everyone to wish to work towards the common good.

Muslims are not free to spread evil, wickedness, abuse or offence—which are matters of tyranny, and hurtful to others. This is why Muslims consider films, plays or books about Jesus 翔 or the Prophet Muhammad 鑾 which they judge to be abusive or blasphemous (such as the infamous book 'The Satanic Verses' by Salman Rushdie, or the film 'The Life of Brian') to be a misuse of the right of freedom of expression.

Abdullah ibn Masud reported: 'You must encourage what is reputable, prohibit what is disreputable, prevent the wrongdoer, bring him into conformity with what is right... or Allah will mingle your hearts together and curse you as he cursed them.' (Tirmidhi and Abu Dawud)

Freedom of expression and opinion should not be employed as a means of spreading anarchy, corruption and falsehood. Islam approves any opinion so long as it remains consistent with public benefit—it does not condone the sort of 'freedom' in which anyone has the right to impose a wrong or damaging opinion.

9.   THE RIGHT TO FREEDOM OF ASSOCIATION

As with freedom of speech, Muslims are free to join any organisations or parties, provided only that this allegiance is not evil or offensive to Allah and to others.

10.   THE RIGHT TO FREEDOM OF CONSCIENCE

No attempt should ever be made to force people to act against their own consciences, so long as they are true to whatever seems the most right course of action for the welfare of humanity, and their act does not harm others even though they think it right by their own standards.

However, the conscience is a very good guide, and should be listened to—for it brings the stirrings of Allah's will.

Abu Umamah reported that Muhammad ﷺ accounted a person as a believer 'when your deed pleases you and your evil deed grieves you.' He was then asked what sin was, and replied: 'When a thing disturbs (the peace of) your heart, give it up!' (Ahmad)

11. THE RIGHT TO PROTECT RELIGIOUS SENTIMENTS

It is impossible to force people to believe what they do not believe. As Allah has allowed a free mind and the ability to reason to all humans, therefore in Islam all religious sentiments are given due respect, and missionary work should not be such that it causes offence to those who are following different faiths. There is no need to hurry faith. It will come, whenever it is to come.

'There should be no coercion in the matter of faith.' (2:256)

'If it had been your Lord's will, everyone on earth would have believed. Will you then compel humanity against their will, to believe?' (10:99)

'God forbids you not, with regard to those who fight you not for faith nor drive you out of homes, from dealing kindly and justly with them; for Allah loves those who are just.' (60:8)

The fact that the Qur'an orders no coercion or force is particularly important when considering the rights of people who live in societies which have a strong Muslim majority. It is totally against the spirit of Islam for any Muslim to harass another person, whether male or female, to try to make them feel inferior, or even unsafe. This must be remembered by some Muslim zealots who feel they have the right to 'look down their noses' or regard themselves as superior to other

Muslim men and women who do not, perhaps, conform to their particular ways.

Allah makes it clear in the Qur'an that the Muslim's duty is simply to show and remind people of their responsibility to exercise their mental faculties:

> 'Remind them, for you are but a reminder; you are not to be a warder over them.' (88:21-22)

> 'If they submit, then truly they are rightly-guided; but if they turn away, it is your duty only to convey the message to them.' (3:20; see also 5:92 and 9:129)

True Muslims should not be always on the lookout for the things that other Muslims do 'wrong'. The real spirit of Islam is gentleness, and the 'covering' of faults.

> 'Kind words and the covering of faults are better than charity followed by injury.' (2:263).

> 'It is part of the mercy of Allah that you deal gently with them. If you are severe and hard-hearted, they will break away from you; so pass over their faults and ask for God's forgiveness for them.' (3:159)

Abu Dharr recorded: 'Look at your own faults; this will prevent you from finding faults with others. Never be in search of the faults of others. It is sinful on your part to detect those faults in others which exist in you.' (Bayhaqi)

12. THE RIGHT TO EQUALITY BEFORE THE LAW

Muslims insist that every citizen must have completely equal rights. People of vastly different social positions can sue each other and expect impartial justice. The principle of equality is the cornerstone of justice in Islam. No individual should ever be above the law, no matter how powerful they are; or beneath the law, no matter how humble.

Yahya b. Husayn recorded: 'If a slave is appointed over you and he conducts your affairs according to the Book of

Allah, you should listen to him and obey.' (Muslim 4528)

The hadith record a very famous incident when a woman of high social standing committed theft and various people interceded on her behalf. The Blessed Prophet ﷺ said:

'Some of your predecessors were destroyed because they freed the noble men among them who stole, and punished the powerless commoners. By Allah, if Fatimah bint Muhammad (his own daughter) stole, I would cut her hand off.' (Bukhari and Muslim).

Everyone had equal rights, for they are all born equal.

'God brought you forth from the wombs of your mothers knowing nothing, and gave you hearing, sight and hearts that hopefully you might given thanks.' (16:78)

'Abu Hurayrah recorded: 'Your God is one and your father is one. All of you belong to Adam, and Adam was created from dust. Those who fear God most are the most noble. An Arab has no superiority over a non-Arab, or a non-Arab over an Arab, or a black person over a white, or a white over a black person, except by being more righteous.' (Ibn Asakir)

'People are all equal like the teeth of a comb.' (Bukhari)

Justice should be impartial, even if it involves making decisions against members of one's own family:

'O believers, be staunch in justice, witnesses for Allah, even though it be against yourselves, or (your) parents or (your) kindred; whether (the case be of) a rich man or a poor man, for Allah is nearer them both (than you are), so do not follow emotion lest you lapse (from truth), and if you lapse or fall away, then lo! God is ever informed of what you do.' (4:135)

Personal animosity should never interfere with proper justice:

'O believers! Stand out firmly for God, as witnesses to fair dealing, and let not the hatred of others to you make you swerve to wrong and depart from justice. Deal justly, that is next to piety; and fear God, for lo! God is well acquainted with all that you do.' (5:9).

Needless to say, any judge who was open to bribery or could be threatened and give false judgement through fear—either of personal physical hurt or of something in his private life being revealed that he would rather keep secret—is not acting as a Muslim. No true Muslim would give in to threats, bribery or corruption, or trade their earthly position for their reward in the Hereafter, as if they thought God could be fooled or kept in ignorance of the realities.

13. THE RIGHT TO PARTICIPATE IN AFFAIRS OF STATE

Islam teaches that all heads of government and members of ruling assemblies should be elected by free and independent votes of the people. They should never imposed by a clique, or granted power simply for reasons of family power. Dynastic rulers can be given allegiance, so long as their rulings do not break Islamic principles.

Political freedom implies the right of any person, man or woman, to occupy an administrative post if they are competent enough to do so, with the right to express their opinion regarding the conduct of public affairs. The ruler is the servant of the nation, and should not be its 'governor', and all positions of authority should always be carried out with consultation of others.

'Consult them in affairs; then when you have made your decision, put your trust in Allah.' (3:159)

Caliph Abu Bakr gave a splendid example when he said: 'O people, I have been appointed as your leader though I am not the best of you. If you see me following the right path, help me, and if you see me following the wrong way, bring me to the right one. Obey me as long as I obey Allah, and if I disobey God you should not obey me.' (Abu Bakr's first address to the Muslims after his election as Caliph).

No true Muslim would attempt, however, to annul any of Allah's commands or wishes, and if any command in the Qur'an appeared to contradict human interest, priority would be given to the Text—for Muslims believe that it is impossible for there to be a real contradiction between the interests of humanity and the divinely revealed word. Right is right, even if all the people contradict it; and wrong is wrong, even if all the people sanction it.

When seeking office, Muslims should be modest, and not push themselves forward. They should not be ambitious and think of the wealth or money reward for a position of office, but instead should think about whether or not they are capable of doing the job. People who are not talented should not seek to be promoted above their capacities, since this leads to the suffering of others when they cannot cope or begin to make serious mistakes.

Anyone who wants to gain a certain position in order to lord it over others is in fact a slave of that ambition, and not worthy of it. Rather than chase promotion, it is far better if others recognise your worth, and press the position upon you.

Abu Hurayrah reported that the Blessed Prophet ﷺ said: 'You will find that good amongst people are the ones who are averse to positions of authority until they are thrust upon them; the worst among people are those who are two-faced.' (Muslim 6135)

Anas b. Malik recorded: 'If anyone desires the office of judge and seeks help to get it, he will be left (by Allah) to his own devices; if anyone does not desire it nor does he seek help for it, then Allah will send down an angel who will guide him aright.' (Abu Dawud 3751)

Muslims should only step forward and volunteer for promotion if they know there is no-one else qualified, and that if they do not do their duty and take the position, public interest will be damaged. However, once in office, all public officials should do their utmost for the public good and not behave corruptly—no matter how they got the position:

Abu Hurayrah recorded: 'If anyone seeks the office of judge among Muslims until he gets it, but then his justice prevails over his tyranny, he will go to Paradise; but the man whose tyranny prevails over his justice will go to Hell.' (Abu Dawud 3568)

As regards women as rulers, or in positions of authority, there is no sound hadith against it, and certainly no Qur'anic injunction. The Prophet's ﷺ comment that nations governed by women would not thrive was not a ruling on the subject; in fact Islam has become notable for the number of its female rulers in this century. In the Qur'an, the Queen of Sheba was asked to become Muslim, not give up her throne.

In any case, in all walks of life, it is the duty of all Muslims to give their best effort at all times—and whatever they do, to do it for the love of Allah. After all, the real 'boss' of any Muslim is not the superior at the office or factory or farm, but Him whose eye sees all and Who never slumbers nor sleeps.

14. THE RIGHT TO RISE ABOVE THE LEVEL OF ANIMAL LIFE.

Islam supports the principles of the unity of all humankind. This means that human beings, when motivated by Allah, should be free to go beyond all bonds of kinship. They should not be party to racial superiority, linguistic arrogance, or economic privilege. Muslims should feel the invitation to move to a higher plane of existence where the Unity of Humanity can be realised.

To a Muslim, the ideal society is one in which there is justice, peace, love and co-operation, and everyone is free to worship Allah according to their own level of awareness.

There should be no question of a 'chosen race' or nation—of Jew or Gentile, Arab or 'Ajam (Persian), Hindu, Arya-Varta, Turk or Tajik, European or Asiatic, White or Coloured. This is one aspect of Zionism that so many Muslims find offensive. To Allah belong all peoples, whether Aryan, Semitic, Mongolian, African, American, Australian or Polynesian, or any other. To all humanity, and any creatures other than humans who have any spiritual sense, the principles and the rights which Allah has bestowed apply universally.

Abdullah b. Amr recorded: 'Truly, the hearts of all the sons of Adam are between the two fingers of the Compassionate Lord as one heart.' (Muslim 6418). He commented: God turns to any direction He Likes. Then Allah's Messenger ﷺ prayed: 'O Allah, the Turner of Hearts, turn our hearts to Thine obedience.' (Muslim 6418)

The Sanctity of Life

The most precious of the responsibilities that Allah has granted to any living creature is the care of its own life. Muslims believe that no living thing has an automatic right to life; if Allah had not wished it to exist, it would simply never have done so. Every living creature receives its soul as a 'loan' from Allah, to take responsibility for it for as long as Allah wishes. The soul is not the same thing as the body; it 'inhabits' the body, and the body is its vehicle—but it is only a 'visitor', a 'guest'. The length of time a soul occupies a certain body is also Allah's gift, and therefore sacred. Once a life has been given, no human has any right to attempt to terminate it.

> 'Allah fixes the time span for all things. It is He who causes both laughter and grief; it is He who causes people to die and to be born; it is He who causes male and female; it is He who will recreate us anew.' (53:42-7)

> 'Nor can a soul die accept by God's leave, the term being fixed as by writing.' (3145)

DEATH

The decision about the moment for the ending of a life therefore belongs to Allah alone. It is a gross presumption for any human being to attempt to interfere with that decision, no matter how well-meaning.

Allah knows the exact length of any creature's lifetime even before their moment of conception. Some people develop a morbid preoccupation with trying to find out exactly when their moment of death will come—but the knowledge is hidden from them. It is not intended to be known. The ability to live each day as it comes, with grace and gratitude, and to be ready at any moment to return to Allah the soul He 'loaned' to earth, is part of the test of faith.

The Prophet's ﷺ friend, Umm Sulaym, showed admirable faith and endurance when her little son died. She asked the members of her family not to tell Abu Talhah (the father) until she had spoken to him first. When he came home, she gave him his supper, made herself attractive, and even satisfied his sexual hunger. Then, when she saw that he was satisfied in every respect, she said to him: 'Abu Talhah, if some people borrow something from another family and then they ask for its return, should they resist its return? 'He said: 'No.' She said: '(Then) I tell you about the death of your son.' Abu Talhah was actually annoyed that she had not told him before, and went to report everything to the Prophet ﷺ, but he said: 'May Allah bless both of you in the night spent by you.' It so happened that she became pregnant that night, and they were blessed with a new baby. (Adapted from Muslim 6013; see also Muslim 5341).

It is easy to claim that you are a Muslim, submitted to Allah's will—but if you truly are, then you must be prepared to put Him first in every respect, to sacrifice anything you cherish if He demands it, and give Him ungrudgingly anything He asks. No human beings know the moment when their lives will be required by Allah and taken back, but they are all very well aware that the moment will certainly come.

'Every soul will have a taste of death, and only on the Day of Judgement shall you be paid your full recompense.' (3.185)

AWARENESS

There are two odd things for us to consider about our awareness of our mortality. Firstly, it is precisely our awareness of death that makes us different from the other animals; they may see other dead creatures, but so far as we know, they are not aware that this is the certain end for themselves too. Secondly, it is the only event in our own futures that we can be certain will happen—any other thing, success or failure, ambition or accident, we can have no idea about. Unfortunately for us, it is a certain event we rarely feel ready for, not even if we are old and ill and burdened heavily by the pains of this life. For most of us, death will confront us when we are not at all expecting or wanting it; we might be in the middle of unfinished business, or at an unsatisfactory moment in our personal relationships. We might be in perfect health, with all sorts of ongoing responsibilities.

Just like some people are obliged to retire from their lifetime's work just when they feel they are at last getting the hang of it and have it organised, and under control—so we might be obliged to hand back our lives just when we feel we are at last beginning to make sense of it, and are confortable and secure.

There are so many different scenarios, including death from accidents, murder, warfare, natural disaster and so on. And we have no idea when our final moment here will come.

Faithful Muslims will not fear that moment, but will try to live in such a way that if that particular day was to be their last—they will be as ready as they can be to face Allah and answer to Him for the things they have done with their lives.

NOTHING TO FEAR

Islam teaches that although you should fear the Day of Judgement if your life has been full of sins for which you never repented, death itself should not be feared. It is only human nature to shrink from pain and suffering, but Muslims are to do their best to bear all such trials with patience and fortitude. Death is the natural end of human life—it cannot be avoided, and no-one escapes it. Most very old people will tell you that they do not wish to go tottering on for ever, especially when they have firm belief in something to follow in which they will be released from the pains of old age and ill health, and will become vigorous and active souls again, in the happy company of those they love.

It is when facing death that a believing person has such an enormous advantage over a non-believer, for the peace of mind and hope that it brings. It is quite pointless for people who assume (in the face of all the evidence otherwise) that the death of the human body is the end, to try to convince believers they are wrong, or to belittle their beliefs as weakness. Like the freewill to believe in God, the freewill to believe or not believe in Afterlife is one of the things granted to all humans during their time on earth. The moment they 'die' that freewill no longer exists, because they are at that stage either snuffed out into nothingness, or confronted with the reality of the situation of Afterlife and must cope with this new knowledge as best they can.

Even if a person has no belief whatsoever in the Afterlife, it is rather pointless and futile to resent the inevitable end of the human body, and a foolish gamble to assume that all religious teachers who have taught the life to come have been misled by God. Those who have gambled that they could get away with selfish, cruel and arrogant lives, abusing others, confident that death would be the end and there will be no justice or retribution to follow, will be in for a shock.

> 'Do you think that We shall not re-assemble your bones? Yes, surely, yes—We are able to restore even your individual fingerprints!' (75:3-4)

DEATH CANNOT BE PREVENTED

When Allah requires us to move on, there is nothing we can do about it. It is very similar to a birth. Once a woman has conceived and a new life is growing within her, she cannot prevent a moment of birth. Similarly, we cannot prevent our moment of death—which will probably be far easier than birth. The soul can slip out of a body with far less fuss than a new human struggling out of its mother's womb. Some people are so fed up with their lives that they long to be done with it; others are desperately reluctant to let go— just as in childbirth some mothers really suffer in the last stages of pregnancy and long for the 'delivery,' whereas others are absolutely petrified of giving birth.

However, when the moment of death comes, just like the moment of birth, it can no longer be held back, and the individual concerned no longer has a choice but is confronted with an over-whelming personal event that over-rides everything else.

Death is beyond human control. No person can choose the time of their passing unless God sanctions it.

> 'A soul cannot die except by Allah's permission, the life-span being fixed as if by written contract' (3:145)

Many people desperately try to prevent their deaths and pray for Allah to grant them some miracle that will keep them alive—but Nature runs its course and miracles are not granted. On the other hand, many people long to die, because they are so unhappy or in such pain, but Allah requires them to go on living.

> 'If you think you control your own destiny, try to stop your own soul from leaving its body at your hour of death'. (56:81-87)

> 'When your time expires, you will not be able to delay the reckoning for a single hour, just as you cannot bring it forward by a single hour.' (16:61)★

REWARDS AND PUNISHMENTS

No true Muslim should fear death, for they believe the Afterlife will be a time of great joy and reward for all their efforts on Earth, if Allah wills.

> 'For those nearest to Allah, will come rest and satisfaction and a garden of delights, and... peace; but if you are of those who have... gone wrong, then your entertainment will be boiling water and hell-fire. Truly, this is the absolute truth and certain.' (56:88-95)

> 'Those who believe and do deeds of righteousness, We shall admit to gardens with rivers flowing beneath—their eternal home; they shall have holy and pure companions there; We shall admit them to cool and deep shade.' (4:57)

A blissful vision for a person used to the baking sands and blinding light of Arabia!

> 'The true servants of Allah shall enjoy honour and dignity in Gardens of delight, facing each other on thrones. A cup from a clear-flowing fountain will be passed round to them, crystal white, a taste delicious to those who drink it, free from headiness; they will not suffer intoxication from it. And beside them will be chaste women, keeping their

---

★   Many of these issues and topics are raised in Sr. Ruqaiyyah's book *After Death, Life*, Goodword Books, 1998.

glances modest, their large eyes full of wonder and beauty, as closely guarded as delicate eggs. They will turn to one another and ask questions—'I had an intimate companion on earth, who used to ask if I was really among those who bore witness to the truth, and when we died and became dust and bones, would we really receive rewards and punishments?' A voice said:- 'Would you like to look down?' He looked down and saw him, in the midst of the fire, and said... .. 'Had it not been for the grace of God, I should certainly have been there myself!' (37:40-57)

Islam does not try to convince people that everything will be all right for everybody, and all people will be forgiven no matter what they have done. There is a condition attached—the one who has done evil and harm to others is obliged to face up to this and genuinely be sorry for it before their moment of death, and prepared to make reparation for their hurts and injustices as far as is possible for them.

For those who die still unrepentant, arrogantly abusive and damaging others to the last with no fleeting twinge of conscience, a punishing destruction is in store.

'Those who reject our signs We shall cast into the fire; as often as their skins are roasted through We shall change them for fresh skins, that they may taste the penalty.' (4:56)

There are a great many references to the Afterlife, and they are all very graphic, particularly the references to the punishments of hell (of which the idea of the fresh skins growing so that the punishment can continue and people not be just burnt up to oblivion is possibly the most harrowing!)

However, Allah Himself asks us to consider that these passages are to be taken symbolically and not literally.

'In the Book are verses of fundamental meaning, and others which are allegorical.' (3:7)

Since Allah has indicated that we cannot grasp with our limited human intellect what lies ahead of us, it is permissible to keep a very open mind on the subject, and just acknowledge that our Afterlife will be as inconceivably different as the butterfly's life is from the caterpillar, or the oak-tree from the acorn!

> 'Now, no person knows what delights of the eye are kept hidden for them—as a reward for their good deeds.' (32:17)

Abu Hurayrah reported: 'Eye has not seen, and it has not entered into the human heart what things Allah has prepared for those who love Him.' Muslim (6780)

LUST AND GLUTTONY IN PARADISE?

Some people with a peculiar attitude towards women (and please remember that over 50% of the Muslim community are women) have wondered whether women will have the same rewards in Heaven as men; whether there will be sexual relationships; what exactly are Huris, and how women in Heaven will react to seeing their husbands greeted by Huris (beautiful female spirit beings). Some writings have suggested that male Muslims in Heaven will have enormous sexual prowess, and will spend their time in using up one fresh virgin after another—one wonders if this would really be a suitable after-death occupation for a man who had spent his earthly life trying to control his passions and retain his sexuality within marriage! And what will happen to all the poor virgins once they have been used? The quaint notion that once a man dies a martyr's death he will be granted the licence to behave as he likes with 72 virgins has done much to give Islam the reputation in the West of being a faith that abuses women. Unfortunately for 'wishful thinkers,' there is no such reference in the Qur'an!

That the Qur'an uses the masculine reference when it speaks of Allah's reward to believers is no more than a requirement of the Arabic language—as it is in many other languages. Allah makes it abundantly clear that the same rewards will be given to male and female Muslims for the same actions. A few passages really make this clear:

'As for anyone, man or woman, who does righteous deeds and is a believer, him We shall most certainly cause to live a good life; and most certainly We shall grant to such as these their reward in accordance with the best they ever did.' (16:97).

'For all men and women who have surrendered themselves to Allah, and all believing men and women, and all truly devout men and women, and all men and women who are true to their word, and all men and women who are patient in adversity, and all men and women who humble themselves before Allah, and all men and women who give in charity, and all men and women who fast, and all men and women who are mindful of their chastity, and all men and women who remember Allah unceasingly; for all of them Allah has truly made ready forgiveness of sins and a great reward.' (33:35).

This latter passage was revealed after the query from the Prophet's wife Umm Salamah, specifically requesting to know why the Qur'an did not mention women.

The point was that one should read *all* references in the Qur'an that occur in the masculine gender, including those referring to rewards in the Hereafter, as equally applicable in the feminine gender. It would be irritating and pedantic to express it at length every single time.

When the Qur'an speaks of wives for believers in Heaven, incidentally, this may or may not refer to the marriages of this world. Certainly, if a married couple are good believers and they are both admitted to Heaven, they may be together in Heaven if they wish it.

'As for those who have attained to righteousness...(they

will find themselves) amidst fruit-laden lote-trees and flower-clad acacias, extended shade and gushing waters, abundant fruit never failing and never out of reach. And (with them will be their) spouses, raised high; for behold, We shall have brought them into being in a renewed life, having resurrected them as virgins, full of love, equal in age, well-matched with those who have attained righteousness.' (56:27-38).

Verse 34 is the key verse mentioning spouses. Some commentators use the literal translation couches here, and render it 'on raised couches' instead of 'spouses raised high.' However, many of the most outstanding commentators (e.g. Baghawi, Zamakshani, Razi, Baydawi, etc.) support the meaning 'spouses.' They do this for two main reasons—the connecting statement in the next verse (i.e. couches are not created afresh as virgins!), and because 'firash' (lit. bed or couch) in the classical Arabic idiom is frequently used to denote 'wife' or 'husband.' Zamakshani draws particular attention to 36:56 which refers to the inmates of Paradise reclining on couches in happiness, 'they and their spouses.'

What about the Huris mentioned in 56:22 and else-where? (38:52; 44:54; 52:20; 55:72) What are they, and how are female believers supposed to react to them? Will they not jeopardise a wife's happiness? One can read fantasies and theories churned out by presumably sex-starved pious gentlemen who genuinely believe they are in for a really amazing sexual 'good time' with these girls in Heaven.

Sadly for them, they have got it wrong. The 'Hur' of 56:22 might even be identified with the 'spouse raised high' of 56:34. The noun 'hur' (pure companion) is the plural of both ahwar (male) and hawra' (female), either of which terms describes 'a person distinguished by hawar—which primarily denotes intense whiteness of the eyeball and lustrous black of the iris of the eye. In a general sense hawar signifies simply 'whiteness,' or in the moral sense, 'purity' (cf. Tabari, Razi and Ibn Kathir in their explanation of hawariyyun in 3:52.) 'Huri' means 'pure beings most beautiful of eyes.' Razi commented that the use of the word 'eye' here may actually refer to 'soul,' since the eye in a sense 'reflects' the state of the soul. So, it may be that 'hur'in' means 'companion pure of soul' and not necessarily a female at all.

However, most commentators regard it as a feminine thing; many of the earliest understood it to signify the righteous human women raised to Paradise and not a different order of beings to be found in Paradise.

So, what about sex? Sadly for those who hoped otherwise, sex only belongs to the realm of the physical. In the earthly life Allah made sex enjoyable in order to ensure the survival of the species. This is no longer relevant in life in the Hereafter. People in Heaven will not go on giving birth to children and increasing their own numbers. At no time does the description of Heaven given in the Qur'an mention children being born to believers.

What will be the case for those who have had more than one beloved wife or husband? People are frequently very possessive about their spouses, and dislike the thought that a partner could love somebody else as well as themselves. Young people, in particular, with their sentimental and emotional attitude towards romantic love, find this hard to contemplate. However, as we grow older, we all know it is perfectly possible to love any number of children equally, and as we pass through our earthly lives, it is quite possible to love someone and then lose them, and then love again without in any way turning against our love for the first person. No doubt in Heaven, without the jealousies often attached to physical sexual relationships, people who have loved more than once, or married more than once, will be bound by a feeling of close relationship to all of them.

SUICIDE

Muslims believe that since every soul has been created by Allah, and is owned by Him, no person is allowed to damage or attempt to kill any body in which it is the 'guest'. To kill yourself is just as forbidden as killing another person unlawfully.

> 'How can you reject faith in Allah, seeing you were without life and He gave you life; and He will cause you to die, and will bring you again to life.' (2:28)

Thabit b. al-Dhhah recorded that the Blessed Messenger ﷺ observed: 'He who killed himself with steel, or poison, or threw himself off a mountain would be tormented on the Day of Resurrection with that very thing.' (Muslim 202)

Life may be full of hardships and terrible sufferings, but Muslims are taught to accept these as part of their test, and to face them with patience and humility. The real life of a Muslim is that to come in the Hereafter—human life on Earth is just a preparation. Therefore, not even the very worst calamities that could happen in life should make a person commit suicide out of despair if their faith in God is genuine.

Anas recorded: 'None of you should wish for death for any calamity that befalls you, but should say: 'O Allah! Cause me to live so long as my life is better for me, and cause me to die when death is better for me.' (Abu Dawud 3102)

The real point is that the person who commits suicide is demonstrating that they have lost their faith in the reality of Allah and the Hereafter, and think, wrongly, that they are 'ending it all'. Furthermore, they are inflicting a life-time of terrible suffering on those who were not able to prevent their suicide. Many, many distressed people have held back from the brink of suicide by realising how much those who love them would be devastated by their fatal act.

To commit suicide out of shame has been considered honourable in some societies; in Islam, the desired course of action is humble apology followed by attempts to right the wrong, and not suicide.

Of course, a large percentage of people commit suicide as a result of clinical depression and mental illness, and this should not be regarded as the same thing as somebody just defying God's will.

The Law of Shari'ah concurs that if any people in these categories commit crimes they should not be punished; if they make agreements or enter into contracts in that state they should not be valid, and similarly while in that mental state they may not divorce a spouse or free a slave. Therefore anybody who unfortunately commits suicide while the balance of their mind is disturbed is not held responsible by Allah, but is forgiven.

'A'ishah reported the very important hadith: 'There are three (persons) whose actions are not recorded; a sleeper until fully awake, a (person with) disturbed mind until restored to reason, and a child below the age of puberty.' (Abu Dawud 4384)[1]

EUTHANASIA

> 'Do not take life—which Allah has made sacred—except for just cause.' (17:33)

Sometimes life seems such a burden for someone that

---

1. The subjects are discussed in detail in Sr. Ruqaiyyah's book *'After Death Life,'* Goodword Books, New Delhi, 1998.

well-meaning people consider it would be better to end it, in as kind a way as possible. They give serious consideration to what is meant by the phrase 'just cause'. Are some conditions of life so unbearable, that a person would be justified in ending it—either their own or somebody else's? 'Euthanasia' means literally a 'good death' (usually thought of as being 'put to sleep' painlessly).

People who believe in euthanasia argue that sometimes we are kinder to our animals than we are to our people, for we would not stand by and see an animal suffer, but would kill it kindly.

They argue that putting a gentle and easy end to human life should be considered when an infant is born hopelessly deformed, or hopelessly mentally ill, when the prospective lifetime in front of it would be grim. It seems much kinder to the child, and to the family that cares for it and loves it, to let it die peacefully while it is still a baby and has no knowledge of what is to come. Nothing is more heartbreaking than watching a child face up to approaching death, usually with extraordinary courage.

Other people for whom euthanasia is seriously considered are the old and the terminally ill. If a person of any age has become so riddled with pain through incurable disease that they feel they can no longer 'carry on', why should they be deprived of a 'good death'? Would it not be kinder to let them just slip away perhaps by a swift lethal injection? Here, medical science has an enormous burden of decision, for sometimes the 'assistance' the doctors give to an individual actually prolongs a human life way beyond the moment when that person would have been allowed to 'go' in nature. Every doctor knows this dilemma—when 'not to strive to keep officiously alive'.

HELPING OLD PEOPLE TO DIE

What about the old people who have become 'vegetables' and no longer enjoy a real existence? Why should they be obliged to spend the last months and years of their lives sitting helplessly and bleakly in a kind of twilight existence? Often they wish to die, for they have nothing left to live for, and all their friends have gone before.

Once again, should 'absence of medical care' be allowed? Many think that pneumonia (the 'old man's friend') really is a much easier way to die than to be repeatedly operated on and struggle on in great pain past the moment when that person would have died, if left to 'nature'. The whole business of when to give or not to give medical help is the dilemma faced by every doctor who is called upon daily to 'play God'. The doctor cannot avoid this situation—luckily for us, it is not usually something that ordinary people have to make decisions over.

MAKING DECISIONS—'ACTING GOD'

But humans do have to give permission for medical help; they do sometimes have to consider switching off a life-support machine; they do have to accept the knowledge that their elderly relative, or one with an incurable disease, may be given the label NTBR—'not to be resuscitated'.

All these matters are very emotive. It is one thing for someone to sit down and think the issues through coldly and logically, and quite another matter for a person to be requested to end a loved one's life, for whatever reason. We are all aware of harrowing cases reported in the media where distraught relatives have taken such decision-making upon themselves, usually for the most noble of motives, and have remained traumatised by it thereafter.

Herein lies one of the problems of abuse of the whole matter—it would be all too easy to legalise euthanasia for social reasons, resulting in the untimely deaths of all sorts of innocent people who might rather have stayed alive, in spite of their unhappy states. Unscrupulous people might cash in on the wealth and belongings of those they 'put to death'.

MUSLIMS REJECT EUTHANASIA

Muslims reject euthanasia, because the reason for the disability or suffering will be known to Allah, and 'mercy' killing does not usually allow the person concerned any choice in the matter. They are appalled by the idea that any person should be put to death out of social convenience.

Muslims regard every soul as being perfect, even though the body it has been born in may be damaged for some reason. They also believe that Allah has decided how long anyone is to live, so it is not the personal choice of the individual anyway. It is Allah alone who knows the reasons for our sufferings and our tests. These tests may indeed seem very unfair to us when we do not know the reasons—but Muslims believe that all will be revealed in due course, and that Allah is never unfair.

The notion of killing somebody in order to give them 'the right to die with dignity' are understandable but misguided. It is quite wrong to suggest that a person struggling with pain or illness lacks dignity; to speak of euthanasia is really a condemnation of a modern society that is unwilling to help adequately.

It is better to pray for strength and courage, and to try to develop inner peace, and accept that Allah will grant death to an individual when it is 'better' for him or her.

Umm Salamah recorded that the Messenger ﷺ said: 'If any Muslim who suffers some calamity says what Allah has commanded—'We belong to Allah and to Allah we shall return; O Allah, reward me for any affliction, give me something better in exchange for it'—then Allah *will* give something better in exchange: (Muslim 1999).

Anas recorded: 'None of you should wish for death for any calamity that befalls you, but should say: 'O Allah! Cause me to live so long as life is better for me; and cause me to die when death is better for me.' (Abu Dawud 3102, Bukhari 70.19.575).

A most important point to consider is that Islam teaches that when people bear their pains without losing faith, it is *not* pointless or useless and meaningless suffering, but *it will be counted for them towards the forgiveness of their sins.*

Umm al-Ala recorded that the Apostle ﷺ visited her when she was sick. He said: 'Be glad, Umm al-Ala, for Allah removes the sins of a Muslim for his (or her) illness, as fire removes the dross from gold and silver.' (Abu Dawud 3086).

Aishah recorded that she told the Apostle of Allah ﷺ that the most severe verse in the Qur'an was: 'If anyone does evil, he (or she) will be requited for it.' He said: 'But do you not know, Aishah, that when a believer is afflicted with a calamity or a thorn, it serves as an atonement for his (or her), evil deed.' (Abu Dawud 3087, Bukhari 70.1.544).

Abu Sa'id al-Khudri and Abu Hurayrah recorded: 'No fatigue, nor disease, nor sorrow, nor sadness, nor hurt, nor distress befall a Muslim, even if it were (as small as) the prick of a thorn, but Allah expiates some of his (or her) sins for it.' (Bukhari 70.1.545).

CAPITAL PUNISHMENT

Many of the standard practices of the times before Islam were not actually forbidden in the Qur'an, but were drastically curtailed; and their continuance only tolerated under certain stringent conditions.

Of these, the death penalty, slavery, polygamy and divorce are probably the most notable.

Prior to Islam, these four practices were widespread and carried out with scant regard for the circumstances of the poor and oppressed. Slavery, polygamy and divorce issues are dealt with elsewhere in this book (see pp. 82, 201 onward and 225 onward).

As regards the death penalty, it is perhaps worth commenting that a person could be hanged in the U.K. for a crime as trivial as stealing a loaf of bread, right into the twentieth century.

In Arabia, there was little sympathy for the thief, and at the same time raids—with opportunities to kill or be killed—were commonplace. The spilling of too much blood was curtailed by the system of tribal vengeance that could take life for life.

In desert conditions, it would often be impossible to locate and arrest murderers and bring them to justice. The awareness that some other innocent person from your tribe might be made to suffer or be killed because of you was an excellent deterrent to an honourable person. However, it is hardly fair on the victim, especially since not all people are honourable.

Allah, in the Qur'an, commanded a more equitable and merciful code of conduct.

> 'Do not take life except for just cause. If anyone is wrongfully killed, We give his heir the right to demand

retribution or to forgive; but let him not exceed bounds in the matter of taking life, for he is bound by the law.' (17:33)

'The law of equality is allowed for you in cases of murder' (2:178)

In Islam, there are two crimes which are considered 'just cause' for giving the death penalty, murder and openly attacking Islam in such a manner as to threaten it, having previously been a believing Muslim.

In the case of murder, the Prophet accepted the justice of taking a life for a life, although individuals are not allowed to take the law into their own hands by seeking revenge. The execution of a murderer can only be carried out after a proper legal trial.

In some societies, the death penalty can be pronounced if the accused person admits they are guilty publicly, four times before the court. This might be considered open to abuse if no-one knew the conditions that had led that person to make those confessions. On the other hand the confession might indicate the strong influence of conscience, and therefore be appreciated.

The Blessed Prophet ﷺ, however, was extremely reluctant to pass the death sentence on anybody.

When he did so, it was either in the case of someone being judged according to the existing law (based on the old Testament Book of Deuteronomy—as in the matter of the execution of the traitors of Khaybar), or it was the case that a Muslim sinner insisted himself or herself on the death penalty in order to face their Hereafter with a 'clean sheet.'

What the Qur'an and the Prophet's sunnah taught clearly was that mercy was always preferable in the sight of God. If a murderer was found guilty, the just penalty was death, but the preferred course of action was for the victim's family to forgive, if it was possible.★

The question of an ex-Muslim actively turning and attacking Islam was the grounds used by the Ayatollah Khomeini of Iran when he put money on the head of the apostate Muslim writer Salman Rushdie in 1989, and invited the people to take the law into their own hands. However, most of the world's Muslim scholars did not agree at all with this fatwa, and felt that the judgement of this writer was better left to the decision of Allah.

As for the suggestion that Muslims are condemned to death if they simply forsake the faith this is a nonsense. Sadly for Islam, multitudes of born Muslims *do* leave the faith, for some reason or another. Other pious Muslims leave the faith in the sense that they misunderstand it to such an extent that they even *reverse* its spirit. None of these are condemned to death, but left for the mercy of Allah and the hope that they might revert, so long as they still live on earth. No-one can be forced in the matter of faith. If a person loses faith, the believers who love them should try to support them with prayer and bring them back, and not seek to punish or enforce.

SLAVERY

Slavery is included in this section because slave-owners had the power of life and death over those they owned, and in any case, when a person became a slave their right to life was seriously affected.

★ We have had in 1997-98 media interest in three cases involving female murderers: the case of two nurses in Saudi Arabia, whose death sentence was commuted by payment to the victim's relative; a case of a pregnant woman in Chechenya, whose sentence was commuted by payment of 100 cows; and by comparison, the case of a woman in Texas, USA, who was convicted in 1983 and finally executed without mercy in 1998!

Although slavery was not abolished by the Qur'an as a direct command, it was stringently curtailed.

Slavery was shown to be wrong by both Qur'an and hadith, which demanded emancipation, benevolence, grace and ransom:

'Who will tell you what the ascent is? It is to free a slave.' (90:13)

'Feed with food the needy wretch, the orphan and the prisoner.' (76:8)

Sometimes people entered slavery by choice in order to pay off debts. Sometimes they were born as slaves in a household, and knew no other home. Frequently, slaves were prisoners of war.

The Qur'an made the freeing of slaves one of the main purposes of the zakah tax on a Muslim's money. To set people free was regarded as one of the highest and most noble acts of charity, and the Sunnah of the Prophet ﷺ and his companions was to free as many as they possibly could. Having been freed, many of those who had served in the Prophet's ﷺ household then refused to leave, and continued to work for him.

'I am the opponent of three people on the Day of Judgement... a person who takes an oath by Me and then betrays it, someone who sells a free person and denies him (or her) his due, and the one who hires a labourer, receives all that is required from that person, and then refuses to pay their wages.' (Hadith Qudsi)

'Visit the sick, feed the hungry, and release the suffering.' (Ibn Majah)

It is a fact that when the Blessed Prophet ﷺ married Juwayriyyah bint al-Harith of Banu'l-Mustaliq, a captive woman who would have been sold into slavery, the victorious Muslim army then felt they could not themselves enslave anyone from her tribe. After the battle of Badr, the Muslims accepted ransom for their captives and after the victory at Makkah the Prophet ﷺ said to the captives: 'Go, you have all been set free.' (Bukhari).

He said: 'Your slaves are your brothers over whom God has given you control. So, he who has a brother working for him should feed him from what he eats and clothe him from what he wears.' (Ahmad, Bukhari and Muslim)

There is a famous story of the Caliph Umar, one of the Blessed Prophet's ﷺ closest companions, entering Jerusalem on foot while his slave rode the camel.

Slaves were granted many rights in Islam, including the right to earn and save money, to marry, and—perhaps most significant for female slaves—not to be used for sexual purposes against their will. This was an enormous reform.

There is still debate over whether or not it was permissible for a Muslim man to take a concubine but the Qur'an makes it crystal clear that no Muslim human should have a sexual relationship outside marriage. A master was free to marry a Muslim slave-woman, 'those that his right hand possessed,' and in their cases to marry them and grant their freedom was counted in lieu of dowry to them.

Slavery has now been abolished legally throughout the civilised world, but that does not mean that the nature of certain people to be tyrannical, abusive, or unjust has been wiped out. Scandalous behaviour of both male and female employers towards the staff in their households and estates puts them well outside the spirit of Islam.

Women's Rights

Males and females are two halves of a whole. For centuries males had regarded themselves as superior because of their greater 'punch-power,' and because women were unable to exercise much control over the 'annual rite' of pregnancy and childbirth until the last half of this century. Allah's revelation brought that clear Reminder to those who were interested in justice that males and females are equal. This is the Divine Plan. All living animals were created 'in pairs' or 'zawaj'.

'Glory to Allah, who created in pairs all things that the earth produces.' (36:36)

'O humanity! We created you from a single pair of a male and a female.' (49:13; see also 35:11 and 49:13)

WOMEN IN THE FOREFRONT OF ISLAM

It should hardly need saying that men and women have equal spiritual worth in the sight of Allah, but please excuse this female author pointing out that some incorrigible males have the feeling of superiority as opposed to responsibility so ingrained into them (usually the fault of doting mothers and grandmothers who have spoiled them!) that they need this simple fact spelling out to them!

Every instruction given to Muslims in the Qur'an refers to both male and female believers! They have been given the same religious duties and will be judged according to exactly the same criteria. Women are expected to live and work actively alongside men, and should try to gain all the knowledge and skills which they will need to succeed.

> 'For Muslim men and women, for believing men and women... for men and women who are patient and constant, who humble themselves, who give in charity, who fast, who guard their chastity, who engage in the praise of Allah—for them Allah has prepared forgiveness and a great reward.' (33:35)

Islam is often accused of keeping its women in a subservient role, but whereas there are certainly abuses of women in some supposedly Islamic societies, truly Islamic women are by no means servile nor second-class citizens! There are several factors to consider. Firstly, a domestic life is not regarded by a Muslim woman as being subservient, but of vital importance to the well-being of her family. Most Muslims are educated in the first instance by their mothers.

Secondly, being a 'covered lady' out of devotion to Allah is accepted by Muslim women out of modesty and not because they see themselves as inferior. However, because of the emphasis in Islam on modesty, consideration and good manners within the culture of any society, it sometimes happens that practices or customs which purport to be Islamic are in fact customs and procedures from the culture that existed there before Islam. It is all too easy to mix up the natural culture of a people with the commands laid down in the Qur'an.

In many of these cultures the women are not encouraged to go out to work, or mix with any males who are not family members. They are expected to cover themselves up completely so that no strangers can see them, and so on. It is a very common misconception that these practices are

Islamic, when in fact they are not at all. (See woman scholars on p. 105-106).

THE RIGHT TO WORK

Muslim women have the right to be provided for, and their men should not force them to go out to earn money. However, there is no text which prohibits a woman from seeking work if she wants to, or specifies work that is 'permitted' or 'prohibited' to women simply because they are female. The restrictions are the same as for the men. (see pp. 110-113) The Prophet's wife Khadijah was herself a successful trader and business-woman, and Muhammad ﷺ was very glad when he was a young man to be employed by her, and later to encourage her and further her success. His later wives Umm Salamah and Zaynab also earned their own money throughout their lives.

At the same time it is quite wrong to 'look down on' the woman who chooses to put all her energies into creating a loving home environment, the housewife. Muslims cannot understand why some people regard work done outside the home as a 'career' while that done within the home is looked down on. Why should a woman who stays at home to cherish and care for her household be regarded as inferior to a woman who cooks in a restaurant for strangers? Being a housewife is as much a 'job' as any other—after all, she is 'on call' 24 hours a day, and a husband would be bankrupted if he had to pay her 'proper wages'. Allah does not 'look down on' those who choose to be housewives, but they are to be praised for their love and care.

Abdullah b. Amr b. al-As recorded the Prophet's ﷺ opinion: 'The whole world is a place of useful things, but the best thing of this world is a virtuous wife.' (Muslim)

It is a sad fact that when women go out to work they are often exploited by their male employers. Any employers claiming to be Muslim must remember that if they are exploiting their staff and keeping them barely above subsistence level, this is hardly in keeping with the spirit of Islam, or the Blessed Prophet's 變 teachings on the dignity and worth of any person who earns their own living.

Injustices done by males to females were commented on by the Blessed Prophet 變 in this way:

'Allah will definitely enforce the settlement of the dues of those entitled to recieve them on the Day of Judgement, even the wrong done to the hornless goat (i.e. female) by the horned goat (i.e. male) will be redressed!' (Muslim)

THE RIGHT TO BE PROTECTED

'Men are the protectors and maintainers of women, because God has given them more strength... therefore righteous women are devoutly obedient, and guard in the husband's absence what. God would have them guard.' (4:34)

Although women are equal to men, Allah points out the physical differences between the sexes, and makes thoughtful allowances in order to protect women and make them comfortable. A Muslim woman married to a Muslim man expects consideration because of her biology—men do not have to put up with menstruation, pregnancy, childbirth and suckling children. Men are not usually harassed because of their attractiveness, or forced to accept sex in order to 'get on', or not lose a job.

The fact that there are powerful urges of nature is not blindly ignored in Islam—but when a woman chooses to be Muslim she has the right to expect that Muslim men will see to it that she passes safely through the stages of being a protected virgin unmolested by strangers or by any male member of her own family, a beloved wife, a respected mother and a cherished grandmother. Moreover a truly Muslim society does not like to see a woman obliged against her inclination to live alone, or without protection or help, or a natural sexual relationship.

Allah urges each Muslim woman to go to her marriage untouched by any man, and to give herself to her chosen partner for life. In return, she has the right to be cared for at times of physical pain and discomfort, for example during her monthly periods, throughout pregnancy, and while rearing her children.

It is a world-wide problem that many men simply do not realise or have any sympathy for 'women's problems.' A good Muslim man remembers that the Prophet ﷺ urged those who wished to be 'the best of them' to be 'best to their families.' This does not just mean a man's parents and his children—it perhaps refers *most* to his care of his wife. In his Final Sermon, the Prophet ﷺ reminded Muslim men— 'Remember that you have taken them as your wives only under Allah's trust and with His permission.'

Husbands should know and understand what happens to female hormones before and during menstruation, pregnancy, and following childbirth, and realise that most of the moaning and groaning, tears and tantrums, fears and irrational behaviours, are caused by real pain, exhaustion and hormonal inbalance.

The hardest time for women is probably the last stages of pregnancy and the first six months after childbirth. In my own case, I swelled up from dress size 14 to size 24 (not counting the actual pregnancy!), and my weight shot up from 9 stones to 15 stones. I was covered in nasty purple stretch marks. My legs never recovered from dropsy-symptoms afterwards. My babies never seemed to sleep at night, and I could never snatch more than 3 hours without being woken. One was sickly for a long time, and I spent long hours doing laundry. Moreover, I had been cut during the delivery and my stitches did not heal properly.

If this sounds like a horror story, I'm sorry to tell male readers it is fairly normal, and nothing out of the ordinary.

Women going through similar experiences need a lot of support, nurturing and sympathy—not men who disappear at the sound of a tear, or who resent the fact that their pretty wives have perhaps turned fat or ugly, are always exhausted, and perhaps reluctant to re-establish physical intimacy.

These three key Islamic qualities become absolutely vital—compassion, patience and love.

THE RIGHT TO MODEST DRESS

A Muslim women has the right to be looked after by her husband and not be obliged to go out to work; but she also has the right to go out to work if she wishes. In the workplace, she hopes to get on with her career without sexual harassment in her employment, and she does her best to safeguard this hope by dressing modestly.

Zayd b. Talhah reported: 'Every religion has a characteristic, and the characteristic of Islam is modesty.' (Ibn Majah)

This should never be a matter of force or co-ercion. In societies where we observe the phenomenon of 'religious police' and harassment of non-Muslim women, or even Muslim women who are considered to be lax in their dress code, it is because the authority is trying in an over-zealous way to maintain values of purity in societies becoming increasingly corrupt. Any physical harassment, humiliation or compulsion is the opposite of the principles of Islam. Presumably it is a matter of community law. In fact, Muslim women out on the street or at business do not want to draw attention to themselves, but have made the decision to live a modest life. Therefore they will not dress in a flashy manner, and if they happen to catch a man's eye, they should not stare at him provocatively, but look away.

The question of what is and what is not Islamic dress has caused a good deal of controversy, through misinterpretation and over-zealousness. In fact, Muslim behaviour is far more important than Muslim dress! As regards the men, they should not attempt to see more of a women out in public than her face and hands. Any other sort of looking is immodest. As regards the women, one can often find a woman dressed according to a non-Muslim culture who nevertheless behaves with complete modesty; and one can find women who are completely veiled with only the eyes showing, but their eyes give a powerful sexual invitation. The Holy Qur'an says:

'We have given you clothing to conceal your modesty, and splendid garments; but that which is best is the raiment of restraint from evil.' (7:26)

'Say to believing men that they should lower their gaze and guard their modesty...and that believing women should lower their gaze and guard their modesty; that they should not display their ornaments except as is normal, that they should draw their veils over their bosoms and not display their beauty except to their close male relatives.' (24:30-31. The surah gives the precise list of these relatives).

The part of the female anatomy that should not be flaunted but covered, was so much not the hair but the *bosom*. The head-veils normally worn by women were decorative, and usually hung gracefully down her back and did not hide either hair or bosom. Another relevant passage is:

> 'Believing women should cast their outer garments over themselves when out: that is most convenient, that they should be recognised as such and not molested.' (33:59)

This reference was specific advice to women who lived in a culture where men felt free to cat-call and harass female passersby. It was positively unwise for a woman to go alone to places where she might be propositioned or even abused. Slave-women were particularly at risk. Allah's advice to women was to cover up, and make it clear that they were religious women and not interested in such encounters.

Although it is true that some men are 'turned on' by women trying to show they are inaccessible, on the whole most men of loose morals are attracted to those who make obvious display of their charms, and who *look* available.

Hijab (more properly called satr) indicates modesty in dress and behaviour. It does not prevent any woman from going out on business, or taking active part in society.

Muslim women in hijab usually cover their heads with some kind of scarf or veil, and cover their arms to the wrists and legs to the ankles, although the Quranic verses do not specifically demand this. There is no such thing as a single Islamic style for woman's dress—or for men's either. It is quite wrong to regard a shalwar-qameez as more Islamic than a long dress, for example; or an Iranian black chador as more Islamic than a shalwar-qameez. Some Muslim women seem to wish to adopt a kind of uniform, but this is neither required or necessary.

What modest women wear generally follows the tradition of acceptable modesty in their own cultural society, and the request of the Blessed Prophet ﷺ. 'A'ishah reported that when her sister Asma came to the Prophet ﷺ dressed in immodest clothing, he said to her:

'O Asma, when a girl reaches puberty it is not proper that anything on her should remain exposed except this and this.' And he pointed to her face (or head) and the palms of her hands.' (Abu Dawud)

Incidentally, although male scholars almost universally regard the first pointing as referring to her face, he could equally well have been pointing to her whole head, or for that matter, her nose or her chin! the real point is that her *body* should be completely and modestly covered.

The Qur'an verses do not specify the covering of the hair, but the 'veiling of the gaze' (for men as well as for women!), and the covering up of a woman's cleavage—the most convenient method being to put on an 'outer garment', be it a coat or veil.

At no stage did either Allah or His Messenger ﷺ require women to cover their *faces*. It is obvious from the hadiths that his female companions never did so. If a Muslim woman chooses to do this it is presumably out of modesty and not because she wishes to imitate the haughty veiled ladies of the non-Muslim societies of the Prophet's ﷺ time, who put veils on for reasons of pride and class distinction!

What is against the spirit of Islam is for any other person to try to *force* her to veil her face. There is no Islamic basis for this.

As regards covering her hair, this is a subject that has recently caused upset to many Muslim women, for all sorts of reasons.

In recent years some Muslim women have given up even wearing a head-scarf. Other Muslims feel that this is quite wrong, and the covering of the hair makes an important (and sometimes political and defiant) statement. To many women, the head-veil is one of the most important ways they have to publicly express their submission to Allah.

The Muslim ladies who do not wear a scarf argue that the point of Islamic dress is *modesty*, and that the detail of the head-scarf was only relevant as modest dress specifically in the culture and century in which the Blessed Prophet lived. They maintain that the vital quality to be maintained is the modesty, and not the piece of cloth, and just as millions of Muslim men have discarded the beard (which was also the Blessed Prophet's sunnah and recommendation, but similar to the head-veil, not compulsory) without jeopardising their eternal reward in any way, so the same attitude should apply to the ladies' head-scarf.

There will always be those who do more than is required, in any aspect of life and religion, just as there will always be those for whom the bare minimum is a struggle; the person who excels in one field may fail miserably in another. Some Muslims regard every Sunnah (recommendation) as fard (obligation) without accepting that there is a difference.

In the early days of Islam, Caliph Umar apparently punished some Muslim slave-girls who used to cover their hair in imitation of free-women. (Dr S.H. al-Darsh, *Hijab or Niqab*, Dar al-Dawa, London, 1997)

However, whatever their outdoor clothing practice, *all* Muslim women were required to always cover their heads *for prayer*. Aishah recorded: 'The Messenger of Allah said, 'Allah will not accept the prayer of a woman who has reached the age of puberty unless she covers her head.'

Aishah was quoted by Ibn Hanbal as saying that when she once stayed in the house of Safiyyah, she saw some girls praying there without covering their heads, and she told them they should not do so.

What is certain is that Muslim women *were* required by Allah to cover their *bodies* completely, and not to make display of their 'awrah' or 'ornaments'.

Unfortunately, this leads to some confusion, for there is actually considerable discussion as to what is meant by these 'ornaments'. One interpretation is that the verse should be taken literally, and was intended to discourage the kind of pride and arrogance that makes a woman desire to show off with expensive jewellery. This is certainly against the spirit of Islam although it seems to be traditional for a lot of Muslim women to wear excessive numbers of gold bracelets and rings, and so forth. Western women are often amazed to discover that all the necklaces, bracelets, rings and ear-rings of their eastern sisters are frequently solid gold!

Another interpretation of the verse is that a woman's 'ornaments' are not her flashy jewellery, but include any part of her that could be regarded as pleasing to a man—and therefore the extreme view is that she should cover her whole self up under an all-enveloping garment. In some countries, women will not even show their faces or even their eyes, but cover these as well—although this was not the practice of the Blessed Prophet's female companions, and causes a lot of unnecessary suffering when it is forced on women in very hot countries.

It certainly seems to be the case that some Muslims have become obsessed with the details of ladies' clothing, and miss

---

Some interesting cultural 'beautifications' carried out by ladies in the time of the Prophet ﷺ included tattooing their faces, plucking hairs from their faces (their eyebrows?) making spaces between their teeth, and wearing false hair. The Blessed Prophet ﷺ disapproved of all these false aids and practices, and regarded it as 'cheating.' (see Muslim 5301-5309).

entirely the point that Allah intended three things; that women should not be ostentatious in their wealth, immodest in the showing of their bodies or the way they walked and talked, or brazen sexually in their attitude to men.

It may well be the case that some Muslim women are less exacting than others in regard to the Blessed Prophet's sunnah on female dress; but men should not be too obsessed with this, and neglect other matters of the sunnah that apply to themselves. If they dislike something, or feel offended by it, it is their duty only to warn, and no more. A father has the duty to teach his daughter as best he can, but once women reach adulthood it is far more fitting that men examine their own lives and social morality to make sure they are not transgressing the sunnah themselves in some other respect. It is particularly important to emphasize this in a society where 'fundamental' Islamic Law has recently gained success, because there is a grave danger of over-zealousness leading to repression and cruelty. Some women wearing perfectly acceptable Islamic dress are punished by their religious authorities because it is not a particular style. This is a gross abuse of true Islam.

A Muslim woman's standards of behaviour and dress should never be from pressure of relatives, or the social norms of society, but simply because she herself has a desire to please Allah. In fact, in some countries some Muslim women wear hijab in spite of opposition from husbands, or secular governments, and can actually run into harassment and violence and abuse simply for wearing a headscarf.

MODESTY

The sorts of clothing which are not acceptable for Muslims are those which are not modest—they are too attention-seeking, either by being too revealing, or too tight or too short, and so on.

Muslim women are no more nor less ugly than other women, but they reject the urge to flaunt their attractions. They certainly do not wear clothes so revealing, low-cut, short, transparent or tight as to leave nothing to the imagination. To dress in such a way is to be regarded as 'naked' even though you are wearing clothes. The only object in dressing like that must be to stir up the passions of men, which is neither fair nor kind nor sensible. Muslim men should not be available for these tantalising women. They are expected to try to control their passions and desires, and remain faithful to their wives and families. Women who flaunt themselves and stir up trouble should therefore be avoided as far as possible, and certainly a Muslim man should never seek to be alone with such a woman.

Hazrat Umar reported: 'When any man meets a woman in solitude, then the third person is Satan.' (Tirmidhi)

Abu Hurayrah recorded that 'Modesty is part of faith and faith is in Paradise, but obscenity is part of hardness of heart and hardness of heart is Hell.' (Ahmad and Tirmidhi)

Muslim women are always very surprised to discover that sometimes people who do not understand Islam think that covered women are being regarded by their men as sex-objects, who cannot show even a piece of hair on the forehead or an ankle without attracting sexual attention from over-lusty men. All this really shows is how far a fixation on sexuality has warped male minds in the 'west.' The object of Muslim dress for women is always modesty. When they see the kind of clothing that reveals naked limbs, is transparent, or clings very suggestively to the female figure—they regard *that* as dressing like a sex-object, simply to attract the attention of men. If the man happens to be their own husband, one can see why they might get angry and disapproving of a tantalisingly clad female in the vicinity!

Some Muslims are so modest that they will never even dress or undress in front of their own husbands or wives, and dislike being seen naked even at intimate moments.

Muslim women expect to be appreciated for their characters and minds, and not just for their bodies. Modest dress does not degrade a woman, but the very opposite—it deprives the lustful male of a lot of free entertainment. Muslim women can be smart or colourful, and their styles vary according to the traditions of different countries—but they should never be indecent or vulgar. In fact, Muslim women regard Muslim dress as the very opposite of 'female repression'—it is really 'liberation'.

THE HAREM

Muslim houses usually have a public room where guests can be entertained without intruding on the privacy of the women. The rest of the house is the harem, the section which belongs exclusively to the family—wife, mother, children—and where outsiders should not intrude unless invited. It is related to the concept of 'haram' or 'forbidden'. It is not intended to be a place where wives are locked away, even though at certain times and places in history some so-called Muslims kept their concubines and mistresses in corrupt luxury. That sort of thing is totally different from the way a real Muslim behaves.

Muslim men who have more than one wife do not usually have them sharing the same living space if they can afford not to, unless the wives themselves wish it.

The notion of a man reclining on silken sheets enjoying the sexual attentions of four glamorous young women simultaneously, is an erotic fantasy, and has nothing to do with Islam.

In happy polygamous marriages, the wives usually regard themselves as sisters, and they normally have separate quarters for themselves and their children. If the wives are not respected and given equal treatment and resources, they may certainly seek redress and justice, if not divorce.

SUPPRESSION OF WOMEN IN ISLAM

It is a serious tragedy that there are several customs in supposedly Islamic societies which actually ignore, misinterpret or deny the rights given to women by Islamic Law, and it will take very brave Muslim women to get the situation put right. Five customs are particularly significant, and have caused many Muslim women untold suffering, deprivation, lack of fulfilment, and boredom.

First and foremost comes the practice of 'purdah' or the seclusion of women; secondly the attempt by some men to restrict or prevent women from going out, even to the Mosque. Thirdly, some very strict Muslims have tried to insist that the voice of a woman should be included amongst her 'awrah' or ornaments, and therefore be forbidden to a stranger. Fourthly sometimes daughters are being given in marriage without their consent. Last but not least, Muslim women in certain parts of the world are circumcised as children, sometimes in appalling conditions.

The first three of these restrictions were presumably based on the following Qur'anic passage—which was given specifically to the wives of Muhammad ﷺ. Devout Muslim ladies seek to follow their example, even though they were not given the command. It is a matter of choice and preference and not compulsion. In Islam, nothing should be done out of compulsion, only for love of Allah—a genuine love.

> 'O wives of the Prophet! You are not like ordinary women. If you fear Allah, don't be too casual in your speech, in case someone with an unsteadfast heart should be moved with desire... And stay quietly in your houses, and do not make a worldly display as in the times of ignorance; establish regular prayer and give regular charity, and obey Allah and His Apostle.' (33:32-33)

PURDAH

Contrary to public opinion, purdah is a practice of seclusion which has nothing to do with Islam, but was used extensively by Hindus, Persians, Byzantines and even some Christians, who did not allow their women equality. The word purdah is nowhere to be found in the Qur'an.

In certain parts of the world ladies hide their faces from strangers and yet are not devout Muslims, and elsewhere devout Muslim ladies do not veil because this would be regarded as odd, or attention-seeking—which defeats the whole object.

At the most holy moments of a Muslim woman's life— at the times of prayer, and when she is on Hajj—she is actually required to show her face to all, no matter what the usual custom is in her society.

Purdah usually involves making women live separate lives from men, and cuts them off completely from public view on the streets. It is often achieved by the wearing of a full-length black veil or chadar (as in Iran or Saudi Arabia) which also covers the face except the eyes. In the North-West Frontier Province of Pakistan the ladies often wear a 'shuttlecock burqa', a strange garment that completely covers them and just leaves a little mesh grid to peer through.

If a woman *wishes* to go about in purdah, that is all well and good. Where Muslim women are reluctant to talk to strangers, wearing a chadar gives complete privacy. They can get on with their business without being disturbed, flirted with, or made the object of unwanted attention. Since they cannot be recognised, they can ignore people they do not wish to meet or spend time with on the streets—even their own husbands!* (Of course, they are easily recognised if they wear an easily-recognisable burqa. For example, someone once gave me a gift of a burqa in purple silk).

Wearing a veil is supposed to mark a woman out as virtuous and modest, and not the type to welcome attention from male strangers who are not her business. Amongst family and friends, and in female company, the black veils come off! It is pointless to veil a woman who *does* seek attention.

True Muslim hijab is not like purdah—intended to segregate women from society—but allows women to play a full and active part in it without fear of sexual harassment or unfair treatment.

GOING OUT

The idea that Muslim women should be kept prisoner, or confined to their homes, is also quite wrong. The Quranic verse 'Stay in your homes and do not bedeck yourselves as in the days of ignorance' simply encourages pious women to concentrate on creating a warm and loving household rather than desiring to waste time 'hanging around on street corners' for no particular purpose.

---

* It has been known for men to wear burqas in order to avoid being known. One example in 1998 was a gunman who shot a man going into court in Karachi.

As with the question of dress, Muslim women take it for granted that the attraction between the sexes can be very strong, and that opportunity for deliberate arousal should be discouraged. Therefore, Muslim women out on the street or at business will always behave modestly, and if they catch a man's eye, they will look away and not encourage him.

Some critics of Islam point out that all this deliberate awareness of sexual attraction, put together with the deliberate suppression of it, might defeat the object by heightening the temptation—like someone on a diet longing for a creamy cake. Muslims reply by pointing out that a person who prays five times a day and remains consciously aware of Allah throughout the day is also aware of the need for self-control, and will not give in lightly to temptation.

One sensible recommendation made by the Prophet 🕌 was that if a man (or woman, presumably) was suddenly struck by a strong sexual urge for someone while out in public, he (or she) should hurry home and enjoy intimacy with his (or her) own partner and satisfy that urge honourably. (recorded by al-Ghazzali).

There are no instructions in the Qur'an or universally accepted sayings of the Prophet which restrict women from going out. Women were certainly not prevented from going to the mosque if they wished—it was normal practice. The hadiths give full support.

Ibn Masud reported one hadith that the Prophet 🕌 said about women, that 'it was more excellent to pray in the house than in the courtyard, and better to pray in the private chamber than in the house.' (Abu Dawud 570). This is the one hadith so frequently used to keep women out of the mosque in some chauvinistic male societies. However, the following hadith tones that down:

Ibn Umar recorded: 'Do not prevent women from visiting the mosques; but their houses are better for them (for praying).' (Abu Dawud 567, Muslim 884).

All the other hadiths make it crystal clear that in Madinah it was the *normal* practice for the wives of the Prophet and other female Muslims to attend the mosque regularly. A *vast number* of hadiths support this; it was even regarded as normal for the Prophet ﷺ to leave the pulpit while preaching and walk down to the women's rows when he wished to address them.

'A'ishah for example, recorded that she 'set out towards the mosque and observed prayer along with Allah's Messenger ﷺ; and I was in the row of women which was near the row of men.' (Muslim 7028)

Abu Hurayrah recorded: 'Do not prevent the maidservants of Allah from visiting His mosques; but they may go out having not perfumed themselves.' (Abu Dawud 565)

Abdullah ibn Umar reported: I heard Allah's Messenger ﷺ say: 'Don't prevent your women from going to the mosque when they seek your permission. Bilal b. Abdullah said: 'By Allah, we shall certainly prevent them!' On this, Abdullah b. Umar turned to him and reprimanded him so harshly as I have never heard him do before.' (Muslim 885). He said: 'I am saying that the Messenger of Allah ﷺ said this, and you say: 'We will not allow!' (Muslim 888, Abu Dawud 568)

Incidentally, in later years, after the Prophet's ﷺ death, 'A'ishah was not very impressed by the behaviour of some women. They did dress up, wore perfume and chatted to each other. She expected Muslim women who attended the mosque to have the same high standards as the men.

Amra, bint Abd al-Rahman reported that she said: 'If the Messenger of Allah had seen what new things the women have introduced, he would definitely have prevented them from going to the mosque.' (Muslim 895)

As for going out elsewhere, women took part in every aspect of life, even supporting their men on the battlefield!

Of the many warrior women named in the hadiths, two famous examples were Nusaybah bint Ka'b (Umm Umarah)— one of the first women to take the Pledge—and the Prophet's ﷺ aunt Umm Sulaym. Nusaybah was wounded by Ibn Qamiah when he tried to kill the Prophet ﷺ. The Prophet ﷺ said of her: 'To left and right, in whatever direction I turned, I saw Umm Umarah fighting in my defence.' (Seerah ibn Hisham, vol. 3, p. 29; Tabaqat Ibn Sa'd, vol. 8, p. 301). In the later battle of Yamamah she received twelve wounds and lost a hand. Many women companions did not fight, but went out with armies to support them, tend the wounded, and supply water.

WOMEN'S VOICES

The notion that it should be forbidden for a stranger to hear a woman's voice is a nonsense, an idea possibly created by persistent male over-enthusiasm for keeping their women out of the way! If it had been forbidden, then the warning given by Allah to the Prophet's wives in 33:32 would have been totally unnecessary.

Many male scholars of Islam received their knowledge from prominent women scholars, including especially 'Ai'shah! She certainly did not instruct them 'voice-lessly' so as not to sexually arouse them!

Urwah b. al-Zubayr recorded in Tashkirah al-Huffaz (vol. 1, p. 27) that he had not seen a greater scholar than 'A'ishah in the learning of the Qur'an, fard duties, halal and haram matters, poetry and literature, Arab history and genealogy. Many scholars and sahaba came to consult her on matters ranging from checking the hadith to medicine and matters of law, especially inheritance (Mustadrak, vol. 4, p. 11).

Many of the other wives of the Blessed Prophet ﷺ were also consulted, and many of the female sahaba were scholars. There is the famous incident of a woman publicly rebuking Caliph Umar in the mosque on a point of Shari'ah in which he had erred. Instead of shutting her up, he praised her and exclaimed: 'Umar is proud of the women of Madinah who are learned enough to guide even the Caliph!'

Examples include Amra bint Abd al-Rahman. Her narrations had so much importance in the sight of Umar b. Abdul Aziz that he ordered Abu Bakr b. Muhammad b. Hazm to write them down. Scholars of the fame of Imam Zuhri and Yahya ibn Sa'id went to her for knowledge.

The famous jurist Qasim b. Muhammad once said to Imam Zuhri: 'Shall I point out to you one who is full of knowledge?' Zuhri said: 'Yes, certainly.' He said: 'Go into the assembly of Amra bint Abd al-Rahman and don't leave it, for she was nourished and educated by 'A'ishah. Zuhri said that on his recommendation he went to her assemblies, and found that she really was a 'boundless ocean of knowledge' (Tadhkirat al-Huffaz, vol. 1, p. 106).

The Prophet's ﷺ wife Umm Salamah was not only famed herself for her knowledge and intelligence, but so were her daughter Zaynab and her maidservant Umm al-Hasan.

Abu Rafai Sa'i said: 'Whenever I speak of the women jurists of Madinah, at once Zaynab bint Abu Salamah comes to my mind' (Al-Isaba fi Tamyiz al-Sahabah, vol. 4, p. 317). Umm al-Hasan regularly did the work of da'wah and preaching (Ibn Sa'd, Tabaqat, vol. 8, p. 350. See also 'Role of Muslim Woman in Society'—Afzular Rahman, Seerah Foundation, London, 1986 for many more examples).

The circle of Aishah bint Sa'd ibn Waqqas included Imam Malik, Ayyub Sukhtiyani and Hakim b. Utaybah (Tahdhib al-Tahdhib, vol. 12, p. 436). Imam Shafi'i sought knowledge from Sayyidah Nafisah, the Prophet's ﷺ great grand-daughter (Wafayat al-A'yan of Ibn Khallikan, vol. 2, p. 129). Incidentally, it is a fact that Nafisah actually led his funeral prayer.

FORCED MARRIAGES

It is quite contrary to the practice of Islam for a father to force his daughter into a marriage arrangement she does not want. In Islam a marriage is null and void if the free consent of both parties is not given. It is unfortunately obvious from various reports that this Islamic freedom is still frequently abused by supposedly Muslim men, and that forced marriages do sometimes take place.

Everyone understands parents trying to make the best possible arrangements for their children, but marriage is a very serious business. Forced marriages are nothing to do with Islam, and parents claiming to be good Muslims should bear this in mind, and realise that such a marriage is not valid.

Abu Hurayrah reported: 'A woman without a husband must not be married until she is consulted, and a virgin must not be married until her permission is sought.' (Muslim 3303). 'Ai'shah added that her permission was necessary even if the marriage had been arranged by some guardian responsible for her. (Muslim 3305)

Once a virgin girl came to the Prophet ﷺ and said that her father had married her to a man against her wishes and without her consent. The Prophet ﷺ instantly gave her the right to repudiate the marriage if she chose. The girl then chose to stay with her husband, saying that she was satisfied, but stressed that she had wished to make the point about it. (Abu Dawud)

FEMALE CIRCUMCISION

Female circumcision is one of the practices originating in the times of jahiliyyah that, like slavery, polygamy and the death sentence, was not banned outright. Unfortunately for Muslim women in a few parts of the world, the tradition there recommends the practice as a part of Islam. In some places the clitoris is completely removed and the labia cut away (sometimes in horrendous conditions by people with no medical qualifications and unhygienic equipment— resulting in infection and death) leaving the child only a tiny opening for later menstruation, and in need of further surgery for childbirth to proceed.

This has *nothing to do with Islam* and is not circumcision but genital mutilation. It is totally haram. Allah created parts of the female body whose only purpose is to grant sexual satisfaction for a wife. To remove the clitoris is as traumatic as the removal of the penis would be for the man. He might enjoy something of a sex life afterwards, but it would hardly be what most men would wish.

The whole issue of female circumcision arises out of three things: firstly, the fact that circumcision for *men* is recommended, and has been a part of Allah's revelation since the time of the Prophet Ibrahim ﷺ. It was recommended to be done by the eighth day of a male child's life, if the baby was healthy. This is not the removal of or damage to the penis, but the removal of the *foreskin* of the penis. It does bring health benefits to the male, even though hadiths suggest that in the Afterlife they will be restored to their uncircumcised state.

Secondly, there is one hadith that when the Prophet ﷺ was asked concerning ritual ablution after intimate sexual relations, he replied that it became necessary 'when the circumcised part of the male penetrated the circumcised part of the female.' We can deduce from this that women in the Prophet's ﷺ time were circumcised. (We also conclude, incidentally, that if the male ejaculated without penetrating his spouse, she was not made ritually unclean by this, but simply washed his sperm off her body as she would wash it off her clothing or the bedding).

Thirdly, it is known that the Prophet's ﷺ companion Umm Atiyyah used to perform this operation on female babies and infants. However, the Prophet's ﷺ hadith to her was not to command or encourage, but to *restrict* the practice. 'When you carry out this circumcision do not cut too much; that gives the best fortune to the woman, and is desirable to the husband.'

The statement indicates only permission, not an obligation, and the woman's sexuality was to be protected by not touching her clitoris at all but only any overlapping skin if she had any, just as in male circumcision it is only the overlapping skin and not the head of the penis itself that is cut.

The idea that intercourse is hindered if a woman has a large clitoris is nonsense. (It may be that it could be hindered if a male penis was too large, and the male concerned did not take the steps necessary to relax and enthuse his wife before 'leaping on her like an animal').

Anyone who has witnessed the results of female genital mutilation—both physical and in mental trauma and marital frigidity—could not possibly defend this as being any part of Islam.

If one is talking about the practice of proper surgical removal of any minute piece of overlapping skin that might cover a woman's clitoris (which might presumably bring the same health benefits as male circumcision, and would perhaps facilitate her marital enjoyment in that she would be able to come to climax more quickly and thus reduce the strain on a husband of 'limited performance'), then of the classical scholars Ibn Hanbal and Shafi'i held it to be an obligation; the majority of scholars in the Hanafi, Maliki and Hanbali tradition believed it to be lawful and desirable; and the others that it was allowed but not obligatory.

The object of this would not be to limit or destroy the female libido, but to increase it, and it would give her *more* satisfaction from the sexual relationship, not less.

The modern round of arguments about female circumcision are not referring to this, but to horrendous female mutilation and this is indeed what happens in unsupervised, primitive circumstances in Egypt and the Sudan. This mutilation is not Islam, and is a gross abuse perpetrated on these unfortunate baby girl Muslims.

If any adult woman wishes to have such an operation, that is her right and a matter for her to decide herself.

It is a tragedy and an embarrassment for true Islam that so many Muslim women married to Egyptian or Sudanese men dare not risk allowing their female children to visit those countries lest they are seized and operated on by their misguided relatives.

Work and Wealth

Just as each individual Muslim man and woman strives to live in as noble and selfless way as is possible, so the economic principles of Islam aim to build up a just society in which all people behave responsibly and honestly, and none are just out to grab all they can for themselves. All dishonesty, greed and exploitation was to be spurned by those who worked only to serve Allah.

Hakim ibn Hizam recorded: 'Riches are sweet, and a source of blessing to those who acquire them by the way; but those who seek them out of greed are like people who eat but are never full.' (Bukhari)

Muslims were to strive to be independent, energetic, thrifty and conscientious. Al-Miqdam ibn Madikarib recorded: 'No-one eats better food than that which they have earned by their own labours, and (even) David the Prophet of God used to eat from what he himself had made.' (Bukhari)

Living idle lives in the lap of luxury while others toil is not approved in Islam.

THE ROLES OF MEN AND WOMEN

There is no ruling in Islam to prevent women from going out to work, but in most Islamic societies it is still the responsibility of the men. Women are expected to take charge of the home, and accept the responsibility of providing food for the hungry, refuge for the weary, hospitality for the guest, comfort for the distressed, peace for the troubled, hope for the insecure and encouragement for the weak—basically all the things it means to be a Mother.

The man's role is generally to be the leader of the 'team', and to provide by his toil and effort the means whereby all the above things can actually be achieved. His job is to protect the home, and generally make the mother's role possible.

Since it is generally the men who are responsible in most Muslim societies for bringing in the money, it is therefore their duty, so far as is possible, to be strong, respected and honourable.

Just as the woman's role involves far more than just cooking and cleaning, so the man's involves far more than just following orders and making money. It also includes leadership, responsibility and duty, and an involvement in the world of economics, business, trade and commerce.*

However, the rules and responsibilities regarding the world of work outside the home are not just limited to men.

It must be made clear that in this day and age it is becoming more and more commonplace for women to be the breadwinners and providers for their families. Sometimes the menfolk move away for long stretches of time leaving the women to cope alone. The underpaid or unpaid labour of millions of women on the land feeds half the world. (In Africa, 70% of the food is grown by women; in Asia the figure is 50-60%). A United Nations report estimated that between 30-50% of all households in Africa, the Caribbean and Latin

---

* Where women take on this kind of role, they too must accept the duties and responsibilities.

America depended on women as their main provider. In some societies the employment situation favours giving jobs to women because they can exploit them—they pay women less wages for doing the same work, and therefore make more profit if they employ women. In the West it is almost unusual, these days, to find 'ordinary' men able to support a housewife at home; most homes require the earning power of both husband and wife.

FORBIDDEN WORK

Muslims are not permitted just to earn money in any way they can. Islam makes a difference between what it accepts as lawful and unlawful methods of earning a living. This does not refer to breaking the laws of the land, but the laws of Allah.

Abu Bakr reported: 'No body which has been nourished with what is unlawful shall enter Paradise.' (Ahmad, Darmi and Bayhaqi)

Basically, the Islamic rule is that if someone's means of earning a living hurts another, or results in another's loss, it is haram. If it is fair and beneficial, then it is halal. Obviously, any form of making wealth that involves dishonesty, falsehood, cheating, deceit or fraud; bribery; robbery or burglary; hoarding in order to take advantage of hardship later; exploitation; artificial creation of shortages; anything to do with alcohol, gambling or lotteries; sexual degradation or any immoral practices, or any other means of making profit by exploiting others, is forbidden to the Muslim.

'O believers! Make not unlawful the good things which Allah has made lawful to you (e.g. money). Commit no excess; for Allah does not love those given to excess.' (5:90)

Forbidden professions include:

- any form of activity deriving money from prostitution, pornography, indecency
- any form of drama or dance entertainment that is deliberately erotic or suggestive
- drawing, painting or photography that is sexually provocative
- manufacturing intoxicants and drugs other than medicine, or trading in them
- working in any organisation supporting injustice
- working in a bar, liquor shop, nightclub, dance-hall etc.
- being involved in armed forces fighting against Muslims

Amr ibn Auf recorded: 'It is not poverty which I fear for you, but that you might begin to desire the world as others before you desired it, and it might destroy you as it destroyed them.' (Bukhari and Muslim)

The Prophet ﷺ was most emphatic that people who made a living unlawfully or against the spirit of Islam would gain no benefit from Allah from their religious practices. Their bad livelihood would cancel out any benefits.

Abu Umar reported: 'If anyone buys a garment which is unlawfully acquired, Allah will not accept prayer from him so long as he wears it.' (Bukhari)

This would most certainly apply to anyone knowingly being in receipt of stolen goods, but it also applies to people who make gain out of exploitation, greed, and general dishonesty or unfair dealing.

Abu Hurayrah reported: 'People make long prayers to Allah although their food and their clothes are illegal. How can the prayer of such people be accepted?' (Muslim and Tirmidhi)

A Muslim working in agriculture should not be involved with harmful or forbidden crops such as hashish, or the farming of opium for the illegal market. Tobacco-growing is doubtful; the strictest Muslims regard it as makruh, since it is harmful to the human body, and they would therefore not recommend seeking employment in any part of the cigarette-making industry. (See p. 250).

It is never a valid excuse for a Muslim to argue that the crop is for the use of non-Muslims only. For example, a Muslim may not raise pigs in order to sell them to Christians. It is not lawful for them to sell grapes to others if they know they will be used in wine-making.

Abu Umamah recorded: 'Leave alone what puts you in doubt.' Turn toward what does not put you in doubt.' (Ahmad, Tirmidhi, Nisai, al Hakim and Ibn Hibban).

BEING TRUSTWORTHY

Muslims bear in mind that whatever they do, it is known to Allah, and they will be held to account for it on the Day of Judgement. They will therefore strive to be honest, decent, truthful, and trustworthy.

'He who cheats Muslims is not one of us.' (Muslim)

Moreover, it is patently not all right to interpret this as referring only to other Muslims—as if it was perfectly in order to cheat non-Muslims! Trustworthiness in all things is vital.

The Qur'an gives the story of why Moses' wife sought him for her husband, and not any other man. She said:—'O my father, employ him; truly the best one for you to employ is the strong and trustworthy one!' (28:26).

An excellent example of trustworthiness was that of Abdallah ibn Mas'ud of Zuhra. He was once pasturing his master's flocks when the Prophet ﷺ and Abu Bakr passed by and asked for a drink. Abdallah refused them, because the ewes were not his own, but entrusted to his care. This faithful shepherd became one of the best and most authoritative reciters of Qur'an.

Employed people have a duty to their employers, as well as to the families they are supporting, so they will not cheat on hours for which payment is claimed, or be lazy, or encourage any practices in their workplace which cheats the employer in some way.

Muslims are also trusted not to waste money irresponsibly, carelessly frittering it away. Extravagance and waste are strongly discouraged.

THE IMPORTANCE OF WORK

It is considered very important that a person *does* work, and does not stay idle. Anyone who tries to avoid work for whatever reason (unless they are incapable through illness) is disapproved of—even if the purpose is supposed to be the devotion of one's self to religion. It is the duty of a Muslim man to earn sufficient money for his own and his family's needs, so that he is a not burden to anyone. Muslims consider it dishonourable to be a parasite!

Abdullah b. Masud recorded: 'To try to earn a lawful livelihood is an obligation like the other obligations (in Islam).' (Bayhaqi)

Abu Sayd recorded: 'Accepting charity is forbidden for the rich except for what comes as a reward of jihad, or what a neighbour gives you from sadaqah or entertainment at a feast.' (Abu Dawud 1633)

Anas b. Malik recorded: 'Once a man came begging from the Prophet ﷺ. He asked him: 'Have you nothing in your house?' He replied: 'Yes, a piece of cloth a part of which we wear and a part which we spread on the ground, and a wooden bowl from which we drink water.' He said: 'Bring them to me.' He then took them in his hand and asked: 'Who will buy these?' A man agreed to buy them for one dirham. Then the Prophet 🕮 said two or three times: 'Who will offer more than one dirham? He sold them for two dirhams and gave them to the man and said: 'Buy food with one of them and give it to your family, and buy an axe and bring it to me.' He then brought it to him. The Apostle 🕮 fixed a handle on it with his own hand, and said: 'Go and gather firewood, and sell it, and do not let me see you for a fortnight.' The man went away and did so. When he had earned ten dirhams he bought a garment with some and food with some. The Apostle 🕮 then said: 'This is better for you than that begging should mark your face on the Day of Judgement.' (Abu Dawud 1637, Bukhari and Ibn Majah)

Abdullah ibn Umar recorded: 'The upper hand is better than the lower one.' (Abu Dawud 1644)—the upper being the one that gives, and the lower the one which takes.

It is thought dishonourable for a Muslim to beg, except in cases of extreme necessity. Muslims are expected to safeguard their dignity, develop self-reliance and not have to depend on others unless it is absolutely necessary.

Sumarah recorded: 'Acts of begging are lacerations on a person's face.' (Abu Dawud 1635)

It has become 'fashionable' and convenient for some mosques to support full-time Imams, but whereas this is accepted, it is not really preferred. There is a danger of Muslim men so elevated starting to regard themselves as 'priests'—those who interceded to God on behalf of 'ordinary' people, and offered the sacrifices for them. This is one aspect of Shi'ite

Islam most disapproved by Sunni Muslims. Western media often mistakenly refer to Imams as 'priests,' without realising the theological significance of this. Imams are prayer-leaders and preferably persons of knowledge. In a thriving Muslim community there should be many people able to function as Imams, and thus avoid dependence on one person. Any scholar of Islam should be able to contribute their knowledge without being paid, although obviously any man giving full-time service is entitled to proper remuneration.

'Some people once came to the Prophet ﷺ in the company of a hermit—a religious recluse. The Prophet ﷺ said: 'Who is he?' They said: 'He is a man who has devoted himself to worship.' The Prophet ﷺ said: 'Who feeds him?' They said 'We all do.' He said: 'Then all of you are better than he is.' (Bukhari and Muslim)

On the other hand, whatever work one does for anybody else (providing it is lawful in Islamic terms), it is as if it is done for Allah.

'The Prophet's ﷺ companions once noticed a man's fortitude and perseverance at work and said: 'O Messenger of God—this man would be really wonderful if only his actions were for the cause of Allah.' The Prophet ﷺ said: 'If he goes to work to support his young children, his old parents, or (even) for the satisfaction of his own needs, (then) all his work *is* regarded as a struggle in the cause of Allah. But if he goes to work in order to boast and be proud, it is in the cause of the Devil.' (Bukhari)

TIMES OF NEED AND RIBA

Sometimes, inevitably, there do come situations and times of great need. Disasters, national and private, do occur. People need help with housing or in business. They cannot be blamed if they are forced to ask for help from the government or from an individual. Qabisa b. Mukhariq al-Hilali recorded that the Blessed Prophet ﷺ said to him: 'A man whose property has been destroyed by a calamity that has befallen him is permitted to beg until he gets what will support him.' (Muslim 2271).

Anas b. Malik recorded: 'Begging is permissible for three sorts of people only: one who is in grinding poverty, one who is seriously in debt, or one who is responsible for a debt and finds it difficult to pay.' (Abu Dawud 1637)

Muslims are allowed to make money from fair trade, but not from exploiting the needy. A rich person lending money at interest usually gets the unfortunate borrower deeper and deeper into debt.

Making any interest on loaned money is regarded as a despicable act capitalising on another person's misfortune or need, and is totally forbidden by the Qur'an.

> 'Allah has permitted trade but forbidden usury; those who after receiving direction from their Lord cease the practice shall be pardoned for the past; their case is for Allah to judge. But those who repeat the offence are companions of the fire... ..Allah will deprive usury of all blessing, but He will give increase for deeds of charity, for He does not love wicked and ungrateful creatures.' (2:278-9)

Muslims with wealth are requested to help the needy by tending them what they need without interest.★

> 'That which you lay out for increase through the property of others will have no increase with Allah; but that which you lay out for charity, seeking the Countenance of Allah, (will increase); it is these who will get a multiplied recompense!' (30:39. See also 3:130 etc.)

★   Allah's earlier revelations to Jews and Christians are recorded in Exodus 22:25; Leviticus 25:36-7, and St. Luke 6:34-5.

Abd Allah b. Masud recorded: 'Cursed be the one who accepts usury, the one who paid it, the witness to it, and the one who recorded it.' (Abu Dawud 3327)

Riba, the Arabic term for usury, means not only interest in banking systems, but any unjustified advantage in trade dealings, and has therefore a wider meaning than the English term 'interest'. To be honourable, money has to be used as a facility not a commodity in Islam, or the owners of money gain an unfair advantage over the producers or traders. For example, it would be wrong to wait until merchandise loses value (for example, fruit will only stay fresh for a limited time) and thereby force the merchant to agree to a lower price.

It is also wrong for other commodities to be bought up by those who have the money to afford them, and then hoarded away until they increase in value to take advantage of the 'hard times of others.'

'One who hoards and withholds food for forty days removes himself from the mercy of Allah and has no connection with Him.' (Ahmad ibn Hanbal)

This kind of speculation on the hardship of others is forbidden in Islam; all sources of possible wealth should be in circulation and being used, and not hoarded away for the private benefit of a few.

> 'There are those who bury gold and silver and spend it not in the way of Allah; announce to them a most grievous penalty! On the Day when heat will be produced out of that wealth in the fire of Hell, their foreheads, their flanks and their backs will be branded with it—'This is the treasure which you buried for yourselves!' (9:34-35)

Abdullah ibn Hamzala reported: 'A dirham which a person knowingly receives in usury is more serious a crime than acts of fornication.' (Ahmad and Darqutni)

Abu Hurayrah recorded that the Prophet said it was worse than having intercourse with your own mother. (Ibn Majah)

To regulate this, Islam imposes a tax on all money which is not spent in circulation.

Charging interest forces others into debt and dependency. In Islam speculation and exploitation is intended to be removed, as providers of funds can only share profits provided they are also willing to share the losses.

'If a debtor is in difficulty, give time in which to repay. If you could only accept it—it would be far better if you cancelled the debt altogether.' (2:280)

One of the chief dangers of banks is that those who wish to borrow money for whatever reason usually end up paying enormous sums of interest as well as repaying the loan.

Banks are a business, not a charity. They make their income from the money they loan out. Hence, they sometimes entice people into borrowing money which is going to trap them in debts, sometimes for years or a lifetime.

If the money was borrowed for a business venture that went wrong, a borrower is still saddled with the debt to the bank until all is paid off. Islamic banking should use systems which incorporate the principle of equality of risk. The risks and rewards must be shared between borrower, bank and depositor. In other words, in the unfortunate case of a person borrowing a business loan, if the business failed the bank would be expected to share the risk and the loss, and not just the borrower.

Muslim banks, of course, should not finance any goods or schemes which are themselves forbidden in Islam.

THE DIGNITY OF WORK

The Prophet taught that there was no room in Islam for snobbery. There was no disgrace or humiliation in doing any menial work, or work that was 'looked down on' by those better off—the only shame was in depending on other people for help when you could be helping yourself. The man who acted as a simple porter had as much dignity and worth in the eyes of Allah as the manager of a great business concern. What counts is his dignity, his honesty, and his attitude to the work he is doing.

Since communities need rubbish-collectors just as much as brain-surgeons, nobody need regard any useful employment as being beneath them—David was a metal worker, Noah and Jesus were carpenters, Moses was a shepherd, and Muhammad was a market-trader. Islam gave dignity to many professions which people had previously considered lowly and degrading.

Abu Hurayrah recorded that Muhammad ﷺ once said: 'Allah did not send a prophet without his having tended sheep'. They asked, 'You too, O Messenger of Allah?' He replied, 'Yes, I tended sheep for wages for the people of Makkah.' (Bukhari)

Al-Miqdam ibn Madikarib reported: 'Allah's Prophet Dawud used to eat from what he had worked for with his own hands.' (Bukhari).

The only shame is in depending on other people for help when there is no necessity. So long as a Muslim can be usefully employed, any work or profession or employment is to be commended—so long as it does not involve doing, supporting or propagating anything haram or unlawful in the eyes of Allah.

Abu Hurayrah recorded: 'It is better that a person should take a rope and bring a bundle of wood on his back to sell and be independent of people, than that he should beg from people, whether they give him anything or refuse him. Truly the upper hand is better than the lower hand.' (Muslim 2267)

'Little but sufficient is better than the abundant and alluring.' (Bukhari)

Thauban recorded: 'If anyone guarantees me that he will not beg from people, I will guarantee him Paradise.' (Abu Dawud and Nasai)

COLLECTIVE OBLIGATIONS

Muslims have a duty to develop crafts and industries which are essential and beneficial to the community. Such professions are known as fard kifiyah, or 'collective obligations.' Every Muslim community should try to include enough people engaged in essential sciences and industries to meet its needs.

These areas include:

- ◆ medicine, midwifery,
- ◆ education,
- ◆ science, mathematics and technology,
- ◆ politics, community welfare and leadership,
- ◆ waste disposal,
- ◆ clothing industries,
- ◆ utensil industries,
- ◆ agricultural industries,
- ◆ drainage and waterworks,
- ◆ proper and decent disposal of the dead.

If there is a shortage of personnel, the whole community is held at fault, for it has a duty to see to it that the needs of the people are met, and that nobody suffers.

All productive resources should be brought into use as far as possible, and not left idle or allowed to go to waste. These resources include unemployed manpower, unused land, water or mineral resources.

Individual freedom may have to be sacrificed if it interferes with the good of the community—the people as a whole must come before any private interest or individual's profits! Corrupt and harmful pursuits should be rooted out as far as possible, even if they are highly profitable and are run by powerful 'trade barons.'

On the other hand, Allah will reward the rich merchants and business-people who look after their communities.

> 'The parable of those who spend their wealth in the way of Allah is that of a grain of corn. It grows seven ears, and each ear has one hundred grains. Allah gives enormous increase to whom He will; He cares for all and He knows all.' (2:261)

TRADE AND COMMERCE

Trading is regarded as acceptable employment, providing it is done honestly, and does not exploit anyone. Muslims are not allowed to hoard substances at times of glut in order to make a big profit in times of shortage.

> 'Let not those who covetously withhold the gifts* which Allah has given them of His grace think that it will do them any good; no, it will be the worse for them! Soon shall the

---

* Remember, also, that a person's 'gifts' also includes their talents and skills. These should all be used as far as possible for the good of others, and not wasted or left idle.'

things which they covetously withheld be tied to their necks like a twisted collar!' (3:180)

Umar ibn al-Khattab recorded: 'He who brings goods for sale is blessed with good fortune, but he who keeps them until the price rises is accursed.' (Ibn Majh, Darimi)

Any form of cheating or unfair trading is dishonourable. This includes such things as lying about merchandise or tampering with weights and measures in order to cheat people.

It is just as wrong to 'water the milk' or to have 'weighing stones' which are inaccurate at a road-side pitch, as it is to lie about the carat-value of the gold being sold to a rich tourist in the bazaar. In all these cases, the person buying the goods is at the mercy of the seller and has to take what they say on trust. A Muslim seller should not cheat.

'Give measure and weight with full justice.' (6:152)

'Give just measure and weight, nor withhold from the people things that are their due; and do no mischief on the Earth.' (7:85)

Since the motivating force behind so much trade and business is greed and profit-making, an 'honest broker' is to be treasured and commended. The Prophet himself ﷺ spent much time as an honest merchant, and reckoned that trustworthy merchants who did not take the opportunities they had for cheating people were equal in value to martyrs for the faith!

'An honest and trustworthy merchant will rise up with the prophets, the righteous and the martyrs.' (Tirmidhi and Ibn Majah)

Those who practice dishonesty should heed this warning: 'On the Day of Resurrection Allah will not look at...the person who swears to the truth while lying about his merchandise.'* (Muslim)

KIND EMPLOYERS

In Islam, those who are employers have enormous responsibilities to treat their employees with justice and kindness, and should give them their due without delay and without cheating or exploiting them.

'Give the worker his wages before his sweat dries up.' (Ibn Majah)

It is so easy to exploit people who are desperately in need of work and cannot risk losing their job. Muslim employers should never 'stick their noses in the air' and be arrogant. Don't forget that value in the eyes of Allah does not rest in one's exalted position in humanity, but on one's spiritual work. The humblest sweeper or weaver may be a far greater 'saint' than the wealthy factory-owner or politician.

The noble employer does not exploit or despise, but cares for his or her employees. The Muslim employer has nothing to do with sexual harassment or any form of intimidation.

Workers should be protected adequately from danger in the workplace, and offered sufficient care and attention while working. Exploiting the weak, or making them work long hours to exhaustion in appalling conditions, with no opportunity to take rest or refreshment, and little pay at the end of it, is not the way of Allah.

The Prophet ﷺ said: 'Give your body its due.' (Bukhari)

'An employer should not ask an employee to do anything beyond his (or her) capacity. If that which the

---

* For exploitation in trade dealings see 2:274-5; 3:130; 4:161.

master demands is necessary the master himself should lend a helping hand to the servant.' (Bukhari)

THE WARNING ABOUT THE TEST OF WEALTH

Finally, let the rich Muslim nations of the world who have received abundance in this century because of the oil boom remember the hadith reported by Kab ibn Anayaz:

'For every nation and Ummah there is a temptation or test, and the test for My Ummah is wealth.' (Tirmidhi)

After all, as Abu Hurayrah recorded: 'Richness does not lie in an abundance of worldly goods, but true richness is the richness of the soul.' (Muslim 2287)

In an Islamic state, there should be a Bait-al-Mal, or Ministry of Finance, to help workers earn a decent living without undue hardship.

Muslim millionares have an enormous responsibility, for the eyes of the world's media are on them to see if they behave any differently from corrupt and selfish non-Muslim millionaries. Hypocrisy in high places has never been more open to scrutiny and criticism than it is today.

Any Muslim with wealth has to make room at the table for the famous hadith:

'The one who eats and drinks while the neighbour goes hungry, is not one of us.' (Bayhaqi)

The Duty to Give

A life of charity and righteousness is the only source of true and lasting happiness in this world and the next. Two of the hallmarks of Muslims should be their generosity and their care for others. Clinging selfishly to your wealth will get you nowhere in the eyes of Allah.

Anas b. Malik recorded: 'Even if non-believers possessed all the gold in the earth, they could not buy their price in the Hereafter with it. The true 'ransom' is belief in the Oneness of Allah.' (Muslim 6733-36)

One of the most well-known passages in the Qur'an, that defines the concept of true righteousness for a Muslim, places practical care of others second only to belief in Allah, and in fact mentions it before the fundamental duty of prayer!

> 'It is not righteousness to turn your faces towards East or West; but this is righteousness—to believe in Allah, and the Last Day, and the angels, and the Book, and the messengers; to spend of your substance out of love for Him, for your family, for orphans, for the needy, for the wayfarer, for those who ask, and for the ransom of slaves; to be steadfast in prayer and practice regular charity; to fulfil the promises which you have made; and to be firm and patient in pain and adversity and throughout all periods of panic. Such are the people of truth, those who are conscious of Allah.' (2:177)

Muslims believe they are all one family, therefore there should never be any barriers regarding race, status or wealth.

Muslims should share a feeling of brotherhood and sisterhood, and be eager at all times to help each other when in trouble, console each other when in grief, nurse each other when sick, and send aid to each other when times of disasters strike. If a Muslim can see the distress of another and does nothing about it, he or she has departed from the spirit of Islam.

'You are niggardly at the expense of your own soul.' (47:38)

Abu Sa'id reported: 'If a Muslim clothes another Muslim in his nudity, Allah will clothe him (or her) with the green freshness of Paradise; if he feeds a Muslim who is hungry, Allah will give him to eat of the fruits of Paradise; if he gives a drink he will drink from the fountains of Paradise.' (Tirmidhi and Abu Dawud)

Ibn Abbas reported: 'He who eats and drinks while his brother goes hungry, is not one of us.' (Bayhaqi)

'Taqabbal Allah minna wa minkum'

Needless to say, although we are specifically requested to help other Muslims, a true Muslim helps *all* people in need no matter who they are.

'May God accept the work we have done for His sake.'—Muslim Dua prayer.

SADAQAH

Charity means caring for others. Muslims are expected to be charitable all the time, and never to turn away from those who need help.

Abu Hurayrah recorded: 'An ignorant person who is

generous is nearer to Allah than a devout person who is miserly.' (Tirmidhi)

Acts of charity and compassion should be able to be requested of any Muslim in the sure hope that if it is possible the one in need will be given help. These are the acts known as sadaqah.

Abu Hurayrah reported: 'If anyone removes an anxiety of this world from a believer, Allah will remove an anxiety of the Day of Resurrection from him; if one smoothes the way for one who is destitute, Allah will smoothe the way for him in this world and the next;....Allah helps a man so long as he helps his brother.' (Muslim)

Abu Musa al-Ashari recorded: 'Giving of sadaqah is an obligation for every Muslim.' (Bukhari and Muslim)

It can be small, individual examples of giving—usually when the heart is stirred to compassion by hearing of the plight of someone unfortunate. A little example is like the baker's shop which gives away what it has left on a Thursday night so that no-one nearby need say their Jumah prayers in a state of hunger. On the larger scale, there are numerous world disasters that desperately need our support—some sudden catastrophes like earthquakes, cyclones or floods, others more long-lasting like famine and drought or war. Money can be sent away to many disaster funds.

Anas recorded that the Prophet 卍 said: 'If anyone supplies a need to any one of my people desiring thereby to please him, he has pleased me; and he who has pleased me has pleased Allah; and he who has pleased Allah will be brought by Allah into Paradise.' (Bayhaqi)

Incidentally, the Prophet 卍 had words to say on who the really destitute and bankrupt person was. In the eyes of

Allah, it was not the person who was physically and literally poor, but:

'The really poor person... is the one who will bring good record of salah, zakah and other forms of worship, but who will also have in his record of deeds such sins as reviling and slandering others, stealing someone's property and murdering someone unjustly, etc. The good deeds of this person will be distributed amongst the aggrieved parties— and when all the good deeds are exhausted, the misdeeds and sins of the aggrieved persons will be laid upon him, and he will be cast into hell-fire.' (Muslim—reported by Abu Hurayrah)

Once again, the Prophet ﷺ stresses the importance of right living before Allah rather than a pious person depending on prayers and rituals which are useless without the correct Islamic spirit and life-style to back them up.

Muslims set a very high standard for charity. It has to be done according to the will of Allah, without expecting any reward in this world. It is never to be spoiled by reminders to the act or hurtful references to it, or boasting about it— which might humiliate and injure the recipient.

Abu Hurayrah recorded: 'The valley of grief is a valley in hell.' They asked: 'Who will enter it?' He said: 'The readers of the Qur'an who are ostentatious in their deeds.' (Tirmidhi and Ibn Majah)

Ibn Abbas recorded: 'One who gives in charity and then gets it back is like a dog which vomits and then eats its own vomit.' (Muslim 3957)

False charity, which is really not charity at all but simply ostentatious giving in order to be admired by other people, actually betrays lack of faith in Allah—for the giver has not understood that Allah sees everything and understands every motive.

> 'O believers! Do not cancel your charity by reminders of your generosity or by injury—like those who spend their substance in order to be seen of men, but believe neither in Allah nor in the Last Day. They are like a hard barren rock on which is little soil; when heavy rain falls on it, it leaves it just a bare stone. They will be able to do nothing with what they have earned.' (2:264)

Abu Hurayrah recorded: 'The generous person is near Paradise, near humanity, and far from Hell; but the miserly person is far from Allah, far from Paradise, far from humanity and near Hell.' (Tirmidhi)

Umar recorded: 'Who is boastful, Allah will make him low and he will then be small in the eyes of men but great to himself, till he become more loathsome than a dog or a pig.' (Bayhaqi)

FALSE CHARITY

Charity only has value if it is something good and valuable which has been given, and which has been honourably earned or acquired by the giver. The things given may well include articles which are of use or value to others after the first owner no longer has use for them—for example, discarded clothes, equipment that has been replaced by better. However, if, for example, a superfluous car is given, but its engine is so far gone that it is in fact dangerous, then the gift is worse than useless—it is positively harmful, and the giver is a wrongdoer!

The same principle applies to wealthy firms or individuals who try to give away some of their profits to indulge in fraud. Islam has nothing to do with tainted property, or gains that are dishonest and dishonourable. Some professions or services may be tainted, if they actually lead to moral harm. Muslims should not ever think to acquire them or give them, soothing their consciences with the mistaken notion that they are practising charity!

'O believers! Give of the good things which you have earned honourably, and of the fruits of the Earth which we have produced for you, and do not even aim at getting anything which is bad, in order that out of it you may give away something, when you yourselves would not receive it except with closed eyes.' (2:267)

Charity is so important that it is one of the things that lives on after a person dies:

Abu Hurayrah recorded: 'When a man dies, his acts come to an end except three—regular charity, or beneficial knowledge, or a pious son who prays for him.' (Muslim 4005)

ZAKAH

Over and above the 'feelings of compassion'—which are often brought on by media programmes quite by chance, Muslims are expected to tax their income and wealth as a matter of duty, and to hand over a certain proportion on a regular annual basis to those who are less fortunate. This is not regarded as a matter of choice, but as a religious duty, and is called Zakah.

Zakah means 'to purify' (from 'zakiya'—to grow, be pure, to cleanse). Muslims 'cleanse' their material possessions and money by donating a percentage of it as a compulsory payment of money or possessions to help the poor, needy, sick, imprisoned, or Muslim mission workers. For money, (cash, bank savings and jewellery) it is 2.5% or 1/40th of surplus income (once the Muslim's own and family needs have been taken care of up to a certain limit—the nisab); other zakah examples are 20% of mining produce; 10%

harvest from rain-watered land; 5% from irrigated land; 1 cow per 30; 1 sheep or goat per 40; 1 sheep or goat per 5 camels. Zakah is one of the five pillars, a regular annual duty and not merely charity given out of kindness, which is called sadaqah. (See 2:95, 210, 264, 270; 9:60). The object is to limit the withdrawal of money from being circulated in society. If wealth is just 'saved' for an individual, it is not being used and nobody gets the benefit from it.

The zakah is usually collected and sent off during the fast of Ramadan.

Abu Hurayrah recorded: "Every day two angels come down from Heaven; one of them says 'O Allah! Compensate every person who gives in Your name.' The other says 'O Allah! Destroy every miser!'" (Bukhari and Muslim)

THE FEASTS

There are only two official Feasts of Islam—the Eid-ul-Fitr, which breaks the month-long fast of Ramadan, and the Eid-ul-Adha which falls during the time of Hajj. Both are seen as occasions on which to thank God for all His blessings.

Both feasts involve worship, purity, and thought for others. The whole family of Islam is brought together, to enjoy a time with loved ones and to share this good feeling by remembering all those who are poor or suffering in any way.

The requirements for Feast Days are simple, but good. The first is cleanliness; baths are taken and clean or new clothes worn. The second is prayer; the whole family of Islam gathers together in huge gatherings, to be as one. Thirdly comes thought for one's own family; presents are given, especially to children, visits are made, cards are sent, special meals are served, cemeteries are visited. Lastly comes thought for the wider family of Islam; the zakah-collection is sent off for people who are less fortunate, and strangers are welcomed to share hospitality.

It is recommended that on Feast Days Muslims should go home after the prayers by a different route from the one they take coming, in order to create the largest possible opportunity for meeting other Muslims, and spreading the joy!

EID-UL-FITR

Zakah for Eid-ul Fitr is a special payment of a set amount, the equivalent of two meals. This should be given to the poor on behalf of each member of the family by every Muslim who is financially able to do this. It is traditionally given before the Feast Prayer, so that the poor who receive it may be able to join in the festival. If Muslims are not able to do it beforehand, they should do it as soon as possible afterwards—but in that case it does not count as obligation, but becomes a normal charity.

THE FEAST OF SACRIFICE

Eid-ul-Adha involves the compulsory sacrifice of an animal for the pilgrims on Hajj, and is a voluntary act for other Muslims round the world. The animal must be chosen from healthy stock and be over a year old. Alms equal to the cost of the animal can be given by non-pilgrims.

The animal is dedicated to Allah, then slaughtered by the person best able to do this as painlessly as possible; then it is divided up and shared. Parts of it may be kept or eaten by the person who paid for the sacrifice, but the larger part of it must be given to the poor. Selling any part of it, or giving any party of it to the butcher who slaughtered it as a form of payment, is forbidden. No Muslim should expect to take payment, or to capitalise on his expertise, on this occasion.

FASTING

Fasting, especially during Ramadan, the ninth month of the Lunar calendar, is an act of self-discipline and self-sacrifice. It requires a great deal of effort.

A Muslim may choose to go without some food or other for religious reasons at any time—usually as an act of penitence for some wrongdoing.

The holy month of Ramadan is quite different. During this month, for the entire 29 or 30 days, Muslims must not give in to the urges of the body for food, drink or sex during the hours of daylight, from the moment at early dawn when a black thread can just be distinguished from a white one, to the Maghrib prayer.

THE FASTING MIND

For the Muslim, fasting is much more than just a physical discipline, making the body's needs submit to the will. The fast is quite pointless without a certain attitude of mind.

The person fasting must become peaceful, and calm. They must not bear any grudges, or think harmful or hurtful thoughts. Sexual purity must be maintained, and all flirtatiousness or direct sexual activity must be put out of their mind during the hours of fasting.

If any Muslim fasts with an incorrect attitude of mind, then the effort has been in vain. It is the niyyah or intention that is of prime importance. The going without food or drink are just outward signs.

'The one who goes without food or drink in the wrong attitude of mind gains nothing but hunger and thirst.' (Bukhari)

Abu Hurayrah recorded: 'If a person does not give up lying and indecent activities, Allah does not require that he (or she) should give up food and drink.' (Bukhari)

MUSLIM AID

There are many Islamic enterprises that organise charity on a large scale. The best known in the UK are:

Islamic Relief—19 Rea St, Birmingham B 5 (0121 6055555). This is an international relief organisation, which also helps needy Muslims in the UK as well as abroad.

Muslim Aid—3 Furlong Rd, London, N7 8LR (0171 6094425)—an organisation which does similar work to Islamic Relief.

The Red Crescent (the Muslim equivalent of the Red Cross) carries out acts of mercy ranging from medical care on the battlefield to famine relief.

Muslim Relief Fund—at the Islamic Cultural Centre, 146, Park Rd, London, NW8 7RG (0171 724 3363)

Smaller care organisations include such things as:

Muslim Women's Helpline—(0181-9048193)—an organisation which gives an emotional support service to Muslim women who have various problems. (Service available on Tues, Thurs and Sun between 12 noon-4 pm).

Helpline—(0181 427 1751) offering advice on problems ranging from housing difficulties to racism; an offshoot of the paper Muslim Voice.

Madinah House—146, Gloucester Rd, London, NWI—offers advice on all women's problems, and runs a children's home.

Appeals recently supported by these organisations have included the Bangladesh cyclone appeal, the Lebanese war victim appeal, the Mozambique famine appeal, the Afghanistan war appeal, the Somalia famine appeal, the Bangladesh flood disaster, the Ethiopia famine appeal, the Kashmir war damage appeal, the Sudanese locust famine appeal, the Tranian earthquake appeal, the Kurdish refugee appeal, and The Bosnian war appeal.

> 'Those who spend their wealth day and night in secret and in public have their reward with their Lord; on them shall be no fear, nor shall they grieve.' (2:274)

Usually Muslims do not use non-Muslim media for their appeals, but stick to their own newspapers and other sources of publicity. This has occasionally led people in host countries to suppose that it is only Christian organisations that help the unfortunate people stricken by disasters, and Muslims often face ill-informed criticism. Perhaps the time has come for Muslims to consider a wider use of media, in order to put right misconceptions.

The kind of detailed work done by the Muslim Aid agencies is to sponsor orphans and widows, education, health visitors; to build medical emergency units, to dig wells and erect water-pumps, and to send food, clothes, blankets, multivitamin tablets, baby milk and medical equipment, wherever they are needed.

'Grief-stricken, homeless—thousands of orphans and widows need urgent support now. Remember—your money never decreases because of your charity!' (Islamic Relief Poster).

Jasir Ibn Abdullah recorded: 'God will not have compassion on the one who does not have compassion for others.' (Muslim)

Difficulties Faced by Muslims Living in Non-Muslims Communities

When you realise the full extent of true Muslim commitment, you can see how sometimes venturing out into life in a non-Muslim environment can be full of difficulties and embarrassing situations, a real obstacle course.

The temptations are almost overpowering. For example, some Muslims have come to the West from very poor backgrounds and find themselves surrounded by all sorts of luxuries and freedoms unavailable back home. Others come from very wealthy backgrounds, and can buy anything they want—far more, usually, than an ordinary person in their host community—and this includes all the expensive vices.

Of course, not every person who shifts to a non-Muslim society from the Middle East or Pakistan or further East is a practising Muslim—just as the entire population of Britain, for example, is not practising Christian. Just as the white face is certainly not synonymous with 'Christian', so the brown face is certainly not synonymous with 'Muslim.'

PROBLEMS

Muslims do not tend to mix very much with the non-Muslim society in which they find themselves, but keep very much to their own kind. There are many reasons for this, some of which derive from the ethnic and cultural background of the Muslim community, but others which are specifically 'Muslim problems', which will apply just as much to the increasing number of western converts to Islam. The major difficulties are food problems, the presence of alcohol, and the allowing of unaccustomed freedoms to women and the young.

Some areas that cause particular difficulties are mixed-sex schools, any enforced communal life (e.g. hospital, prison), the availability or otherwise of facilities for Islamic burial, facing aggression and hostility from racist elements in the community, finding suitable lodgings or other accommodation, and the sexual freedom granted to women and the young. One drastic freedom granted to Western women is

the right to divorce their husbands, not only for just cause, but simply because in their opinion the marriage has 'irretrievably broken down.' This freedom, although sanctioned by the Qur'an and several hadiths that show the Blessed Prophet allowing the disentanglement of unhappy marriages, seems to be not available to many Muslim women from various Third World cultures.

FOOD PROBLEMS

Muslims should not eat pork in any shape or form, or any product made with pig fat. Neither should they eat any other meat that has not been killed by the halal method.

> 'O believers! Eat of the good things that we have provided for you, and be grateful to Allah, if it is him you worship. He has only forbidden you carrion-meat and blood and the flesh of pigs, and that on which any name other than the name of God has been invoked.' (2:173; 5:3)

Many animals slaughtered in the West for meat have been killed by electrocution, a method forbidden to Muslims. Muslims have a particular method of slaughter:

Shaddad b. Aus recorded: 'Truly Allah has commanded goodness in everything; so when you kill, kill in a good way, and when you slaughter, slaughter in a good way. Every one of you should sharpen his knife and let the slaughtered animal die comfortably.' (Muslim 4810)

In fact, Allah ordered in the Qur'an that Muslims should 'eat of meats on which God's name has been pronounced, if you have faith in his signs. Why should you not (do this) when he has explained to you in detail what is forbidden to you, except under compulsion of necessity?' (6:118-119).

What is important in halal killing is the sharpness of the instrument used to kill, and the desire that the animal should suffer as little as possible. Therefore, it is worth stressing that if a Muslim killed an animal cruelly, with a blunt instrument or blunt knife, the meat of that animal cannot be regarded as halal. (See the section on hunting p. 280).

This halal food rule drastically reduces a Muslim's ability to mix socially with non-Muslim neighbours. Unless they can get access to halal meat, or unless they follow the ruling of the Maliki School that meat killed by ways sanctioned as humane by Christian and Jewish societies are makruh and not haram, they are obliged to follow a vegetarian diet—although they are not vegetarians.

Non-vegetarians may not realise that this means a whole range of products is forbidden—certain bread, biscuits, soups, chocolate, ice-cream, fried breakfasts—in fact anything that contains animal fat as opposed to vegetable fat, or animal gelatine. One has to examine every packet! Thankfully, in these days of 'rape-seed oil', it is now becoming more common to find that restaurants cook in vegetable oil, and biscuits and cakes rely on vegetable oil only and not the mixed animal fats.

Muslims cannot understand why Christians have ignored completely the example of Jesus ﷺ, who—as a devout Jew—certainly never let pork touch his lips, and left instructions that none of the laws of God were to be broken.

'You shall not eat... the pig, because it parts the hoof and is cloven-footed but does not chew the cud, and it is unclean to you. Of their flesh you shall not eat, and their carcasses you shall not touch, they are unclean to you.' (The original Jewish Law recorded in Leviticus 11:7-8; Deuteronomy 14:8).

'Whoever relaxes the least of these commandments, and teaches people so, shall be called least in the Kingdom of Heaven.' (Teaching of Jesus ﷺ recorded in St. Matthew's

Gospel 5:19).

The Christian decision to relax the food laws, in spite of Jesus' ﷺ specific command, came as the result of a dream experienced by St. Peter. To a Muslim, no dream of any person, no matter how saintly, can be allowed to encourage people to contravene a revealed law of God.

Many Muslim children find they cannot eat the school dinners because of the food restrictions, and are forced into making do with packed lunches. Fortunately, in areas where there is a high Muslim population, the authorities have allowed the inclusion of halal meat, and frying in vegetable oil and not lard, on to their school menus.

Unfortunately it is extremely difficult in non-Muslim societies to be certain that meat pronounced halal in the shop really is halal. The Prophet ﷺ taught that if you genuinely believed it to be halal, you were not held guilty if someone else had perpetreted a fraud on you.

Other Muslims feel that in view of the sanction given in 5:5. 'and the food of the People of Book is lawful to you, and your food is lawful to them' it is allowed to eat meat prepared in Christian or Jewish societies—where meat is certainly not offered to idols, and has been slaughtered in a way judged to be 'not cruel' by the authorities.

When the Prophet ﷺ was unsure if meat he was served was halal or not, he advised to pray over it, and eat.

No doubt, in a non-Muslim society, it is advisable always for a Muslim to pronounce the name of God over any food they are about to eat.

ALCOHOL

Muslims should not only refuse alcohol, they should not even be in a place where alcohol is served. If they do go, to be sociable to a non-Muslim friend, they would be embarrassed if the conversation turned to the subject of religion—for a Muslim should not discuss God or the Quran in the presence of alcohol. The whole subject is discussed elsewhere in the book (pp. 239 onwards).

PRAYER

Performing salah can present a problem for some Muslims. Not all employers are sympathetic if workers want to break off for a few minutes to pray. Often there is no private place for them to go anyway, or facilities to wash first.

Non-Muslims are surprised to see people washing their feet in a high sink, and some even think it dirty—although the opposite is obviously the case!

As a matter of fact, this is not a practice that should really cause Muslims any problem. Prayer times are flexible, and tend to follow the normal breaks in the day; to insist on the clock times when one is in an environment outside the mosque is really over-particular and unnecessary.

However, it is not always easy to find somewhere quiet where one will not be laughed at. In Muslim countries, of course, people just get down and pray anywhere while life goes on around them, and no-one thinks anything of it. Now that Islam is gaining ground in the West, it is no longer impossible to see Muslims praying in a quiet place in a park, for example, although we have yet to see the day when they 'stop the traffic'!

FRIDAY PRAYERS

The performance of the communal salah at midday on Friday presents a problem when Friday is not the cultural day 'off.' Salat al-Jum'ah requires time off to go to the mosque for an hour or so during Friday lunchtime—the length of time one is absent from work depending on one's distance from the mosque. It is expected that young boys should go too, so they often miss some lessons before and after lunch.

It is not obligatory for women to attend the mosque also—although they should never be banned from doing so if they wish. Most mosques, however, have little space for womenfolk, and if all the women decided to attend the lack of space would surely be an embarrassment. It is usually expected that the mosque should be left to the men, and the women should get on with their prayers at home (or wherever they happen to be) and then carry on with organising the family domestic arrangements smoothly. In many families, there is considerable contentment with this arrangement, and no urge to alter it.

The Blessed Prophet ﷺ once told Umm Humayd that although she longed to pray with him in the mosque, her prayer in her own chamber was preferable. (Ahmad, Kanz al-Ummal, Muslim 668).

RAMADAN

Ramadan is the twenty-nine or thirty-day fast carried out each year, when Muslims abstain from all food, drink and sexual activity during the hours of daylight. Muslims who perform this fast are usually very strict—nothing at all must pass the lips from the early light of dawn until sunset. Since the date of Ramadan is based on the lunar calendar, it comes ten or eleven days earlier each year, and thus progresses around the calendar. When it falls in the summer months, it means that not only is it quite likely to be hot, but that the hours of fasting are very long indeed. In England they can be from 2.30 am until 9.45 pm.

'Ramadan is the month in which was sent down the Qur'an as a guide to humanity, and clear signs for guidance and judgement. So every one of you who is present during that month should spend it in fasting, but if any one is ill, or on a journey, the prescribed period (should be made up) by days later. God intends to make it easy for you; He does not want to put you in difficulties.' (2:185)

Non-Muslims who have not experienced fasting can have no idea of the effects this self-denial can sometimes has on people. Some get very irritable and impatient, or light-headed and giggly; many feel faint at certain times; most feel very tired and drained of energy in the afternoons until their bodies get used to the regime.

One of the hardest parts about Ramadan for some Muslims is the lack of sleep, or disturbed sleep patterns. The usual custom is to get up before the break of dawn and eat some food, before the first prayer, and then return to bed. A really devout Muslim will go to the mosque for this prayer. Therefore, it can mean that they are waking themselves up at around 3 am (or whatever time is just before dawn), and not getting back into bed until an hour and a half later, or some such regime.

Many Muslims who are able to adjust their days get round the problem by staying up all night until the fast begins, and then going to sleep until mid-day. This may be all right for students or the unemployed, but it is not possible for those who have to go out to work, or for housewives with small children to look after.

Some people find it impossible to eat at these early times, even when allowed, and become quite weak by the end of the 30 days.

It becomes very difficult to do hard physical work. Teachers sometimes tell Muslim pupils off for being sleepy or lazy, without realising that the pupil is probably very hungry and may have been up until 3 am with the family the previous night! When the teacher himself or herself is a Muslim, it is very hard—the job involves talking for much of the day.

In a Muslim country, the whole system is sympathetic, and one might be able to take it easy, or sleep, during the day.

SCHOOL

School problems fall into four main areas
— immodest dress, especially in compulsory PE lessons
— not separating boys and girls after the age of 10
— unacceptable moral aspects of sexual instruction in the classroom
— religious instruction that actively denigrates Islam, or presents Islam in an incorrect manner.

Muslims prefer that girls and boys should be educated separately as soon as their sexual urges begin—to protect them, and make them concentrate on lessons! There are arguments for and against single-sex schools, of course. Those who have taught both in mixed schools and in single-sex schools find it very obvious that many boys in a single-sex school tend to be much more immature and cruder in manners, attitude and speech than those who had girls growing up around them. Whether or not they work harder is debatable—the girls tended to mature earlier than the boys, and where there are girls in the class the standard of work is frequently much higher from the girls until they reach the age of fifteen or sixteen. It might do boys some good to realise that the 'gentle sex' is not stupid, and could often be superior at the work subjects. It might make them work that little bit harder later on. It is hard to say.

It is not having boys and girls together, supervised, in a classroom that is the problem——it is the unsupervised free times, in the playground and so on. In Islam, young women should not be left unchaperoned in any circumstances where they could be misled or taken advantage of.

Clothing has presented a problem for Muslim girls at school. They should not be forced to wear short skirts. Ideally, the uniform should allow trousers for girls, and shalwar-kameez and hijab if the girls wish it.

Hijab has caused some problems at school, particularly where the girl involved, or her family, is trying to make a statement of 'religious superiority.' The same difficulty arises sometimes when youths insist on being allowed to grow beards in a school where this is not generally allowed. Should young Muslims insist on their 'right' to wear hijab or grow a beard? Or should they politely accept that they are not yet classed as adults in that society, and therefore the sunnahs of Muslim *adults* can wait until they leave school?

In any case, Muslims should consider two things—the 'rights' of other Muslims *not* to put on head-scarves on grow beards; or alternatively, to find out for themselves whether a polite request to the school governors might not bring them the required permission.

If a school has a particularly *secular* ethos, then perhaps Muslims should consider whether it would be better for them to place their children elsewhere, rather than cause trouble in a school environment that is specifically secular.

Clothing for physical education is sometimes blatantly sexual. Muslim girls should request to wear modest track suits, and not have swimming lessons in mixed classes.

Sometimes schools insist on communal showers, usually to the extreme embarrassment of everyone concerned, not only Muslims. Muslims consider nakedness even in front of one's own sex to be immodest and unnecessary, and do not think communal showers in the nude should ever be forced on girls or boys.

Abu al-Rahman recorded: 'A man should not see the private parts of another man, or a woman those of a woman.' (Muslim 667)

Ya'la recorded: The Apostle ﷺ saw a man washing in a public place without a lower garment. So he mounted the pulpit and extolled Allah and said: 'Allah is characterised by modesty and concealment. So when any of you washes, he should conceal himself.' (Abu Dawud 4001)

One possible solution would be to request to be allowed to shower whilst wearing underpants—and perhaps keep a special pair for this purpose, or take a dry pair to change into.

SEX EDUCATION

Sex education is always a controversial subject, even in totally non-Muslim societies. Many parents are only too pleased for their offspring to be taught the facts of life by someone other than themselves—others are horrified at the thought, and disapprove of it strongly. The worst aspect of sex education in schools is that there is little control over what is actually taught or how it is expressed, or the character and presentation of the person teaching it.

Many teachers have no desire whatsoever to put themselves in the position of teaching this subject, and are very embarrassed. Usually they are not obliged to teach it, and a willing member of staff will take their place, but this is not always the case.

Muslims generally feel that sex is not a subject that should be discussed in class, especially in a mixed-sex class, or if taught by some person who does not share the Muslim attitude that sex outside marriage is condemned by Allah. If it is purely the mechanics of sex and reproduction that is to be taught, there are plenty of excellent booklets on the subject, and it is as much the duty of a Muslim to seek knowledge in this area of human concern as in any other. Indeed, a lot of unnecessary suffering is caused in marriage through ignorance of sexual matters, because husbands and wives are too modest or embarrassed to discuss them, or love their partners too much to hurt their feelings by implying that they are criticising them. It is a very delicate matter. The Muslim injunction to 'seek knowledge' should certainly apply here, but in an Islamic way—which is to seek for the greatest happiness of each partner, and thereby turn the act of sexual intercourse from the animal level into sadaqah.★

The moral aspect of sex education in schools presents many problems for Muslims, whose attitude is very straight-forward. Homosexuality, and sex before marriage is wrong and against the wish of Allah. Many of the state educational lectures (and lecturers) talk openly about 'relationships', and often seem to assume that all the young people are having them, or trying to have them. This attitude blatantly condones what Muslims regard as weak and wrong, and puts temptation before their youngsters that are difficult to cope with.

The latest programmes to give explicit sexual education to children as young as seven in the hopes that it will frighten them off being promiscuous and risking catching Aids when teenagers, are quite offensive to Muslims (and, incidentally, to many concerned non-Muslim parents!) Parents' rights to supervise the moral upbringing of their own children is seen,

----

★ Sr. Ruqyaiyyah discusses these matters more fully in *The Muslim Marriage Guide*, Goodword Books, 1998.

rightly, to be under threat by these programmes. It is not fear of Aids that will stop premarital sex in a 'free' society, but love of God, acceptance of duty, and respect for the well-being of other human beings.

Sometimes it is not a specific sex education lession that is involved, but the content material of an English lesson. Muslims in non-Muslim societies cannot really expect their young people never to come across books, TV programmes, videos and so forth, which offend their religious beliefs.

They must make sure young Muslims have a good understanding of Muslim morality, and encourage them never to join in with sniggering smutty behaviour, or behaviour which abuses young women (or boys).

Muslims should not be buying or looking at porno-graphic material, including magazines, newspaper nudes, playing-cards with naked women, and so on. They should realise this is usually offensive to *all* decent women, not only Muslim ones.

If a book was included in a school lesson that could be claimed to be unsuitable, then a protest should be made if possible. There is no need to take an extremist stance—just quietly point out that it is against your faith to read, watch, or be involved in that kind of material.

RELIGIOUS EDUCATION

This can be a problem if it is concerned with Bible material only (since the Muslim interpretation of many passages is different, e.g. the sacrifice of Isma'il and not Isaac), or if it teaches Islam with prejudice, or inaccurately.

Muslims should not mind knowing *about* other reli-gions, but cannot agree with youngsters being 'taught' by teachers who believe nothing themselves, or who actually regard Muslims as non-believers, and try to convert them to Christianity. It is fashionable these day in RE syllabi to present all the world's religions as being of equal value, and no Muslim can accept that.

Muslims are often obliged to withdraw from school worship because they will not pray to Jesus or 'in Jesus' name'; they must also be left out of preparations for Christmas and Easter, and if they try to point out the pagan or inaccurate Christian mythology behind the 'Christmas' story, this can make them appear to be antisocial. (An 'accurate' Christmas means abandoning December 25th, mistletoe, holly, Yule logs, Santa Klaus, elves and reindeer, and most Christmas cards or 'Nativity Plays' which present shepherds, Big Star, three kings all crammed round a stable etc. Incidentally, RE teachers who try to teach factually, and examine the actual Gospel texts, usually get no thanks for it!)

Thankfully, in this day and age people are becoming much more tolerant towards the religious faith of others, and do not try to upset the religious beliefs of others.

Where religion is taught simply in *educational* terms (that is—*what* do various people believe, and *why*, and how do they practise their faith)—there is nothing wrong with this, and Muslims should not deprive themselves of this information.

Muslims have nothing to fear from any comparison; they should have confidence that 'the Truth stands clear from enor.' (2:255)

Parents who withdraw their children from RE lessons should consider the other side of today's efforts to give multi-faith education—it has led to millions of non-Muslim youngsters learning at least an introduction to Islam, and seeds being planted that may well bear fruit later.

MUSLIC

Some Muslims take the point of view that all Music is forbidden, and totally ignore the rich traditions of Islamic music in many countries. The Music that is forbidden to a Muslim is that which incites lust and sexual feelings (a great deal of modern 'pop' music—including, incidentally bangra); that which incites to jingo-istic patriotism; and that which is simply to show off.

There is nothing wrong in the classical music and folk music of most nations, and Muslims would be foolish to try to prevent their youngsters hearing or learning such music.

MEDICAL TREATMENT

It is not thought proper for a Muslim woman or girl to be examined by a male doctor, or vice versa. This is not usually a problem in a group practice, or where you can choose a doctor. The only major problems come when there is no choice of doctor—as sometimes in hospital, and when a Muslim dies in hospital.

Muslims find the 'red tape' difficult to understand or cope with, and expect to be with their relatives when they die, and to take them away immediately for washing, prayers and burial.

Fortunately, there is increasing knowledge of culture, customs and religious sensitivities, and these problems are decreasing.

However, the knowledge of how to properly wash and shroud a corpse in the Islamic manner can easily die out in a non-Muslim host society. Muslim should take care that the knowledge is passed on in their congregation.

They should also make arrangements with local cemeteries for burial facing qiblah—and be aware that it is the face that should face qiblah, not the deceased's feet.

PRISON

The two main problems here are attitudes to crime and prison visitors. Non-Muslims are allowed the visit of a priest—but as there are no priests in Islam, many Imams have no official capacity. Any adult male could be an Imam—and this could include relatives of the inmate, and hence arouse charges of unfair privilege.

If the visit from an Imam is refused, then there is the charge of unfair discrimination against the Muslim. Sending in an inappropriate person can cause enormous ill-feeling. Muslims should consider this matter carefully.

In a perfect Muslim society, we would never find any Muslims in prison at all; it is a great pity that some do fall short of their own high standards and commit crime. It is not good enough to attempt to excuse them on the grounds of the temptations of the West. There are always temptations, in any country—and weakness is weakness, whatever way you look at it.

The Muslim has a strong inner sense of shame, made all the more potent by the awareness that Allah sees everything, even when nobody else has seen, and that every deed done will have to be accounted for on the Day of Judgement. The awareness of the presence of Allah ought to be enough to prevent any Muslim committing a dishonest action, but where faith is weak this is obviously not the case.

CAUSING PREJUDICE AND RACISM

Certain zealots and extremists cause so much damage to the good name of Islam that they really are 'an enemy within.'

Fanaticism, tyranny and competitiveness are not Islamic qualities.

The fact that certain people are naturally more pious and more enthusiastic about religious and ritual practices is as obvious as that certain people are more intelligent than others. None of these characteristics implies greater merit. Allah appreciates our devotion, but He does not place burdens on us (5:90).

Muslim who wish to be thought better than others are suffering from pride and misplaced confidence (31:19). Their intention is wrong, although they might genuinely wish to please Allah by their practices and attitude.

Sometimes those people who seem to be the most devout are actually the most harsh and unforgiving. Those whose hearts are 'wrong' can spend all day fasting and all night praying, but gain only thin bodies and sleepless nights.

In fact extremists, from misplaced enthusiasm, can impose all sort of religious burdens on others that are not at all necessary. Instead of gentleness, tolerance, politeness and consideration for others, their attitude actually drives seekers *away* from Allah. It appeals only to others of their own type.

Islam is for all, not just for those with special endurance or who wish to create limits. Extremism is generally too much for normal human nature to condone or tolerate, and it is very often at someone else's expense—someone else is likely to suffer neglect, hurt or inconvenience as the result of the extremists's pre-occupation with doing more than others.

For example, a man who spends all his time making extra voluntary prayers at the mosque is almost certainly neglecting his wife and family. He just assumes they will 'get on' without him, and treat him with awe and admiration when he turns up. In fact, he is virtually making himself superfluous to the family which is learning to cope without him.

The main characteristics of extremists are ghuluw (excessiveness) tashdid (bigotry), takfir (branding others as unbelievers), and 'hair-splitting.' Exclusivist believers, who often espouse the very worthy causes of combating racism, discrimination and unemployment, often only serve to alienate already poorly integrated groups from their state and society.

Muslims must remember the gentleness, forbearance and tolerance of the Prophet ﷺ. Those who promote hatred, racism, and so forth really cause great harm to the image of Islam amongst people who do not know the truths of Islam.

Suffice it to quote here one key hadith: 'He from whom his neighbour does not feel safe from his harm, is not one of us.'

Friendship and Unity

Anas b. Malik recorded: 'Don't nurse hatred, or jealousy, or enmity, but be companions of each other and servants of Allah! It is not permissible for believers to keep their relationship estranged from other believers for more than three days!' (Muslim 6205, Bukhari)

Abu Ayyub Ansari's record added: 'The better of the two is the one who is first to give greeting.' (i.e. to heal the breach). (Muslim 6210)

There have always been religious people who have sought to escape from the world, to lock themselves away in conditions that satisfied their need for 'purity' or peace. Muslims consider such detachment, or religious seclusion, to be a form of escapism; it can even be seen as a kind of insult towards the rest of human society that Allah has created and loved.

In Islam, individual salvation should not be sought away from society. Islam disapproves of monasticism. It encourages people to mix together, and desires collective actions and co-operation. Therefore, to a Muslim, friends are extremely important, and good conduct when out amongst the general public is extremely important.

Incidentally, one of the things that female Muslims often find quite irritating is the tendency of male Muslims in certain societies to segregate themselves to an unnecessary and excessive extent—thereby encouraging that very atmosphere of 'religion at a man's club' that was disapproved of in monasticism.

The Prophet ﷺ emphasized often that his sunnah included marriage, and encouragement of family life and care and companionship for the female Muslims.

The sort of Muslim man who avoids and shuns all female company would do well to reflect on the enormous number of female persons (aunts, wives, cousins, children and friends) who surrounded the Prophet ﷺ and cherished him.

THE IMPORTANCE OF FRIENDSHIP

We do not chose our families, but we do choose our friends. Although blood is thicker than water, some of our relatives end up with characters we seriously do not like, and would not let past our front doors were they not our relatives.

Friends are a different matter. Once we have made a close friend, it is a relationship that may last for life as a matter of mutual trust, enjoyment, support and love.

Friendship plays a vital role in moulding an individual's mind, thinking and attitude, and also shapes the extent of a person's spirituality and moral well-being, and therefore the well-being of society as a whole. So much depends on the wisdom with which we choose our friends.

'Let not believers take for friends and helpers unbelievers rather than believers; if any do that, there will be no help from God except by way of precaution, that you may guard yourselves from (being influenced by) them. Allah cautions you to remember Himself, for He is your final goal.' (3:28)

'A person is apt to follow the faith of his friend, so be careful with whom you make friends.' (Ahmad and Abu Dawud)

'FRIENDS' TO AVOID

If friendship is based on love of Allah and commitment to the faith, then it will be blessed. Muslims are warned against friendships with people who may take them from the straight path.

'On that day, the wrongdoer will bite at his hands and say—'O would that I had taken the straight path! Woe is me! Would that I had never taken such a one for a friend! He led me astray!' (25:27-30)

Muslims are not expected to mix without caution with people who take faith as a joke, or belittle it. When Muslims see evil in a group, and are able to do something about putting it right, then it is their duty to act in the best way they can. If they cannot do anything to help or improve the situation, then it is better to withdraw, and keep apart and not be tainted by it.

'Leave alone those who take their religion to be mere play and amusement, and are deceived by the life of this world;

proclaim to them this truth—that every should delivers itself to ruin by its own acts.' (6:70)

HOW TO NOURISH FRIENDSHIP

The key quality in a good friendship is unselfishness, thought for others before self. This leads almost automatically to the spreading of love and goodwill. Social courtesies and politeness are important, too. If you are rude to your friends and neighbours, they may forgive you because they love you, but it will leave a bad feeling which may later increase if the rudeness becomes a habit.

You should not ignore your friends, but visit them as often as you can without becoming intrusive or a nuisance, accepting all invitations with a glad heart—because it is a compliment to you and indicates that you are wanted and your presence is cherished. If you refuse an invitation, that is hurtful and shows lack of sensitivity.

Abdullah b. Umar reported: 'When one of you is invited to a wedding feast, he must attend it.' (Abu Dawud 3727). Ibn Umar also recorded: 'If he is not fasting he should eat; and if he is fasting he should leave the food.' (Abu Dawud 3728)

Gatecrashing, however, was certainly not approved of:

Abdullah b. Umar recorded: 'He who does not accept an invitation has disobeyed Allah and His Apostle; but he who enters without invitation enters as a thief and goes out as a raider!' (Abu Dawud 3732)

The good Muslim host should not seek just to impress wealthy friends and people of high standing, but always remember to do good by including the less fortunate:

Abu Hurayrah recorded: 'The worst kind of food is that at a wedding feast to which the rich are invited and from which the poor are left out.' (Abu Dawud 3733)

VISITING

But suppose you make too many visits? How do you know if your visits are really wanted? Are you perhaps becoming a nuisance? You must ask yourself this question, and consider how long you stay with your friends and what it is your visit is 'preventing them from doing.'

Abd Shuriah al-Khuzai recorded: 'The entertainment of a guest is three days, with the most unstinted kindness and courtesy for a day and a night. It is not permissible for a Muslim to stay with his brother until he makes him sinful.' They said: 'Messenger of Allah! How would be make him sinful?' He said: 'By staying with him so long that nothing is left with which to entertain him.' (Muslim 4287)

The Blessed Prophet 🕌 understood very well the problem of the guest who did not realise when 'enough was enough.' On the occasion of his own marriage to Zaynab bint Jahsh he gave a large and generous feast, but some of his guests lingered on in the house long after the meal, preventing him from consummating his marriage to his new wife. The Prophet 🕌 left the feast and visited his other wives, who were very surprised that he had left Zaynab on her wedding night. When he eventually got these tactless visitors out of the house he put up a curtain between the public and private parts of his dwelling, and this was when he received the revelation known as the 'descent of the hijab (veil)—33:53.

'O believers, do not enter the houses of the Prophet unless permission is given to you for a meal... and when you are invited, enter, and when you have taken food, disperse, not seeking to listen or talk.' (Recorded by Anas b. Malik—Muslim 3330)

Any visit made to someone out of love and concern is always appreciated, but if you are only going out of duty, or to cadge a warm fireplace or a free meal, then this may soon be resented.

If you always arrive at an inconvenient time—just as the host or hostess is going out, or is in the middle of important study, or has other plans made, or too late at night or too early in the morning—then this is really rudeness and bad manners, and not good Adab (manners). You do not have the right to expect someone else's family to revolve around you—although if you are a loved guest, you may soon find that you have become 'one of the family.'

The Blessed Prophet ﷺ particularly asked people returning from a journey to try not to arrive late at night without warning. Anas b. Malik pointed out that the Messenger ﷺ would not go back to his own family by night. He would come to them in the morning or earlier in the evening. It was suggested that it was inconsiderate if wives should be taken by surprise; they should be given time to beautify and bathe themselves, preparing their hair and seeing to their intimate cleanliness. (Muslim 4726-7).

It is very important for Muslim men to be sensitive to the needs and feelings of their wives in the matter of hospitality. This is one problem area in the western culture, where the womenfolk do not spend the major part of their lives fussing over their men, or having hospitality ready for visitors at all times. Western women no doubt need to become a little more hospitable and welcoming towards unexpected callers, but the men need to learn how to give forward planning as far as possible, and should learn the technique for caring as much for the wife as for the guest in circumstances when the wife is sick or tired. After all, a man's wife should be his *best* friend.

If a friend has to be put off because it really is not

convenient, then a true friend should not be offended but should understand and be considerate. This is what is implied by the passages in Qur'an and hadith where a person is requested to withdraw and not intrude upon the privacy of a household if there is no answer to his knock. The desired host is not obliged to give the reason why he does not wish to receive a visitor at that particular time; it is Muslim good manners for the unexpected guest to be sensitive and withdraw, without feeling hurt or offended, even if he or she knows the person is really in, and is just not answering.

If a husband realises that his wife has a problem and simply goes off somewhere with his friend and leaves his wife to get on alone, he runs the risk of finding his marriage in difficulties in due course, for having the wrong priorities!

Hanzala reported: 'There is a time for worldly affairs and a time for worship. So long as your state of mind is always the same (at home) as it is at the time of remembrance of Allah, the angels will shake hands with you and greet you on the path with *As-salaam alaikum.*' (Muslim 6624)

THOUGHTFUL ACTS

How else can one show friendship? Little evidences of affection and thought such as the bringing of small gifts are always welcome. Expensive things are not required—it is always the thought that counts.

If your friend has done you some kindness, it is a good thing if you can make some return with a kind deed of your own.

THINGS TO AVOID

The things that spoil friendship are really so obvious that it hardly seems necessary to list them. Any word or action of yours that belittles or mocks another will destroy friendship, even if the mockery is done behind a person's back. Be sure it will soon find its target, and the hurt will be done. A true friend guards the kinds of jokes and personal remarks made, and avoids anything that would hurt another's feelings or be regarded as a taunt.

Abu Hurayrah recorded: 'Backbiting means your talking about your brother in a manner which he would not like.' (Muslim 6265)

Ibn Sayd and Jabir recorded: 'Backbiting is more serious than fornication.' They asked: 'Messenger of Allah, how is this so?' He replied: 'Truly, when a man commits fornication and then repents, Allah returns to him (straight away); but the backbiter is not forgiven until the person talked about by him forgives him! (Bayhaqi)

Backbiting, and spying on friends is bound to be destructive. So is a snobbish attitude and feeling of superiority. Sometimes we hurt our friends by being suspicious, by being so insecure ourselves that we attribute evil motives to our friends' actions.

Jabir reported: 'Those deprived of tender feelings are in fact deprived of good.' (Muslim 6271)

This lack of trust will gradually destroy the friendship. So will any act that threatens Muslim brotherhood, such as drinking, gambling, cheating, secret conversations, corruption, egotism or hypocrisy. So long as all our deeds are in accordance with the will of Allah, we will not go far wrong. Once we begin to encourage the kind of behaviour that is disruptive, unkind and corrupt, the increase of bad conscience and guilt will soon have its effect.

Abu Hurayrah recorded: 'Beware of suspicion, for suspicion is a great falsehood. Do not search for faults in each other, do not spy on one another, nor yearn after that which others possess, nor envy, nor entertain malice or indifference; do not turn away from one another, but be servants of Allah, and brothers to one another as you have been ordered.' (Muslim 6214, Malik)

Abu Hurayrah reported: 'If anyone conceals the faults of a Muslim, Allah will conceal his faults in this world and the next. Allah helps a man so long as he helps his brother.' (Muslim 6267)

Amash recorded: 'Don't sever ties of kinship, don't bear enmity against one another, don't nurse aversion for one another, and don't feel envy against the other. Live as fellow-brothers as Allah has commanded you.' (Muslim 6217)

POSITIVE ACTION

'Forbid evil and enjoin good.' (3:104, 110)

Muslims should co-operate together to do what is pleasing to God and to fulfil their individual roles as trustees on earth. They must take positive steps—just to ignore a situation is no good, and words alone are not enough.

Tariq b. Shihab recorded: 'The messenger of Allah said: If you see an evil action, change it with your hand (i.e. positive action); or if you are not able to do this, then with your tongue; or if you are not able to do this, then with your heart.' (Muslim 79)

For example, if you come across some friends of yours being cruel to an animal, free the animal first and then speak boldly to your friends to encourage them towards kindness. Let them see that you do not approve of their action. Apathy is not the right attitude.

REASONS WHY PEOPLE AVOID ACTION

There are many reasons why people are afraid to speak out, and allow wrong feelings or situations to continue. The first is probably the fear of losing the friend involved. Here you must examine your conscience and work out what is right and what is wrong. Nobody is perfect—your friend is not, and neither are you. You will yourself have plenty of faults that others may point out to you in due course. Sometimes it is necessary to be 'cruel to be kind.' Every parent knows this when dealing with children; sometimes the same principles have to apply towards our friends.

A second reason for keeping out of the business is the fear that perhaps you may be the only one among millions who is crusading against this particular evil, and therefore what possible good can you do? This is not a reasonable argument. I once attended a mass meeting at which all the lights were put out, and people who had matches were asked to produce them. The leader of the meeting struck the match, and it was a tiny little light in that vast space. However, when everybody lit their tiny match, the whole scene was transformed, and there was light.

Sometimes we do not interfere because of apathy, a 'couldn't care less' attitude. What our friends are doing is not really your business. But is that true? Usually what your friends do will soon affect you in one way or another, and if you do not like what they are doing, you will either be expected to condone it or turn a blind eye—and so your own standards will be compromised.

If your friends do not like their weaknesses and wrongdoings pointed out to them—then think about the quality of those friends. The negative attitude is against Islam.

If everyone thought negatively no progress would ever be made. Muslims should do whatever lies within their power, simply to please Allah—and leave the results to Him.

'May God have mercy on anyone who gives me my faults as a gift.' (Saying of Caliph Umar)

Some criminals gain courage because they see people doing nothing to stop them, and so they think they are going along with their evil actions. Islam does not seek heroes, but it does want the general attitude in society to be that evil must be prevented from taking place.

UNITY—THE FAMILY OF ISLAM.

All Muslims belong to the Ummah—the single 'family' of Islam. Muslims believe that Islam is so natural to human reason that all children are in fact born with Fitra—the yearning to submit to Allah. They are born Muslims, and made into followers of other faiths by their upbringing in their parents' homes. It is a common experience that when a non-Muslim turns to Islam, there is a very strong feeling that this is nothing new, but that they are coming home. Such converts are often called reverts.

Abu Hurayrah recorded: 'No babe is born but upon Fitra. It is his parents who make him a Jew or a Christian or a polytheist.' (Muslim 6426)

He also recorded: 'Had his parents been Muslim, he would have remained Muslim.' (Muslim 6429)

THE UMMAH

Ummah extends across all places and ethnic groups, and also links people in different historical periods. Each believer feels they are part of a given community, not only in their own time but also of the community extending from the past—all the followers of the all the prophets from Adam onwards!

The unity of believers takes precedence over all other relationships, including those of family. It is a unity of faith.

Abu Musa recorded: 'Believers are like the parts of a building; each part supports the others.' (Muslim 6257)

Numan b. Bashir recorded: 'If any single part of the body aches, the whole body feels the effects and rushes to its relief.' (Muslim 6258)

And: 'Believers are like one person; if his head aches, the whole body aches with fever and sleeplessness.' (Muslim 6259)

'Muslims are like the structure of a building for another Muslim. One portion of it gives strength to the other portion.' Then the Prophet ﷺ twisted the fingers of one hand together with the fingers of the other.' (Bukhari)

It is unfortunately obvious in our split and suffering world that the family of Islam has a long way to go before outsiders can see evidence of real unity amongst the believers. Far too many issues divide the Muslims of different countries and cultures, far too many insecurities and weaknesses are spoiling the faith.

Mua'dh b. Jabal reported: 'The devil is a wolf to humanity, like the wolf which harries sheep, catching the one which is solitary, the one which strays from the flock, and the one which wanders. So avoid the branching paths, and keep to the general community!' (Ahmad)

Abu Dharr reported: 'He who separates himself a handbreadth from the community has cast off the rope of Islam from his neck.' (Ahmad and Abu Dawud)

Abu Hurayrah recorded: 'Do not envy one another, nor dispute with one another, nor hate one another, nor leave one another in the lurch. Take the servants of Allah as brothers. A Muslim is brother to a Muslim, he should neither oppress him, nor put him to disgrace, nor blame him as a liar... it is an evil deed for a man to hate his brother Muslim.' (Muslim)

Muslims of particular countries have to beware of too much nationalism, which is actually divisive in Islam. Above all, they have to avoid the pitfalls of what is often called 'the Muslim of the Year' competition. This means that many Muslims have been overcome by the kind of attitude that regards 'their' Islam as being 'superior' to the Islam of another person. They have become so self-righteous and so 'devout' in their religious devotions and practices, that there is a tendency to look down on other people who are not 'living up to' their standards.

In short, they are in danger of trying to 'become' God the Judge—and this is totally against the spirit of Islam which seeks always to woo gently and to bring into the fold, and never to criticise, ostracise and cast out. Such Muslims have not yet understood the first lesson about there being no compulsion in religion—for love of Allah, like love of any person, is not a matter that can be ordered or forced.

Nevertheless, the ideal of Ummah is there to be aimed at, and insha'Allah, maybe one day the world will see a truly united Islam.

> 'The believers are but a single Brotherhood, so make peace and reconciliation between two (contending) brothers, and fear Allah, that you may receive mercy.' (49:10)

> 'O our Lord, make us submitted ones (Muslims) unto you, and make of our descendants a community (Ummah) that shall surrender itself unto you; and show us our ways of worship, and accept our repentance.' (2:128)

The Family

Abu Hurayrah recorded: 'Those who show the most perfect faith are those who possess the best disposition, and the best of you are those who are kindest to their wives.' (Tirmidhi and Ibn Majah)

The most important thing a human can possess, after the awareness of the care and love of Allah, is the warmth and affection and support to be found in the loving environment of their own home and family.

A household in which there is love, peace and security is valuable beyond price—but this is not something which comes about by accident. It has to be worked for by all its members, and requires a strong commitment to patience, forgiveness, tolerance, and a keen sense of duty. All these things are regarded as vital.

If any person has suffered a broken family as the result of death or disaster, or maybe because of divorce, then they have truly known a loss and a suffering that those who have grown up in security cannot fully appreciate.

The welfare and stability of any society lies in the value it places upon the institution of the 'family.' If a person's family is insecure or disturbed or unsuccessful in any way, it has a radical effect not only upon the people in it throughout the rest of their lives, but also upon the whole framework of contacts that family is going to make.

Islam teaches that the family is actually the cornerstone of the whole social system, and that society's progress or breakdown can be traced directly to its strength or weakness. The well-being of the family cannot possibly be valued too highly. Moreover, it is not a casual or spontaneous institution, but is divinely ordained. It is therefore to be regarded as noble and sacred:

> 'It is He Who created you from a single cell with a mate of like nature, in order that you might live together.' (7:189)

'The family provides the environment within which human values and morals develop and grow in the new generation. The family system and the relationships between the sexes determines the whole character of society and whether it is backward or civilised.' (Sayyid Qutb)

BASIC OBJECTIVES OF THE FAMILY IN ISLAM

To people who do not value their families, or perhaps regard them as just the assortment of relatives they happened to grow up with, the following ideals and objectives might seem rather strange, but they are regarded as very important in Islam.

The first objective is the preservation of the human race by procreation in happy and secure units. Happiness and security are conditions that cannot be bought. They are not automatic. So often people do not value what they have until it is too late—and this frequently happens in families unless they consciously consider their attitudes to each other as individuals within the family.

LOVE WHILE YOU HAVE THE CHANCE

It is a tragic fact that many people, when a loved one dies, feel strong pangs of guilt because they had not fully appreciated that person while alive, had not done everything they possibly could, had not let them know how much they loved them. It is so easy to be irritated with our nearest and dearest, and to forget that Allah might take back their precious souls that very night, and catch us out! Awareness of Allah, and our mortality and dependence upon Him should make us draw closer to our own loved ones before the experience of bereavement catches us out—because they are not our possessions, only gifts from Allah loaned to us for a time.

One sad story concerning the Blessed Prophet's ﷺ relatives involved his aunt Umm Sulaym. Her son Anas b. Malik reported that while her husband Abu Talhah was away, his son breathed his last.

When he came back he said to his wife: 'What about my child?' She said: 'He is now in a more comfortable state than before.' She served him the evening meal, and he took it. He then came to her, and only when that was over did she tell him to make arrangements for the burial of the child. It so turned out that another child, Abdullah, was conceived that very evening.' (Muslim 5341). (See also p. 64)

OTHER OBJECTIVES FOR THE FAMILY

The family is also regarded as the prime means of protecting the morals of individuals and society, satisfying emotional and psychological needs, providing a secure background for the raising of children, and providing social and economic security.

It motivates individuals to work hard, sacrifice their own welfare for that of others, and be generous. It provides a stable framework for the bringing up of children in the faith of Islam.

Abu Masud al-Badri recorded: 'When a man spends to support his family hoping for (Allah's reward) it is counted for him as Sadaqah.' (Bukhari, Muslim)

WHO IS INCLUDED IN THE FAMILY?

The family is not just the mother and father plus a couple of children, as is so common in the West. Where birth control is limited, there are usually far greater numbers of children born—and where health conditions are primitive, there are far greater numbers of deaths of both young and old. Hard conditions make people aware of mortality, and the fact that death is no respecter of persons. It can strike down the least likely person in a moment. No-one can have the least idea how long they will live; the Muslim tries to be ready at all times to face death and accept it with faith.

This kind of awareness of mortality also encourages a strong bond between family members. The Muslim family, therefore, has a much wider aspect, and includes all the persons who are involved in the 'unit.'

If a tragedy befell any relative, or even a member of a neighbour's family—it would be expected that the family would rally round and give support during the time of need. A stable family can take care of children who have lost their parents for whatever reason. Muslim society places kindness to all children as a very high priority, and whether a child's parents are alive or dead, present or absent, children must be provided for with the best possible care.

'Worship none but Allah, and treat with kindness your

parents and kindred, and orphans and those in need; speak kindly to them, be steadfast in prayer, and give your charity regularly.' (2:83)

CONCERNING FATHERS AND MOTHERS

In Islam, the head of a household should be the father. He is responsible for its smooth running and its financial resources. However, the key person in the household who sets the tone and does most of the work is undoubtedly the mother.

Abu Hurayrah recorded that a person asked Allah's Messenger ﷺ: 'Who among the people is most deserving of the best treatment from my hand?' He said: 'Your mother.' He said again: 'Then who is next?' He said: 'Again, it is your mother.' He said: 'Then who?' He said: 'Again, it is your mother.' He said: 'Then who? Thereupon he said: 'Then it is your father.' (Muslim 6180)

To be a good mother is so important in Islam that she is considered to be the most precious treasure in the world, and her role is the decisive factor in the family. What a pity that so many men do not realise that their wives *are* the mothers of the next generation, and simply take them for granted.

It is vitally important that the father of the family treats his wife with the proper respect and consideration, and does not simply regard her as a servant. A good mother *is* a servant, and a very-hard-working one at that—but she should never be abused or looked down on, or taken for granted as a servant.

Children should be trained from an early age to help and respect their mothers, and speak to them politely. It is a disgraceful thing to see spoiled children ordering their mothers about and being rude to them. Fathers have a most important role to play in this respect—for if they themselves are rude and abusive to the mother, their children will simply copy their example. The mother will no doubt be so depressed and unhappy by what has happened to her that she will have lost the ability to stand up for her rights and redress the balance.

It is a Muslim father's duty to see that the mother of his family (or even a childless wife) is never treated with disrespect or taken for granted, either by himself or by anyone else. He should notice when she is tired or ill or in discomfort, and take steps to alleviate her suffering. He should be prepared to help her and not regard this as being beneath his dignity. It should rather be beneath his dignity to see the wife he is responsible for suffering and losing her joy in life because of his careless attitude.

Homes never stay places of joy and refuge unless all the members work hard to create the right atmosphere. Sometimes Muslim men, in their desire to serve Allah well, tend to forget the people they have responsibility over and spend all available time amongst friends at the mosque. This is really an abuse of their families, and they should be encouraged to see that it is more pleasing to Allah to create happiness amongst their family by serving him in the home, than by selfishly seeking good for their own souls while neglecting their wives and children.

It is a good idea for Muslim men to remember every hadith of the Blessed Prophet's ﷺ concerning love and care and good treatment of one's neighbour, and treat the wife with just as much love and care—for she is, after all, a man's closest neighbour!

CONCERNING CHILDREN

It is natural for parents to hope that their children will be a source of pride for them, but sometimes parents can 'put them on a pedestal', or overestimate their talents and capabilities—and this can cause enormous stress. Parents should therefore be on their guard against anything which might spoil or distress the child.

The Prophet 變 was once approached by some Bedouin who were surprised when he kissed his children. 'Ai'shah recorded that they said: 'By Allah! We do not kiss our children.' Thereupon Allah's Messenger 變 said: 'Then what can I do, if Allah has deprived you of mercy? (Muslim 5735)

Abu Hurayrah recorded: 'He who does not show mercy (towards his children), no mercy will be shown to him.' (Muslim 5736)

Parents should avoid being over-protective, over-indulgent or too proud of their children. They should not push their children beyond their abilities, or be disappointed with them if they cannot do all the things they had hoped.

No single child in a family should be made the favourite, but all should be treated equally, and with firm but fair discipline.

An-Numan ibn Bashir reported: 'My mother asked my father to present me a gift from his property, and he gave it to me after some hesitation. My mother said that she would not be satisfied unless the Prophet 變 was made a witness to it. I being a young boy, my father held me by the hand and took me to the Prophet 變. He said to the Prophet 變: 'His mother requested me to give this boy a gift.' The Prophet 變 said: Do you have other sons besides him?' He said: 'Yes.' The Prophet 變 said: 'Do not make me a witness for injustice.' (Bukhari)

Moreover, favouritism should not be shown to sons above daughters. The Prophet ﷺ insisted that Muslims should not act as in pre-Islamic times, but should value their girl-children.

Ibn Annas recorded: 'If anyone has a female child and does not bury her alive (one pre-Islamic method of birth-control was to put a new-born baby face down in the sand before it had drawn breath), or slight her, or prefer his male children to her, that will bring him to Paradise.' (Abu Dawud 5127)

Abu Sayd al-Khudri recorded: 'If anyone cares for three daughters, trains them, gets them married, and does good to them, he will go to Paradise.' (Abu Dawud 5128)

ALL ARE INDIVIDUALS

Muslims are expected to treat all people as individuals, and not to try to force their children to be something they are not. They should accept their natural qualities, encourage their good points, and gently steer them away from bad characteristics.

The most important thing a parent can do for a child is to set a good example, so that the child grows up devout, kind, independent, and able to help others.

They should give the child the best possible education, not just to be clever but so that they may be able to earn a living and be independent. They should help them to make happy marriages, so far as it lies in their power. They should neither be negligent nor over-protective, but train them in a good way of life.

Ibn Abbas reported: 'He who has no compassion for our little ones and does not acknowledge the honour due to our elders, is not one of us.' (Tirmidhi)

Incidentally, the Blessed Prophet ﷺ also praised the woman who was bereft of male support and did her best to bring up her fatherless children on her own:

Awf b. Malik al-Ashjal reported: 'I and a woman whose cheeks have become black shall be like these two on Resurrection Day (pointing to middle and forefinger). (Abu Dawud 5130)

CONCERNING OLD PEOPLE

Muslims should love and cherish their parents and look after them unselfishly; they should also train their children to cherish them in their turn.

Muslims should never regard old people as a burden or a nuisance. All people are travelling along the same road towards old age. Today's old people were yesterday's providers and heroes, and have a right to be respected. Therefore a Muslim family should take the best possible care of its own old people, be they actual parents, or uncles and aunts who have grown old.

In Muslim families age comes first, and the grandparents should take priority over the children, who should be taught to be respectful and considerate. Muslims should treat their parents with great honour and respect, and behave towards them with tolerance and understanding.

'Your Lord orders that you... be kind to parents. If one or both of them attain old age with you, do not say one word of contempt to them, or repel them, but speak to them in terms of honour... and say, My Lord, bestow Your mercy on them, as they cherished me when I was a child.' (17:23-24)

Muslims are forbidden to be disrespectful, even if the parents are non-Muslims and try to turn them against Islam.

'Be grateful to Me and to your parents... If they try to make you (go against Me) do not obey them; but keep company with them in this life in a kind manner, and follow the way of them who turn to Me.' (31:14-15)

There is obviously a very special relationship between children and parents, and this bond grows stronger as the children become adults and elderly themselves. Parents will never cease to feel like parents towards their offspring—they continue to nag chide, 'bully', criticise—no matter what the age of their children.

As people become old, they do not regard themselves as old. They are the same people they always were, but they often become confused, or bad tempered, or suffer from diseases, aches and pains. It is human nature for them to think that they are always in the right, and always superior to their children, even if they are in the wrong, and even if the children themselves are in their sixties!

The 'children' should be aware that there will inevitably come a time when perhaps the parent's judgement may be clouded, or they may not be able to cope. They should be aware of their increased physical weakness and possible mental weakness, which may be accompanied by impatience, lack of energy, increased sensitivity and misjudgement. An increase of patience and kindness on the part of their family is what is required to cope with this.

'Serve them with tenderness and humility, and say 'My Lord have mercy on them, just as they cared for me when I was a little child.' (17:23-24)

In this day and age, many people of child-bearing age decide *not* to have children for various reasons. Women who choose to remain childless perhaps took notice of how their mothers were treated, and how they had to cope to the point of exhaustion without much support. Other women prefer a career, or to create a beautiful home without the 'mess' children create.

Young women who deliberately choose childlessness must bear in mind that they may see things totally differently when they hit their forties and not only have no joy of grandchildren but are probably too late to produce offspring themselves.

Moreoever, remember that the day will come when these people, perhaps childless though selfishness, will have to rely on the kindness and nursing abilities of other people's children.

SOME PRACTICAL INSTRUCTIONS

Muslims should always be patient, compassionate, respectful and kind towards their parents. It is considered impolite for a child to call his parents by their first names, or to do in front of them things which they disapprove of—smoking, for example. Don't walk in front of them, or sit down before they do. Never interrupt them or argue with them—you can always think your own thoughts! Help them without being asked, and avoid doing anything that irritates them.

If your parents ask for something you cannot afford, or have wishes you cannot fulfil, then you should not be impatient but apologise in a polite manner. If you draw attention to the care or support you are giving your parents, or what you spend on them, you will make them feel a burden, or feel guilty.

Parents are much more sensitive to any act of discourtesy towards them from their own children than from any other people. Hurtful behaviour or speech from their own children hurts them more than anything else.

Abu Bakr reported: 'Allah defers the punishment of all your sins until the Day of Judgement except one—disobedience to parents. For that, Allah punishes the sinner in this life before death.' (Bayhaqi)

It is considered unthinkable for Muslims to pass over the care of their parents to a stranger unless there is no alternative. Just as the mother expects to bring her own child into the world and nurse it until it reaches independence, so the Muslim 'child' is expected to care for parents who are approaching the end of life, and to nurse them safely into the next life.

Abu Hurayrah recorded: 'May his nose be rubbed in dust who found his parents approaching old age and lost his right to enter Paradise because he did not look after them.' (Tirmidhi)

In fact, the Blessed Prophet ﷺ thought care of parents so important that no personal religious devotion should ever be used as an excuse for neglecting them.

Abdullah b. Amr recorded that a person came seeking permission to participate in jihad, but the Prophet ﷺ found out that he had parents living, and sent him away saying: 'Go back to your parents and look after them.' (Muslim 6186)

CONCERNING ORPHANS

The Prophet ﷺ knew from his own experience the sorrows of being orphaned. His father died before he was born, and his mother while he was a toddler. He was brought up first by his beloved grandfather Abd al-Muttalib, and then by his kind uncle Abu Talib, and his aunt Fatimah of whom the Prophet ﷺ said that she cherished him even more than her own children. Later in life, the Prophet ﷺ repaid some of this kindness by bringing up this uncle's son, Ali, as his own. He also adopted his slave Zayd ibn Harithah.

'By the glorious light of morning, and the stillness of
night—your God has never forsaken you, and He is not
angry with you. Did He not find you an orphan, and gave
you shelter?' (93:1-6)

Abu Hurayrah recorded: 'I, and the one who raises an
orphan, will be like these two in the Garden' (his middle and
index fingers). (Muslim 7108, Abu Dawud 5131)

The Qur'an teaches that any orphaned or abandoned
child should be looked after by a welcoming family as an act
of compassion, and given shelter, food, clothing and anything
else they need. This is regarded as an important charitable act
for which Allah promises great rewards.

No fostered or adopted children should ever be misled
about their true parentage, or allowed the rights of children
born into a family. Mere human words or contracts cannot
make a parent's blood run in the veins of an adopted child,
or produce family affection and loyalty, or bestow genetic
characteristics.

'He has not made your adopted sons your real sons; that
is simply what you call them... Call them by the names of
their fathers; that is more just in the sight of Allah. But if
you do not know their fathers, they are your brothers-in-
faith and your wards.' (33:4-5)

Islam insists that the identity of the real parents should
be kept clear. Adopted children should always be told the
circumstances of their upbringing. This becomes important
when considering marriage, or inheritance.

Abu Bakra recorded: 'If someone claims a person as his
father with the knowledge that he is not his father, the
Garden will be forbidden to him.' (Bukhari)

'Raised' sons are not allowed the freedom of a 'true' son
with the women of the family. A man's wife is not an adopted

son's mother, nor is his daughter an adopted son's sister.

However, caring for orphans is regarded as a vital act, and the helpless status of children who have lost parents is never to be taken advantage of.

> 'To orphans restore their property (when they come of age); do not substitute your things of less value for their valuables; do not use up their inheritance by mixing it up with yours.' (4:2; see also 4:6 and 4:10)

> 'Come not near the orphan's property except to improve it.' (17:34)

To the amazement of the Arab tribesmen who had previously done very well for themselves by appropriating the rights of orphaned girls—the Prophet's ﷺ words applied as much to female orphans as to male ones!

MILK BROTHERS

If a baby is given to another woman to breast-feed on a regular basis, that child would be regarded as brother or sister to the suckling mother's own children, and future marriage between them would not be allowed.

Uqbah b. al-Harith recorded: 'I married Umm Yahya bint Abu Thab. A black woman entered upon us. She said she had suckled both of us. So I came to the Prophet ﷺ and mentioned it to him. He turned away from me. I said: 'Messenger of Allah! She is a liar!' He said: 'What do you know? She has said what she has said. Separate yourself from her (your wife).' (Abu Dawud 3596) (The evidence of a single woman, the one who suckled the child, is held by most scholars to be sufficient evidence. Malik and Abu Hanifah hold that two women are necessary, and al-Shafi'i thought three other women should back up the original witness— Awn al-Mabud III, 336).

This milk-feeding did not apply to casual situations, someone feeding a friend's baby on one or a couple of occasions.

'A'ishah recorded: 'One suckling or two do not make (marriage) unlawful.' (Muslim 3414)

There is opinion that there was once an injunction in the Qur'an that it had to be over five sucklings to make the child a 'milk-brother', (see Surah 4:23), but jurists have divergent opinions over this. If a man was intimate with his wife and swallowed some of her milk, it would not affect his status.

There are reports of Aishah sending some of her milk so that she could speak privately to various men, but it is hard to see where this milk came from, since she never had a child.

WHEN NOT TO OBEY

Finally, Muslims must remember that the most important 'person' in every family is not any of the family members as such, but Allah Himself. So long as He comes first and His will is sought after by each family member, then success will come to that household.

But if any family member tried to turn another away from Allah, then this is the one case when their wishes should not be respected.

'O believers! Take not for protectors your fathers and your brothers if they love infidelity above faith. If any of you do so, you do wrong. Say: If it be that your father, your sons, your brothers, your friends, or (any of) your kindred... are dearer to you than Allah or His Apostle, or the striving in His cause—then wait until God brings about His decision. He guides not the rebellious.' (9:23-24)

We have enjoined on humanity kindness to parents; but if they strive (to force) you to join with Me anything of which you have no knowledge, obey them not. (29:8)

The Qur'an gives the warning from the story of the Prophet Noah ﷺ, whose son turned away from belief and thus perished in the flood.

'Noah called upon his Lord and said: 'O my Lord! Surely my son is of my family! And your promise is true, You are the most just of judges.' He said: 'O Noah! He is not of your family, for his conduct is unrighteous.' (11:45-46)

Marriage

Sex is a gift of pleasure and comfort from Allah which should not be abused or misused. Marriage is the institution ordained by Allah to bring sexual happiness (amongst other blessings) to humanity.

> 'And among His signs is this, that He created for you mates from among yourselves, that you may live in tranquillity with them; and He has put love and mercy between your (hearts). Truly in that are signs (about the nature of Allah) for those who reflect.' (30:21)

The Blessed Prophet ﷺ disapproved of the idea of celibacy, or living without sex, as an ungrateful and unnatural

way of life. People who deliberately abstain from sex, for a multitude of reasons, often develop a view of human life which most people would not accept as being normal. Since the only proper way for a Muslim to take part in sexual activity is within marriage, the commitment to a good life-partner and the building up of a successful relationship together is of vital importance, indeed, it is 'half the faith.'

Anas b. Malik recorded: 'Whoever has married has completed half of his faith; therefore let him be conscious of Allah in the other half of his faith.' (Bayhaqi)

Abdullah ibn Masud recorded: 'O young men, those among you who can support a wife should marry, for it restrains eyes and preserves one from immorality.' (Muslim)

Marriage is not regarded as a mystical sacrament 'made in heaven' between two perfectly attuned souls, but as a social contract which brings rights and obligations to ordinary men and women, and which can only be successful when these are mutually respected and cherished, and both partners are 'pulling in the same direction' and for each other's benefit—not against each other. Just putting two people together in a house does not make a marriage—but a great deal of hard work, sympathy, humour and patience does! The Blessed Prophet himself had a delightful, earthy humour about wives:

Jabir b. Abdullah recorded that the Prophet ﷺ once commented with a wry humour that there were more women than men in Hell. When asked why, he said: 'Because you (women) grumble (more) often, and are ungrateful to your spouses!' (Muslim 1926)

In fact, there is no difference of value between male and female Muslims—they are equal in every respect. They were created from a single soul, and are complementary—one sex is not more important or cherished by Allah than the other.

However, the notion of 'role-playing' is important in Islam as one of the fundamental ways in which happiness and contentment can be achieved on earth.

Many women will recognise the 'truth' that they are regarded as 'people' or 'individuals' so long as they remain single, but once they marry, a subtle change of identity occurs. A woman becomes 'someone's wife.' This change may or may not be satisfactory to the couple. If it is not satisfactory, a lot of problems arise. Husband and wife adopt different roles, which should be complementary, and which are only successful if there is no resentment.

Muslims believe that it is the duty of the husband to be the head of the family, the 'boss', and that if this is not the case friction is bound to arise.

'The man is the ruler over his wife and children, and is answerable to Allah for the conduct of their affairs. The woman is ruler over the house of her husband and she is answerable for the conduct of her duties.' (Bukhari)

Muslim men have been granted the role of head of the family as their God-given right. If a wife is rebellious, or finds that she cannot accept this situation, the marriage is not going to be very successful. Therefore it is vital that a Muslim woman should take very great care to marry a man whom she really does respect and who is worthy of her—for there is nothing more irritating than being obliged to accept graciously the orders of someone who really is not 'up to the job.' On the same lines, just as a Muslim man should not seek advancement at work that he is not capable of performing well, he should be realistic in his choice of wife and try to avoid trouble by choosing a life-partner who will be compatible to him.

The Blessed Prophet, who dearly loved his wives (especially Khadijah and 'A'ishah), knew very well what made for happiness in his marriages. He enjoyed feeling welcomed by his wives, and appreciated the knowledge that they did so many things to please him—the mere sight of them made him happy; he knew that they respected his wishes and would not go against him; and he knew that he could trust them not to let him down in his absence.

Umar recorded that he once said: 'Shall I tell you about the best treasure a man can have? It is a virtuous wife who always pleases him whenever he looks at her, who obeys him whenever he orders her, and who guards herself when he is absent from her.' (Abu Dawud, Ibn Majah)

The husband should regard himself and his wife as a team, in which the wife is highly dependent upon him. A good Muslim husband is obliged to treat the wife just as he would treat himself, for example in such things as spending on food and clothing.

Mu'awiyah recorded: 'You shall give her food when you take your food, and you shall clothe her when you clothe yourself.' (Abu Dawud)

If the husband is miserly and reluctant to see to her expenses out of his wages, and does not willingly provide adequate maintenance, the wife is entitled to take money from him without his consent. 'A'ishah reported that Abu Sufyan's wife Hind once complained to the Blessed Prophet on this very subject:

'A'ishah recorded that Hind said: 'Abu Sufyan is a miserly person. He does not give adequate maintenance for me and my children, but I take from his wealth without his knowledge. Is this a sin on my part?' Thereupon Allah's Messenger said: 'Take from his property the usual amount that would suffice you and your children.' (Muslim 4251)

The Blessed Prophet ﷺ knew that men sometimes became irritated with their women, but he knew very well that it was wrong to try to force women to change their characters and be different, and pointless to be frustrated by things that were not going to change.

Abu Hurayrah recorded that the Blessed Prophet ﷺ said humorously: 'Treat women kindly. Women have been created from a rib. (The rib is a crooked bone) and the most crooked part of it is the upper region. If you try to make it straight, you will only break it; and if you leave it as it is, it is bound to remain crooked (and will therefore continue to annoy you)! So treat women kindly.' (Bukhari and Muslim)

The Blessed Prophet ﷺ was quite clear that no matter how provoked a man might feel, he should never strike his wife on the face or speak to her abusively, or rudely neglect her whilst out in public.

Hakim b. Mu'awiyah recorded: 'You shall not slap her on the face nor revile her, nor leave her alone except within the house.' (Abu Dawud)

A wife was to be cherished, treated kindly and protected.

'If the wife performs her five daily prayers, restrains herself from adultery, and obeys her husband, she will enter Paradise through whichever of its doors she wishes.' (Abu Dawud and Ibn Majah)

ARRANGED MARRIAGES

In the Muslim world there is little free contact between young men and women because chastity and modesty are strongly emphasized. It is the chief loving duty of a Muslim parent to help the young person choose a good life-partner.

All parents hope to see their offspring happily set on their path to married life, so therefore great care is usually taken in the choice of a spouse.

Sometimes the proposed person will be a known member of the family, perhaps a cousin. In all cases the parents should examine and he guided by the family background and known character of the young person of their choice, and not just choose somebody for convenience, or to oblige other family members. Indeed, when an individual marries a relative, it can lead to enormous family trauma if the marriage fails and the partners seek to divorce. The Prophet did marry one of his cousins, Zaynab bint Jahsh, but she was his seventh choice and nowhere near his first choice!

The ideal of an arranged marriage is that young people should have been kept chaperoned from the opposite sex in order to maintain their purity and modesty into young adulthood. It is quite important that they do not get attracted to other youngsters, or begin to 'suffer the pangs' of teenage romance—(usually nothing more than a very powerful sexual urge created by something which catches the youngster's fancy—like the person's face, figure, or even the clothes they wear). Muslims are far more concerned with more lasting matters—the character of the young husband and wife, whether they will be compatible and suitable for each other.

They look to see if the chosen partner will be kind, good humoured, tolerant, honest, generous, hard-working, and so forth. What the youngster looks like is of very secondary importance. It is not good Islam to despise a person because Allah happens to have given them a face or figure which is not considered attractive. That attitude only causes endless hurt to the so-called 'unattractive' person. Islam places its values quite differently—what makes a person attractive is not their face of figure, but their inner character.

This is why parents assume such large responsibility—for they are often in a far better position to judge such matters than the young people involved, and if they are doing their job properly, they will get to know the proposed marriage partner as well as possible, and find out as much as possible about him or her from those who are in a position to know, in order to judge their character and their qualities and see if they will be suitable for their own child to marry.

Having made a choice, it is then up to the Muslim parents to present this choice to their son or daughter, to see if they react favourably or unfavourably. If, for example, a girl sees a proposed young man and feels that she could not possibly marry him, then the marriage plans should proceed no further—unless she is given the chance to change her mind at a later date when she has had time to reflect, and she does change her mind. Similarly, a young man may be introduced to a young women and feel the same kind of aversion.

For this reason, these meetings are usually arranged very tactfully, so that retreat is possible without people feeling hurt or snubbed. This is particularly important if the suggested spouse is a cousin, for it is wrong in Islam to put pressure on young people to marry those they do not wish to, simply because the family would like it and would find it difficult to refuse an uncle's request.

The usual meeting-ground of Muslim young people from eastern cultures is at family gatherings—perhaps someone else's wedding, where the young man and young woman, although never left alone, will at least be given the opportunity to have the proposed partner pointed out to them, and perhaps to observe them tactfully.

Nobody should be forced to marry—the parents can set the whole thing up, but it should be the young couple themselves who make the final decision. Occasionally parents do feel that they know better than the youngsters involved, and have seen so many other 'protesting brides' settle down and become happy wives that they do not take the objections too seriously. Nobody can ever guarantee that a marriage will work—but it is worth commenting that in the UK, where youngsters have unlimited opportunity to see and know (even intimately) the eventual marital partner, the marriages are not successful and the divorce rate is at present running at around 50%!

In some societies the bride and groom do not see each other at all before marriage, but this is actually against the teaching of the Blessed Prophet ﷺ.

Abu Hurayrah recorded that when the Prophet ﷺ was told of a certain man who had arranged to marry, he asked him straight away: 'Have you had a look at her?' When the man said he had not done so, the Prophet ordered him to go to see her. (Muslim 3314)

Jabir b. Abdullah recorded: 'When one of you asks a woman in marriage, if he is able to look and see what makes him wish to marry her, he should do so.' Jabir said: 'I asked a girl to marry me, and I used to look at her secretly, until I saw why I wanted to marry her.' (Abu Dawud 2073)

'A'ishah recorded that she asked the Prophet ﷺ about the marriage of young girls whose guardians arranged matches for them. Was it necessary to consult the girl involved, or not? He said: 'Yes, she must be consulted.' (Muslim 3305)

If a girl does not object to the match but is too shy to speak, her silence is taken as consent—but she has to be given a genuine opportunity to voice her consent or refusal. Parents who avoid giving their offspring the opportunity to see each other first, often take this attitude because they do not want the couple to be influenced just by physical appearance—which is bound to assume some importance when people meet briefly. Sometimes marriages are arranged in which (usually) wives are brought to a new land from the male Muslim's country of origin (if he is an immigrant), and it would be too expensive and difficult to arrange for them to meet beforehand.

Sometimes these are regarded as 'fake' marriages, by people who do not understand the cultural background of the people involved. In the West, it seems almost incredible that boys and girls can grow up with so little contact—but in many Muslim cultures this is the way of life.

No Muslim should ever try to force another to marry someone they do not wish to, although we do hear of sad cases where the parents have abused their position and sent their daughters off very much against their will, hoping they will come to accept it and settle down. Many are very unhappy as a result, although as the parents know, sometimes it does work out. In a society where divorce is possible to put right marital mistakes, such wrong decisions are not the end of the world, but in places where divorce is usually denied to the woman, such arranged and enforced marriages are totally against the spirit of Islam.

Most Muslim young people, therefore, do not marry 'under the influence of love'—which is regarded as rather a dangerous influence since it clouds the judgement—but on the whole they are happy to accept the guidance of their parents, who love them, and have had the chance to see and get to know their intended partners long enough to make a decision. For many of these couples real love comes after the marriage—when they have got to know each other—and not before.

PARTNERSHIP IN MARRIAGE

In Islam, marriage is a partnership. A husband is not a master—Muslim women accept only Allah as their Master, and have the right to over-rule him or disobey him if he wants them to do anything against the wishes of Allah. Therefore Muslim wives do not consider themselves to be inferior to a husband.

'And the believers, men and women, are friends of one another. They enjoin good and forbid evil'. (9:71)

Islamic marriage is a legal and binding contract between two people who accept each other with a mutual commitment to take no other sexual partner, and to live together according to the teachings of Islam. If either husband or wife departs from Islam, and life becomes uncomfortable for the other partner, then divorce is considered permissible.

Abdullah b. Umar recorded: 'Every one of you is a shepherd, and is responsible for his flock. A ruler is a shepherd and is accountable for his domain. A man is a shepherd in charge of the inhabitants of his household. A woman is a shepherdess in charge of her husband's house and children, and she is responsible for them; a man's slave is a shepherd in charge of his master's property, and he is responsible for it.' (Bukhari, Abu Dawud 2922)

MALE DOMINANCE IN MARRIAGE

'Men are the protectors and maintainers of women, because Allah has given the one more (strength) than the other, and because they support them out of their means.

Therefore the righteous women are devoutly obedient,
and guard in (the husband's) absence what Allah would
have them guard.' (3:34)

For a marriage to work successfully, one person usually
takes on the role of 'head of the family.' Most women, when
they fall in love with a man, are happy to look after him and
see to his needs and the needs of his children—on the
understanding that the man keeps his obligation to provide
for them and not take his wife for granted.

Umar recorded: 'The best of treasures is a good wife.
She is pleasing in her husband's eyes, looks for ways to please
him, and takes care of his possessions while he is away; and
the best of you are those who treat their wives best!' (Abu
Dawud) (See the section on Mothers and Fathers in the
chapter on the Family p. 171).

In Muslim marriage, the roles of males and females are
regarded as equal, but different. Both came from a single soul,
and are intended to be complementary.

'O humanity, be careful of your duty to your Lord, Who
created you from a single soul and from it created its mate,
and from the two of them spread abroad a multitude of men
and women.' (4:1)

Many men think that their dignity requires them to
issue a multitude of orders, and that it is enough to be
provider—their wives should be content to get on with their
business efficiently without bothering them too much. These
husbands are missing out on a really happy relationship in
which man and wife work together in love and fulfilment,
and are really seeking a servant, not a wife!

Most women are content to do an enormous amount
of work under considerable strain, so long as their men
appreciate when they are doing and do not take them for
granted.

Unfortunately, many men seem to forget the encouragement of the Blessed Prophet ﷺ that a good Muslim husband should treat his wife in the best possible manner. They seem unable to grasp the simple skill of 'rewarding' their wives with encouragement, little words of love, and keeping an eye open for when their wives look tired or under strain. No woman particularly wants her man interfering in her kitchen or other domestic arrangements—but to be noticed, and invited to sit down, and be made a fuss of from time to time would be the opening of the flower in many marriages that have stayed 'nipped in the bud.'

Al-Aswad said: 'I asked 'A'ishah—what did the Prophet ﷺ used to do in his house?' She said: "He used to work for his family, that is, serve his family; and when prayer (time) came he went for prayer.' (Bukhari)

THE RIGHT TO COMPATIBILITY IN MARRIAGE

Abu Hurayrah recorded: 'A woman is sought in marriage on account of four things—her property, her family, her beauty and her piety. You should seek to win one for the sake of piety.' (Muslim 3457, Abu Dawud 2042)

Abdullah b. Umar recorded: 'Do not marry only for a person's looks; their beauty might become the cause of moral decline. Do not marry for the sake of wealth, as this may become the cause of disobedience. Marry rather on the grounds of religious devotion.' (Tirmidhi)

The only compatibility that really matters in Islam is piety. It matters far more than equal financial, social or educational status. The Blessed Prophet ﷺ permitted marriages between people of vastly different social status and financial backgrounds (and his own marriage with Khadijah was an excellent example), knowing that it was not these factors which made for compatibility, but what they were like in their hearts.

The most important ingredients in a Muslim marriage are shared values and beliefs, so that even if the couple come from totally different cultures and backgrounds, they possess the same basic view of the universe, and attitudes and habits which will bind them together.

> 'A slave who believes is better than an unbelieving woman,
> even though she attracts you.' (2:221)

The aim in marriage is that the partner should also be 'best friend' and 'closest neighbour', the one who shares the concerns and responsibilities of life, who offers peace, comfort and rest, and who helps to bear difficulties which would be too much to be faced alone.

THE RIGHT OF BEING A HOUSEWIFE

Muslim women have the right to run their own households without the strain of having to go out to earn wages. In fact, Islam raised the status of the housewife as no other religion or society has ever done before or since, even giving a mother the right to charge her husband for breast-feeding his baby. Being a housewife or 'house-mother' is regarded as the most valuable of all occupations, for it safeguards the next generation, and gives comfort and support to the existing family members. A wise man loves and cherishes the mother of his family above all else.

Abu Hurayrah recorded: 'A man came to the Prophet ﷺ and asked: 'Who among all people is most worthy of my good company?' The Prophet ﷺ said, 'Your mother.' The man again asked: 'Who next?' He said: 'Your mother.' The man again asked: 'Who next?' Again the Prophet ﷺ said: 'Your mother.' Only next did he say: 'Your father.' (Bukhari,

Muslim 6188, Abu Dawud 5120)

Don't forget that the word 'housewife' frequently means 'unpaid cleaner, cook, gardener, nurse, child-minder, chauffeur, teacher, secretary, etc. It would cost a husband a fortune to replace what his wife does with hired staff.

.BIRTH CONTROL

Muslims believe it is only Allah who controls when births and deaths take place; if a child is born to a couple in spite of their attempts to prevent conception, it is due to Allah's will.

Abu Sirma recorded that once the Muslims were on an expedition and wished to have sex with some women without making them conceive (by using the withdrawal) method; this incident took place before the cancellation of the tribal traditional 'mutah' or temporary marriages). The Prophet 鄘 retorted: 'It does not matter if you do not do it (i.e. withdraw), for every soul that is to be born up to the Day of Resurrection will be born.' (Muslim 3371)

However, the Prophet 鄘 apparently did not object when his friends and supporters told him they practised the withdrawal method of contraception, so some scholars deduce from this that methods which prevent fertilisation from taking place are not 'hidden killing', but those which destroyed a foetus after conception were not allowed.

Abu Sa'id al-Khudri reported: 'When Allah intends to create anything, nothing can prevent it.' (Muslim 3381)

Jabir recorded one incident when a person reported to the Prophet 鄘 that he practised the withdrawal method because he did not wish to make the woman pregnant. The Prophet 鄘 said: 'Practise 'azl (withdrawal) if you like, but what is decreed for her will come to her.' The person eventually came back and said: 'She has become pregnant.' Whereupon he said: 'I told you what was decreed for her would come to her.' (Muslim 3383)

Jabir made it quite clear that: 'We used to practise 'azl during the lifetime of Allah's Messenger ﷺ. This reached him, and he did not forbid us.' (Muslim 3388)

A man may not practise birth-control by withdrawal without the consent of his wife, since it might deprive her of her right to full sexual satisfaction. Neither husband nor wife should practise any form of birth-control secretly, without the consent of the other partner.

ABORTION

In Arabia, before the time of the Prophet ﷺ the usual way to regulate the size of a family was not by birth control, but by allowing conception and pregnancy to happen naturally, then to take the unwanted babies (usually girls) and bury them face down in the sand immediately after birth—almost like the practice of drowning kittens or puppies before they have drawn breath. This practice was totally forbidden by the Qur'an.

'Slay not your children... the killing of them is a great sin.' (17:31)

Muslims do not accept the argument that population growth must be controlled to avoid overcrowding the earth, or because of poverty.

'Do not slay your children because of poverty—We will provide for you and for them.' (6:151)

Some Muslim scholars used to argue that the breath of life, or spirit, of an individual did not enter the foetus until the end of four months of pregnancy, and therefore abortion in those early days was not forbidden.

Abdullah b. Mas'ud recorded: 'The creation of each one of you is brought together in your mother's belly for 40 days in the form of a seed, then you are a clot of blood for a like period, then a morsel of flesh for a like period, then there is sent to you an angel who blows the breath of life into you.' (Muslim 6390, Abu Dawud 4691).

So, if the soul enters the foetus after 120 days, if an abortion is absolutely necessary it should clearly be done before that time. After the fourth month, abortion would be unlawful killing.

However, others maintain against this that no-one really knows the nature of the soul or spirit, and that when the Prophet ﷺ asked to define it he was instructed by Allah to say that knowledge of it belonged to Allah alone. Therefore, the foetus represents a potential life from the very moment of conception, and should be protected and given all the rights of human life, in the same way as any other person.

This point of view is totally backed up by the modern ultrasound equipment which can show the life, activity, and changes in the foetus from the very earliest moments. The baby is developing, feeling and moving long before the mother is aware of it at around the 16th week.

It is certainly the case that a foetus has developed enough to be regarded as fully human by the *sixth* week, when its sensory and motor nerves are functioning, and it reacts to painful stimuli.

One hadith indicates six weeks as a highly important moment in the development of a foetus: 'When forty-two nights have passed over that which is conceived, Allah sends an angel to it, who shapes it, makes it ears, eyes, skin, flesh and bones; then the angel says: 'O Lord, is it male or female?'

and your Lord decides what He wishes, and the angels record it.' (Muslim 6396).

In modern support of this, ultra-sound scanners *can* detect in the sixth week whether the foetus is male or female.

Most people who see the films taken by ultrasound of an abortion, and realise what is actually involved, very quickly realise how serious and terrible a matter abortion is. It is the taking of a life. Women who have abortion maybe adjust at the time, but the trauma of what they have done never leaves then for the rest of their lives.

Abortion is only lawful in Islam in a case where the life of the mother is genuinely at stake, on the principle that the life that already exists (the mother) takes precedence over the life that is still only potential (the unborn child). The tree trunk is saved at the expense of its branches.

Some women argue that it is a woman's right to decide what she does with her own body. They insist that she has the right to choose whether or not to give birth to a child. Muslims maintain that this means the woman has conveniently forgetting her unborn child, the separate living person with its own body that is temporarily within her. The Qur'an reminds these mothers that on Judgement Day infants will want to know why they were killed.

> 'When the souls are sorted out; when the female infant buried alive is asked for what crime she was killed;... .when the World on High is unveiled... then shall each soul know what it has sent ahead.' (81:7-9, 11, 14)

TEMPORARY MARRIAGE

The origin of the idea of temporary marriage, or mut'ah, was to put an end to illicit sex. Under this arrangement, a man and woman may live together as husband

and wife for a specified period and under specified conditions, at the end of which time they are automatically separated. In support of this custom, surah 4:24 is cited:

> 'Then as to those from whom you derive profit *(famastam-ta'tum)* give them their dowries as appointed.'

In fact, when put in context it is clear that the real meaning of the full verse is that a man should pay a fixed dower to those whom he did marry, the payment of the dower being a sign of proper wedlock.

> 'And lawful for you are (all women) besides those (listed in previous verses), provided that you seek (them) in marriage, not committing debauchery. Then, as to those from whom you derive profit, give them their dowries as appointed.' (4:24)

Mut'ah was an established custom in Arabia before the advent of Islam, and it seems that the Prophet ﷺ had not revoked permission at first. Later, however—either after the conquest of Makkah or the victory at Khaybar, he did issue an order of prohibition. This order was continued after his demise.

For example, Caliph Umar declared he would cancel, annul, prohibit and punish Mut'ah-al-Hajj and Mut'ah an-Nisa. (Muslim). He once declared from the pulpit: 'Should I know that someone had contracted mut'ah, I shall straight away charge him with adultery, and mete out the punishment.'

Those who support mut'ah sometimes quote Abdallah ibn Abbas who gives the hadith: 'Mut'ah in a time of distress is as much permissible as are dead meat, pork and animal blood.' However, Ali reprimanded him for expressing this opinion and told him the Prophet ﷺ had definitely forbidden mut'ah on 'the day of Khaybar.' He was backed up by Urwah ibn Zubayr.

The question was actually put direct to Aishah, and she advised those seeking knowledge to refer to the Qur'an, and recited the following verse:

> 'And those who restrain their sexual passion, except with their wives and those whom their right hands possess, for such, in certainty, there is no blame. But whoever seeks to go beyond that, these are transgressors.' (23:5).

Polygamy

'Marry women of your choice, two, three or four; but if
you fear that you shall not be able to deal justly with them,
then only one.' (4:3)

Many non-Muslims have the fixed notion in their heads
that Muslims all marry a vast number of wives. This is a
nonsense. In pre-Islamic times, polygamy was unrestricted,
a man taking as many wives as he wished. Indeed, a wealthy
man who limited himself to only one wife was considered
ungenerous. Feelings of individual women were not taken
into consideration. That there was a good deal of unhappi-
ness, jealousy and friction is amply illustrated in the pages of
the Old Testament.

The revelation of Islam did not forbid polygamy, but
drastically curtailed it and allowed it only under certain
stringent conditions.

In fact, the ideal Muslim family is monogamous—
except in situations where there is an unfortunate surplus of
women who are not provided for, and no-one to support
them, as we shall see in a moment. In normal circumstances,
if any man wishes to take on more than one wife, there are
all sorts of restrictions to consider, and the most important
of these is whether or not his existing wife is able to accept
the arrangement happily. One of the most basic rules of Islam

is that no one Muslim should ever deliberately hurt another, male or female equally. It is patently obvious that in the vast majority of cases no woman is going to want to share her husband with another woman, so the question of polygamy will not arise.

However, it is neither prohibited nor unlawful for a Muslim man to have more than one wife in certain circumstances. Islam did not introduce the practice. On the contrary, polygamy had been the normal practice of most countries in the ancient civilisations for centuries, usually for the very practical and pragmatic reasons that there were no welfare states or benefits for women who could not support themselves.

As regards the practice of the Prophet ﷺ himself, we have two sunnahs to consider. The Prophet ﷺ married for the first time when he was around 25 years old, and remained faithfully married to just this one wife until she died 25 years later. In the last ten years of his life, the Prophet ﷺ married a series of women, all widows and divorcees except 'A'ishah, the daughter of Abu Bakr.

It is a well known fact that the Prophet's ﷺ first marriage was somewhat unusual in that his wife was his employer, a woman some 15 years older than himself. The vast majority of men marry women younger than themselves. If the Prophet ﷺ had done so, and had died before she did, then there would only have been the sunnah of his monogamy.

The encouragement to polygamous marriage was only given after the battles for the sake of Islam left many widows and orphans with no-one to support them. In those circumstances, charitable men and women were asked to consider taking another woman into their households. Some men might have extended their generosity to marry, and over-burdened themselves—so the request was limited to four.

Western society tends to be rather hypocritical in its attitude to polygamy. It condemns men who seek to have a sexual relationship with more than one woman while at the same time there can be very few Western men who can honestly say that they only ever had a sexual relationship with one woman in the whole of their lives. Affairs before marriage are increasingly accepted as normal, and divorce for adultery is far from being uncommon! One of the reasons for polygamy in Islam is that sexual activity outside marriage is considered dishonourable and is forbidden, so Muslims should not have affairs, keep mistresses, and so on. (The idea of a harem with numerous glamours concubines has nothing to do with Islam, and is the very opposite of Muslim practice!)

The Blessed Prophet ﷺ was well aware that even the happiest of married people can suddenly fall subject to physical temptation—especially if they are sexually hungry at the time. If a Muslim suddenly became strongly attracted physically to someone outside the marriage, the Blessed Prophet (ﷺ—ever practical!) did not sanction giving in to the urge, nor did he recommend pointless agonies of suffering. Instead, he recommended taking immediate action to quell the desire.

Jabir recorded: Allah's Apostle ﷺ saw a woman (and wanted her) and so he came to his wife Zaynab, while she was (busy) tanning leather, and had intercourse with her... He told his companions: 'When one of you sees a woman (i.e. physically wants someone he has seen), he should come to his wife (straight away), for that will repel what has stirred in his heart.' (Muslim 32340)

Although the practice of men having more than one wife is referred to as polygamy, in fact it should be called polygyny—since true polygamy, in which a woman could also have more than one spouse, is not allowed.

SOCIAL REASONS FOR POLYGAMY

Islamic polygamy is based on morality, practicality and kindness, and not on the lust to have more than one woman at once!

In any society where there is a greater number of women then men, strict monogamy means that many women will have no chance of marriage at all, and could therefore be tempted into immoral relationships. A widow or divorcee whose prospects of marriage were small might prefer to be a second wife rather than face the rest of her life in a lonely struggle on her own. What matters most in these cases is the reaction of the prior wife in an existing marriage—for she has the right not to be hurt or displaced by her husband's decision to care for a second woman.

It is interesting to note that in Munich, Germany, in 1948, after the Second World War caused an imbalance in the ratio of men to women, polygamy was included among the recommended solutions to the problem caused by the death of so many young men.

Wives can suddenly become incapacitated through mental or physical illness. Islam considers not only the plight of the lonely widow or divorcee, but also the plight of a husband who might have lost his physical relationship with his wife for some reason (the plight of Mr. Rochester in Charlotte Bronte's famous book 'Jane Eyre'). Should he be expected to manage without sexual comfort for the rest of his life—the alternatives being to keep mistresses, or to divorce the unfortunate wife at the very time when she most needs his help? He would hope that a second wife, if he chose well, might become a second mother to his children, look after the household and, if necessary, help to look after his first wife.

Widows and their children need to be protected from destitution in times when many men might be lost through warfare or plague or natural calamity. This again is regarded as good grounds for allowing polygamy.

Finally, if a person becomes overwhelmingly attracted to another after marriage, it is considered that the existing wife in a marriage should not just be cast aside and divorced (usually after having given the husband 'the best years of her life'!), but has the right to continue respected, honoured and provided for as a wife, if she prefers this to divorce.

DISADVANTAGES OF POLYGAMY

There are four huge disadvantages to polygamy, and these are reasons why it is discouraged except in the above circumstances of kindness towards women in need. They are jealously, inequality, disharmony and conflicts between the children of different wives. Each of these must be taken very seriously when considering polygamous marriage.

It is never the intention in Islam for one Muslim to make another Muslim unhappy, or suffer unnecessarily—particularly not the 'wife of one's youth.' A man who goes ahead with a polygamous marriage against the consent of an existing wife is breaking the spirit of Islam and will have to account for it and his motives on the Day of Judgement.

Even though the Blessed Prophet's ﷺ wife 'A'ishah was his third wife, and knew that she was the true love of his last few years of life, she still suffered from jealousy when he decided to take other women in marriage for various reasons and had to struggle to overcome it.

'A'ishah recorded that one night the Prophet left her apartment during the night, and she felt jealous. Then he came, and saw her agitated state of mind. He said: "A'ishah, what has happened to you? Do you feel jealous?' She said: 'How could I not be jealous in regard of a husband like you?' He said: 'It was your devil which came to you.' (Muslim 6759)

However, no Muslim man should underestimate the tremendous feelings of sacrifice and self-control that polygamous wives are obliged to summon from the depths of their hearts. If the position was reversed, and the men were asked to share their beloved wives with other men, they would realise straight away the depths of emotion and control involved.

The Blessed Prophet was certainly aware of all this, for he defended his daughter Fatimah when her husband Ali ibn Abu Talib sought to take a second wife, and refused him permission to do so.

Al-Miswar b. Makhramah recorded that he heard the Apostle of Allah ﷺ say from the pulpit: 'Banu Hisham b. al-Mughirah sought permission from me to marry their daughter to Ali b. Abu Talib. But I do not permit, again, I do not permit, again, I do not permit, unless Ibn Abi Talib divorces my daughter (in order to) marry their daughter. My daughter is part of me; what makes her uneasy makes me uneasy, and what troubles her troubles me.' (Abu Dawud 2066)

Ali b. al-Husayn recorded that Ali b. Abu Talib asked for the hand of Abu Jahl's daughter in marriage after his marriage to Fatimah. I heard the Apostle of Allah ﷺ say, while he was addressing the people about this matter on the pulpit... : 'Fatimah is from me, and I am afraid that she will be tried in respect of her religion.' (Abu Jahl was one of the leading enemies of Islam) (Abu Dawud 2064)*

It was also well known that the Blessed Prophet's fifth wife, Umm Salamah, the beautiful widow of his cousin Abu Salamah, was very reluctant to marry the Prophet ﷺ at first because she already had children by her first marriage, and was afraid that she would not be able to accept the polygamous situation. In the end, she did agree to marry the Prophet ﷺ, but the traditions reveal that she was never fully at ease with his earlier wives (Khadijah had died; his next three wives were the widow Sawdah, and the daughters of his best friends— 'A'ishah bint Abu Bakr and Hafsah bint Umar).

Polygamy, therefore, should never be undertaken lightly.

EQUALITY IN POLYGAMY

If a man taking a second wife commits any injustice, that marriage can be declared illegal and against the principle of Islam. The permission to marry more than once is conditional on his good behaviour and good faith. The man must deal justly with all his wives. He should give them the same quality and amount of food, clothing, medication, leisure, living space, time, compassion and mercy.

Abu Bakr b. Abd al-Rahman recorded that when Allah's Messenger ﷺ married Umm Salamah and he visited her, when he intended to leave her she caught hold of his cloth; whereupon he said: 'If you so desire, I can extend the

---

* After Fatimah's death, Ali went on to marry other women, and fathered a further 24 children!

time of my stay with you; but then I shall have to calculate the time (that I stay with you, and shall have to spend the same time with my other wives).' (Muslim 3445)

It was considered normal for a polygamous man to spend three nights with a new wife who had been previously married, and seven nights with a virgin bride, before reverting to the practice of spending a night with each wife in turn. The Blessed Prophet was perfectly pleased with the thought of spending a full week with Umm Salamah, but by breaking the normal practice this meant he would have been obliged to spend a full week with all his other wives afterwards, and it would have been a very long time before he returned to Umm Salamah again. She settled for the three days.

In some households, more than one wife manage to live quite contentedly together. In other instances the man has to provide separate establishments for them. He must always be fair and considerate.

As the Blessed Prophet ﷺ has said: 'A man who marries more than one woman and then does not deal justly with them will be resurrected with half his faculties paralysed.' (Ahmad)

The only area where complete justice is obviously impossible is in the way that the man loves his wives emotionally, for this is something over which no human being has control. However, it is very bad manners to show this emotional favouritism in any way that would cause hurt to any of the wives.

'The Prophet prayed: 'O Allah! This is my justice in what I could control; do not blame me for what You control and I do not control.' (Abu Dawud, Tirmidhi, Nisai)

Should polygamy be abolished? Some argue that since Surah 4:129, a verse concerning divorce settlements, states

'You will never be able to do justice,' therefore polygamy is effectively prohibited. The complete verse is:

> 'You are never able to be fair and just between women, even if it is your ardent desire; but do not turn away (from a woman) altogether, so as to leave her hanging (in the air). If you come to a friendly understanding and practise self-restraint, God is Oft-Forgiving and Most Merciful.' (4:129)

However, using this ayah as an argument against polygamy is not well-founded, since it is a fact of history that the Prophet 鷺 and all his companions practised it, and it is unthinkable that they should have done so in violation of the sanction of Allah.

POLYANDRY

Some people claim that Islam is being unfair to women and does not grant them equal rights, because they do not have permission to have more than one husband as is the norm in certain societies where men drastically outnumber women. The reason for this used to be the prior right that all human beings have the right to know who their fathers are, and this used to be impossible if women were married to more than one man. Modern technology has now removed that objection, of course. Also, since males usually take on the role of leader in the family, there would be competition and possibly violence if a woman had more than one husband, so it is not regarded as a practical proposition.

MIXED FAITHS

Muslim men are allowed to marry not only Muslim women but also Christian and Jewish women, since these are also believers in the One God. They are not allowed to marry Hindu or Buddhist women, however, as their religious beliefs are so different it would inevitably cause conflict and friction.

> 'Do not marry unbelieving women until they believe; a slave who believes is better than an unbelieving woman, even though she allure you... .' (2:221)

> 'Lawful to you in marriage and chaste women who are believers, and chaste women among the People of the Book.' (5:6)

The Blessed Prophet's ﷺ own marriages set the precedent. One of the Blessed Prophet's ﷺ wives was a Christian (Maryam the Copt), and two were Jewish (Safiyah, Rayhanah).

It is not allowed, however, for a Muslim woman to marry a non-Muslim man. This restriction came about because it was recognised that a non-Muslim husband would probably object to the way of life of his Muslim children and might actively seek to stop them or undermine their faith, and this would cause too much conflict for a true Muslim woman to be able to cope with successfully. Wives normally take the nationality and status of their husbands, so the conflict of loyalties would arise immediately.

Sex

Sex is a very important aspect of human behaviour. All humans have three parts to their personality—spiritual, intellectual and physical—and have urges to satisfy the needs of all three. In Islam, the only qualification is that they should be satisfied according to the commands laid down by Allah— that is to say, in a wholesome and pure manner, without excess, and without causing suffering. This applies in particular to sex, because it is such a basic and fundamental urge in humans, the fulfilment of which can cause the greatest joy and happiness, and the failure of which can cause the greatest despair and hurt.

Abu Hurayrah recorded: 'When a husband and wife share intimacy it is rewarded, and a blessing from Allah; just as they would be punished if they indulged in illicit sex. (Muslim)

Abu Dharr recorded: 'Having sexual intercourse with one's wife is sadaqah (loving charity).' (Abu Dawud 5223)

Muslims do not believe that sex is unclean and should therefore be resisted and suppressed. On the other hand, they do not accept that sexual pleasures can be pursued regardless of moral considerations. Muslims maintain that both these extremes go against human nature which requires that sexual desires are satisfied, but that the individual and the family are protected from dangerous consequences. If any society does not keep a watch on its sexual morality it does not take long before preoccupation with sex, the development of sex as a business, and the various forms of abuse of sex begin to proliferate.

CELIBACY

Islam actually disapproves of the idea of celibacy, or living without sex, regarding it as a kind of 'ingratitude' and misuse of Allah's gifts, which might even lead to a dangerously stressed, perverted or repressed personality. (Living with sex also has its pitfalls, of course, as multitudes of people might be too shy to affirm, but it is true nonetheless!)

Sa'id b. Abi Waqqas reported: 'Uthman b. Mazun decided to live in celibacy, but Allah's Messenger ﷺ forbade him to do so.' (Muslim 3239)

This was a mercy and restrained over-zealous fanaticism. The same hadith commented that 'if he had permitted him, we would have got ourselves castrated'!

The powerful urge to enjoy sex is part of Allah's design to give people pleasure and contentment, as well as to continue the human race—therefore there is something perverse in seeking to survive without fulfilling these natural longings.

Abdullah b. Masud recorded: 'O young men, those among you who can support a wife should marry, for it restrains the eye and preserves one from immorality; he who cannot afford it should fast as a means of controlling sexual desire.' (Muslim 3233)

At times, people have a fierce need to be relieved of sexual tension. Islam regards relieving oneself as a weakness, but it is tolerated by the jurists Ibn Hanbal and Ibn Hazm under two conditions—the fear of committing sex outside marriage, (perhaps when one marital partner is unable or reluctant to satisfy the other), or when a person has not got the means to marry. In some societies, the burden of finding a dowry is so grievous (and totally against Islam!) that young men have to wait a great many years before they are able to marry.

The Prophet was well aware of the temptations of those unable to marry for some reason. His advice was to practise frequent fasting, in order to improve will-power and self-control.

PERMISSIVENESS

Muslims have observed with horror how the West has virtually done away with traditional morality, with catastrophic consequences for child-rearing and the break-down of families, leading to stress, depression, crime and suicide.

It often comes as a shock for non-Muslims to discover what Muslims think of their 'freedom.' Europeans, for example, have become used to regarding themselves and their opinions as superior, although the need for a re-examination of morals and standards is becoming increasingly obvious.

There are six things which are expressly forbidden to a Muslim—premarital sex, adultery, alcohol, gambling, making or borrowing money at interest and eating forbidden meats. The object of these rules is to prevent Muslims becoming slaves to cravings and selfish instincts, and damaging society by breaking up the family unit. In Muslim eyes, the permissive societies of the West have become so tolerant of sex outside marriage, illegitimacy, exploitation and greed, plus the behavioural patterns associated with drinking, drugs and gambling, as to be actually guilty of encouraging them!

Permissiveness leads not only to the obvious instances of breakdown in society, but also to selfishness, rape, lying and deception, lack of responsibility, drug addiction, theft, and even murder. If Muslims are God-conscious, they should be able to resist temptation, and know right from wrong.

SEX BEFORE MARRIAGE

Umar recorded: 'Let no man be in privacy with a woman who is not lawful unto him, or Satan will be the third.' (Tirmidhi)

Islam prohibits any type of privacy between couples who are not married to each other. They do not believe that sexual freedom before the marriage commitment contributes anything to the future stability of that marriage; the assumption that the couple will have 'tried each other out' and so will 'know' each other is incomprehensible nonsense to a Muslim.

It is patently obvious that in societies where sexual freedom is tolerated many marriages go wrong, and divorce is at a very high level. Muslims would not welcome marriage to a partner who had experienced many previous 'trial encounters', because they might quite easily seek other 'trials' even after the marriage.

However, it is not true that Muslim couples are prevented from seeing each other before marriage. The Prophet ﷺ actually commanded that bridegrooms should go and see the prospective brides, so that the first seeds of love, companionship and closeness would be planted. However, they should not be left on their own, but be chaperoned.

Abu Hurayrah recorded: 'There came a man and informed Allah's Messenger ﷺ that he had contracted to marry a woman of the Ansar. Allah's Messenger ﷺ said: 'Did you have a look at her?' He said: 'No.' He said: 'Go and see her.' (Muslim 3314)

A woman should be approached through representatives and not by anyone else until she has either consented or refused to take the matter further. If she agrees to meet the man, and then to marry him, the marriage can be contracted even though it may not necessarily be consummated straight away.

Any such agreement should not take place within the waiting period after a woman's divorce, in case the couple can be reconciled. It should also be quite clear that the woman involved is not pregnant.

It is disrespectful, and even offensive, to court widows during their period of mourning.

SEX OUTSIDE MARRIAGE

Adultery is regarded by Muslims as a form of theft, of the worst possible sort.

'Have nothing to do with adultery, for it is a shameful thing, and an evil opening the way to other evils.' (17:32)

Stealing another person's marriage partner is considered to be the most serious crime, and giving in to someone who attempts to seduce you away from your marriage partner is an act of betrayal so fundamental that few marriages can survive the shock. Not only is the marriage-trust irreparably damaged, but adultery is responsible for the breaking up of at least one entire family unit, and possibly more than one.

'The man or woman guilty of adultery or fornication, flog them with a hundred stripes; do not be moved by pity... and do not let any person guilty of these sins marry any but others similarly guilty... ..unless they repent and change their ways' (24:3-5)

If the husband (or wife) saw a person and felt a sexual urge that became a temptation for them, the Prophet's ﷺ advice (as reported by Jabir) was to 'go to his wife and have intercourse with her, for that would repel what he had felt.' (Muslim 3242, Abu Dawud 2146)

If a couple no longer love each other, and do not wish to continue in marriage together, honourable divorce is the answer and should be arranged. It is not Islamic to force either wife or husband to remain a prisoner of a failed relationship, if it really has failed. Families and friends should do everything possible to try to save the marriage, but if it cannot be saved then the break should be done in such a way as to cause the least amount of damage to the respective families. Giving in to the urge to have casual sex outside marriage is despised in Islam, and seen as a major weakness and dishonour.

HADD PUNISHMENT FOR ADULTERY

The punishment for adultery is quite clear and unambiquous in the Qur'an—a hundred lashes, on the condition that the adultery was witnessed by four person who were in the position to identify both parties with certainty.

In other words, allegations against a woman's chastity should supported by evidence twice as strong as would ordinarily be required for business transactions, or even murder.

In cases of one spouse catching another in the act of adultery, four witnesses—or even one outside witness— would be impossible by the very nature of things. The matter is then left to the honour of the spouses (24:6-10).

The cases of stoning to death sanctioned by the Prophet ﷺ related to a Jew and Jewess in one case (Bukhari 23:61) and others that apparently occurred before the revelation of 24:2.

That stoning to death was never contemplated by Allah as punishment for adultery is made quite clear in 4:25, when it is expressly stated that the punishment in the case of married slave-women is half that inflicted on free married women. Stoning to death cannot be halved.

Stoning to death was the Law of Moses, and not the Law of the Qur'an. The Prophet ﷺ made it clear that his words could not cancel the World of Allah, but Allah's Word could cancel his—if what he said was contrary to the Qur'an. The Prophet ﷺ never intended to *add* to the Qur'an of 'improve' on it.

> 'If he had added against Us certain sayings, We would certainly have seized him by the right hand and cut off his heart's vein.' (69:44-46).

HOMOSEXUALITY

Islam prohibits all illicit relationships and sexual deviations. Homosexuality is not regarded as a normal variation on the way things are, but as an activity which is against the laws of nature.

There is nothing new about homosexuality. Lot the nephew of Ibrahim lived among a community of people addicted to it.

> 'Of all the creatures in the world, will you approach males and abandon those whom God created for you as mates?' (26:165-166)

Homosexuality is not regarded as an acceptable variant to normal sexuality, but as a depraved practice which makes people slaves to their lusts. It robs them of decency in matters of taste, morality and dignity.

> 'If two men are guilty of lewdness, punish them both. If they repent and change their ways, leave them alone...

Allah accepts the repentance of those who do evil in ignorance and repent soon afterwards... of no effect is the repentance of those who continue to do evil.' (4:16-18)

In Islam, the only form of sexual activity that is regarded as permissible is that which takes place within the framework of a marriage. Therefore, it can be argued on these grounds alone that homosexuality is unacceptable.

Several societies in history condoned homosexuality and accepted it as virtually normal—notably the Greeks and the Romans. It was even suggested that a man's love for his male friend was in a way more noble than his love for a woman. Male lovers were placed beside each other in battle, so that they would fight better and defend the loved one.

In this century, a lot of discussion has arisen over the reasons for homosexuality. Some argue that it is a case of genetics—the homosexuals are victims of their genes and not guilty of any offence. If this is the true case of the homosexual then one can accept that it is not the fault of the individual concerned. However, rather than strive to find genetic or hormonal cures, we are urged to be more tolerant and accept variant sexuality as within the range of 'normal.'

Others feel that the general sexual liberation in the West that was vastly increased by the freedom from pregnancy conveyed by the contraceptive pill raised the expectancy of sexual satisfaction, especially for women. This led to many women becoming increasingly dissatisfied with men who did not know how, or could not, or did not take the trouble to satisfy their needs. Women know how to satisfy each other, without embarrasing explanations that come across as criticism to the sensitive male ego. Hence the rise of lesbianism.

At the same time, women becoming more demanding and aggressive posed greater problems and effort for selfish men; some preferred homosexual relationships that were free from hassle, pregnancy or commitment.

One price for all this lack of willingness to make an effort with the opposite sex has been the rapid spread of AIDS, although this has now gone for beyond the homosexual.

In societies where homosexuality is openly admitted, people are asked to be tolerant, but are usually disturbed and uncomfortable in the presence of homosexuals, and frequently hostile, abusive and vindictive towards them. Less hostility and embarrassment, and more honest research are what is urgently needed.

As far as the Prophet ﷺ was concerned, he declared that women should not even wear male clothing, nor vice versa; they should not imitate the opposite sex in speaking, walking, dressing, or moving.

'Three persons shall not enter Paradise—the one who is disobedient to parents, the pimp, and the woman who imitates men.' (Nisai, al-Bazzar, al-Hakim)

Ibn Abbas recorded: 'Allah has sent down curses on those men who try to adopt the semblance of women, and those women who try to adopt the semblance of men.' (Bukhari)

SEXUAL HAPPINESS WITHIN MARRIAGE

A good sexual relationship is one of the chief joys and satisfactions of married life, and can bind a man and woman together in a deeper sense than any other. As in all walks of life, it is the Muslim's duty to 'seek knowledge' in order to pursue the marriage relationship in the best possible way, that will make for the happiness and contentment of both partners. As Muslims are naturally shy and modest, it is doubly important for a husband to understand the needs of his wife, and how to fulfil them. He may know how to satisfy himself, but have no clue how to satisfy a woman. If he makes no effort to learn, and ignores his duty to grant her pleasure and satisfaction, then his sexual relationship with her will not be sadaqah at all, but painful, frustrating and, in short haram.

The Prophet ﷺ recommended that a couple should consciously and deliberately aim to give each other happiness rather than concentrate on self-gratification, and when their intimate relationship was carried out in the best and most unselfish and loving way, bearing the will of Allah in mind, then it would be successful.

He recommended that all intimacy should be commenced in an atmosphere of prayer:

Ibn Abbas recorded: 'If any of you intend to go to his wife, he should say: 'In the name of Allah, O Allah protect us against Satan and keep Satan away from the one You have bestowed upon us.' Then, if Allah has ordained a child, Satan will never be able to harm it.' (Muslim 3361, Abu dawud 2156)

Muslims were allowed to carry out loving relations with their wives in any position they liked, except one. There had been discussion amongst the couples of Madinah because apparently the Jewish citizens there had superstitions regarding intercourse in any position other than face to face. It was in response to queries about this that the following revelation was received:

'Your wives are as a tilth to you, so approach your tilth when and how you will; but do some good act for your souls beforehand; and fear God, and know that you are to meet Him (in the Hereafter). Give good tidings to those who believe. And make not God's name an excuse in your oaths against doing good, or acting rightly, or making peace between persons; for God is One Who hears and knows all things.' (2:223-224).

The revelation implies that a couple may choose whatever method of intimacy pleases them. The 'good act' to be done beforehand has been interpreted by some scholars as the necessary loving acts between husband to wife before male satisfaction that are so vital to help a wife to achieve her full marital satisfaction, such as kissing and stroking, and telling the wife that she is loved. It is unfair to call this 'foreplay before sex', as for most women this part of the intimacy *is* the part which brings satisfaction, and not male ejaculation.

Only when the intimate relationship is fulfilling to both partners is 'peace' made between them. It is not Islamic conduct for a man to seek his own satisfaction and ignore the needs of his wife—even if he thinks he is 'being religious' by abstaining from helping her. That is patently not 'doing good or acting rightly', and on the Day of Judgement when all books are opened, his lack and her suffering will all be revealed and held to account. One hadith recorded by al-Ghazzali stated that: 'He is not one of us who satisfies his need for her before he has satisfied her need for him.'

The one form of intimacy not condoned by the Prophet ﷺ was intercourse through the anus.

Abu Hurayrah recorded: 'He who has intercourse with his wife through her anus is accursed.' (Abu Dawud 2157) It is horrendous to realise that some misguided Muslim men have used this way as a method of birth-control, or have used their women in this way because their vaginas became stretched after bearing their children.

In a truly Islamic marriage, neither partner should try

to force the other one to do anything which is distasteful or unpleasant or painful to them. Marital rape should never take place, or abuse of the wife.

Cleanliness on the part of both husband and wife is also vital. In pre-Islamic times women who were menstruating were regarded as unapproachable and were left untouched. The Sunnah of the Blessed Messenger ﷺ was to expect his wives to protect themselves (and him) adequately from any flow of blood, but having done that they could lie together and enjoy any intimacy short of full intercourse.

Thabit narrated from Anas: 'Among the Jews, when a woman menstruated they did not dine with her nor did they live with them in their houses...the Messenger of Allah ﷺ said: 'Do everything except (full) intercourse.' (Muslim 592)

There are numerous hadiths recorded by the Blessed Messenger's ﷺ wives revealing that this was indeed his sunnah. (See Muslim 582-592). Once he found that one of his companions had separated his bed from his wife's and ordered him to replace it next to hers.

Before intercourse the Blessed Prophet ﷺ recommended ten acts of physical cleanliness, including the shaving of the pubic hair, and the keeping clean of fingers, breath and armpits. After intercourse a full bath was necessary before prayer could be resumed, and the Prophet's ﷺ wives 'A'ishah and Umm Salamah both recorded how they and the Prophet ﷺ used to bathe from the same vessel. (Muslim 581).

At the time of a woman's menstruation she should be particularly careful about cleanliness, and the Prophet ﷺ recommended the use of sweet scent. (Muslim 647-651).

Abdullah b. Abul-Qays reported: I asked 'A'ishah about the prayer of the Messenger of Allah ﷺ and... then I said: 'What did he do after sexual intercourse? Did he take a bath

before going to sleep, or did he sleep before taking a bath?'
She said: 'He did all these. Sometimes he took a bath and then
slept, and sometimes he performed ablution only and went
to sleep.' I said: 'Praise be to Allah Who has made things
easy.' (Muslim 603)

The Prophet ﷺ also recommended taking a bath if
either husband or wife had experienced orgasm in a sexual
dream. (Muslim 607). Also, of course, sexual organs should
always be washed after going to the toilet.

Husband and wives were requested not to hurt each
other by refusing loving requests:

Abu Hurayrah recorded: 'When a woman spends the
night away from the bed of her husband, the angels curse her
until morning.' (Muslim 3366 and Abu Dawud 574), and 'By
Him in Whose hand is my life, when a man calls his wife to
his bed and she does not respond, the One Who is in the
heaven is displeased with her until her husband is pleased
with her.' (Muslim 3367)

Since wives have the same rights in marriage as
husbands, the same principle would apply if the husband
refused the loving requests of his wife.

The Blessed Prophet ﷺ disapproved of either men or
women being so excessive in their religious devotions that the
marriage relationship was damaged or pushed into the
background. On one occasion he asked the wife of Safwan b.
al-Muattal not to fast without her husband's permission, and
not to spend too long in prayer, as Safwan appealed 'I am a
young man, and I cannot withhold myself.' (Muslim 2435).

Marital relationships should always be discreet, and
intimate details should never be divulged to any outsiders—
a matter which would be extremely hurtful to the partner
concerned.

Abu Sa'id al-Khudri recorded: 'The most wicked of the people on the Day of Judgement is the man who goes to his wife and she comes to him, and then he divulges her secret.' (Muslim 3369, Abu Dawud 1358)

As before, the same applies if a wife divulges private details about her husband.

The important thing is that both couples realise that a loving and unselfish intimate relationship with their spouse is regarded as sadaqah, and worthy of earning merit.

Abu Dharr recorded: 'In every declaration of the glory of Allah there is sadaqah; and every takbir is sadaqah; and every praise of Him is sadaqah; and every declaration that He is One is sadaqah; and encouraging good is sadaqah; and forbidding that which is evil is sadaqah; and in a man's sexual intercourse with his wife there is sadaqah.' They said: 'Messenger of Allah, is there reward for him who (simply) satisfies his sexual passions?' He said: 'If he were to devote it to something forbidden, it would be a sin on his part. If he devotes it to what is lawful, he shall have a reward.' (Abu Dawud 2198)

This area of human life is so important and vital to the well-being of Muslim marriage that the Blessed Messenger ﷺ actually listed it alongside the chief Muslim acts of religious acts of piety.

Muslim sex is therefore a whole world apart from the business of a man flinging himself upon a woman and satisfying himself like an animal. It should be a precious, religious, and unselfish act between the two people involved.

---

*   Many issues regarding sexuality and general marital well-being are discussed in Sr. Ruqaiyyah's book 'The Muslim Marriage Guide,' Goodword Books, 1998.

Divorce

Of all the things Allah has allowed out of concession to human weakness, but which He is most reluctant to grant, divorce is the most serious. It is like a death, but in some ways worse than a death. If a spouse dies, at least he or she can be honourably mourned and their memory cherished. In divorce, the spouse has gone but is still alive, and the target of all sorts of traumatic feelings—despair, regret, hatred, vengeance, sometimes even horror and loathing, or perhaps unassuageable grief. It is a terrible trauma for the man and woman involved, whatever the cause. And apart from the suffering of the husband and wife it is like a great hole opening up in the life of their children as they watch the two people they love most split apart and go to live in separate places.

'The most detestable act that God has permitted is divorce.' (Abu Dawud and Ibn Majah)

THE HURT FAMILY

Usually children are aware of the bitterness and bad feelings that have caused the break-up, and sometimes they blame themselves for it. They think that perhaps it was all their fault, that they upset their parents too much or put too much stress on them; if only they had done (or not done) this or that thing, if they had behaved better, then maybe Mum and Dad would still love each other and would not be leaving.

A worse hurt is that they think the parents cannot really love *them*, for if they did, surely they would be able to make peace with each other enough to stay together if only for their sakes. It all seems a terrible nightmare, and the child—who is usually quite innocent—is hurt and damaged sometimes beyond repair.

Divorced people also hurt their own parents, who are obliged to watch everything taking place without being able to give much help or to stop it, and who sometimes suffer the terrible loss of all contact with their much loved grandchildren. When a grandmother sees her child and grandchild suffer, it is usually a worse feeling than actually suffering herself. She feels so frustrated and helpless.

For divorce is not so much something between a man and his wife, but the breaking apart of two complete families.

THE CAUSES

Since divorce is so devastating, why does it happen? For a start, it should never happen lightly. Even though Islam permits divorce it is treated as a very serious matter, and should be only a last resort. A Muslim couple should never split apart without genuine attempts at counselling and trying to find a solution to the problems first.

> 'If you fear a break between the two, then appoint two arbiters (reconcilers), one from his family and the other from hers; if the couple wish for peace, Allah will cause them to reconcile; for Allah has full knowledge and is acquainted with all things.' (4:35)

It is only after all persuasion and appeal has failed that divorce is reluctantly agreed to.

'If they disagree and must part, Allah will provide
abundance for all from His far-reaching bounty. For Allah
is He Who cares for all, and He is wise.' (4:129)

It is obviously a great deal easier if it is a young couple
involved, who have not yet had any children to add to the
heartache. Even then, divorce should not be rushed into—
but in such cases the complications are far less. What is not
any less is the hurt caused to the man and woman who have
experienced the death of their love, and the conscious intent
of a partner they had once vowed to share their lives with
now actively rejecting them.

The hurt of rejection is one of the most savage pains that
humans can know. How tragic that some people behave so
badly that their partner has no choice but to reject them, in
order to safeguard their physical and mental well-being!

If two people have entered into a marriage contract to
remain faithful to each other, and take care of each other no
matter what their circumstances, then that is usually what
they genuinely intend to do. They have no intention
whatsoever of abandoning a partner simply because he or she
might be struck by poverty or illness. If a husband or wife
tried to divorce a partner for such a reason, we would have
nothing but contempt for them.

No, the cause of divorce is really the breakdown of love,
of the relationship upon which the bargain was struck. And
this is seen in law as being reasonable cause—because humans
are very well aware of the hell that can be created when one
person is forced to live with another who does not love them.

AVAILABILITY OF DIVORCE

In some societies divorce is forbidden completely,
resulting in much distress; in others it is too freely available,

and there are no checks on its abuse. Neither of these extremes are helpful in solving the problems that go along with divorce. Human beings sometimes choose to ignore, abuse or defy the laws of their societies.

Although Islam emphasizes the sanctity of marriage and the need for its continuance and permanence, it also recognises that human nature is such that not every marriage will be successful. Rather than condemn people to lifelong misery, Islam makes provision for legal divorce, as a last resort—although it is highly discouraged.

> 'If a wife fears cruelty or desertion on her husband's part, there is no blame on them if they arrange an amicable settlement between themselves; and such a settlement is the best way.' (4:128)

When a husband simply withdraws from his wife and deprives her of sexual intimacy for a period of four months, this is known as 'Ila, and is forbidden in Islam

> 'Do not turn away (from a woman) altogether, so as to leave her hanging (in the air). If you come to a friendly understanding and practise self-restraint, God is Oft-Forgiving, Most Merciful.' (4:129)

THE LAST RESORT

Some people mistakenly think that divorce is an easy matter in Muslim societies, and that all one has to do is to pronounce the fateful phrase 'I divorce you' three times, and that is that. This is to grossly misunderstand Islam. Just because Islamic procedure is not cluttered up with bureaucracy does not mean that it is taken lightly (although obviously, some people who claim to be Muslim do abuse the system). It should always be the last resort, after all attempts to put things right have failed. A long series of procedures should have gone before the pronouncement of divorce.

'Divorced women shall wait concerning themselves for three monthly periods, nor is it lawful for them to hide what God has created in their wombs, if they have faith in Allah and the Last Day. And their husbands have the right to take them back in that period, if they wish, for reconciliation. And women shall have rights the same as the rights against them, according to what is equitable; however, men have a degree of advantage over them. (2:228) (This is usually related to their financial situation or means of support).

The Prophet ﷺ said: 'Marry and do not divorce; undoubtedly the Throne of the Beneficent Lord shakes due to divorce.' (Kashfal Khala, Tafsir al-Qurtubi)

Although it is unfortunately possible for a woman in some societies to discover that she has suddenly been divorced without her knowledge, and her belongings are being put out of her husband's house. This has nothing to do with Islam and is totally against its teachings.

Neither is the business of a man refusing to allow his wife a divorce if she really wants one.

'Either keep your wife honestly, or put her away from you with kindness. Do not force a woman to stay with you who wishes to leave. The man who does that only injures himself.' (2:231)

GROUNDS FOR DIVORCE IN ISLAM

These are very reasonable. Any action of the spouse which has caused the loss of love or respect of the other is considered seriously. If a spouse neglects or abuses the partner or their children, or is cruel, or behaves shamefully, then divorce can be considered. It is harder for a woman to divorce her husband in most Third World societies, and in some it is still virtually impossible, but this is not the teaching of Islam.

Muslim women have the same rights as the men, and the following things are considered reasonable grounds for a woman to ask for and be given divorce in Islam—if her husband leaves Islam; if he is unable or refuses to maintain her; if he abuses or mistreats her; if he is impotent; if he contracts some incurable, repulsive disease such as leprosy; or becomes insane; if he deserts her, or has gone away and has not communicated for an unreasonable time (say two years?); if he has been sent to prison for a very long period; if it was discovered that he deceived her when they were drawing up their marriage contract, or concealed important information concerning the marriage. The only proviso is that the reason should be genuine:

Thauban recorded the Apostle of Allah ﷺ as saying: 'If any woman asks her husband for divorce without some strong reason, the scent of Paradise will be forbidden to her.' (Abu Dawud 2218)

DIVORCE BY MUTUAL CONSENT

Husbands and wives can agree amongst themselves to terminate their marriage, and agree the financial arrangements which will follow.

If the wife has a genuine grievance against her husband she can obtain divorce from him by returning his marriage gift to her in return for the dissolution of the marriage. This type of divorce is called Khul'. A woman came to the Blessed Prophet ﷺ and said: 'I hate my husband and I want separation from him.' He asked: 'Would you return the orchard that he gave you as a dower? She replied: 'Yes, and even more than that!' The Prophet ﷺ said: 'You need not return more than that.' (Bayhaqi)

On the other hand, the husband seeking divorce may not *demand* his gifts back, unless he finds his wife guilty of clear immorality.

> 'It is not lawful for (men) to take back any of your gifts, except when both parties fear that they would be unable to keep the limits ordained by God. If you do indeed fear (that) there is no blame on either of them if she gives something for her freedom.' (2:229)

CONDITIONS NECESSARY FOR THE DIVORCE TO BE VALID

For a divorce to be valid in Islamic law the husband must be sane, conscious and not under pressure from some outside party; the divorce must be clear and unequivocal, and not ambiguous or couched in vague language; and the husband must not be under the influence of alcohol, drugs, or so angry that he did not fully appreciate what he was saying.

WHEN DIVORCE IS NOT ALLOWED

Sometimes divorce is forbidden in Islam, to safeguard the justice of the situation. This is usually when the woman is having her period, or when she is in her post-natal rest period.

At these times it would not have been likely that the husband would have approached his wife for intimate relations, and this might have been a source of tension leading him to make a hasty, ill-judged decision.

If the couple have had intimacy, they must wait until after the next monthly cycle, in case of pregnancy.

THE WAITING PERIOD, OR IDDAH.

This is usually 3 months, although it can be as long as 9 months if the woman is pregnant. The wife is entitled to continue living at the home, even if she has been divorced, and is also entitled to full maintenance and to receive good treatment; she should not be forced out.

If a reconciliation occurs, there is no need of remarriage if it is during the iddah. If the couple seek remarriage after the expiry of the waiting period, they may remarry, but with a new contract. Such remarriage is allowed a second and third time. However, when the 'waiting period' is over, the woman has no further claim on her ex-husband. What she has been paid in that time is in consideration of the fact that she cannot marry anyone else in that period—it is a time in which both parties are given time to think again.

If a wife is divorced three times from her husband, it is clear there is a serious problem, and in this case they are not allowed to remarry until after the woman has been properly married to some other person.

'A'ishah recorded that the Apostle of Allah ﷺ was asked about a man who divorced his wife three times and she married another who, however, divorced her before having intercourse with her. Was she lawful to the former husband? The Prophet ﷺ replied: 'She is not lawful to the first husband until she tastes the honey of the other husband and he tastes her honey.' (Abu Dawud 2302)

It is not permitted in Islam to 'cheat' by arranging such a marriage falsely in order to remarry the ex-husband. It is a Sunnah for there to be at least one month between each of the divorces.

After the waiting time, no-one is allowed to prevent the woman from marrying whoever she chooses. No-one has the right to interfere—not her ex-husband, father or guardian. In some societies, the woman's family might try to prevent her from remarrying a disappointing husband from whom they felt she was well rid, but this is not allowed in Islam.

> 'When you have divorced women and they have fulfilled the term of their iddah, either keep them honourably or let them go honourably; but do not retain them in order to injure them, for this is sin, and whoever does this has wronged his own soul. Do not mock the revelations of Allah... Be conscious of Allah, and know that He is aware of everything.' (2:231; 65:1-2)

> 'Do not prevent them from marrying their former husbands if they agree among themselves in an honourable manner.' (2:232)

DIVORCE SETTLEMENTS

> 'For divorced women, maintenance (should be provided) on a reasonable (scale). This is a duty on the righteous.' (2:241)

It is not normal practice in many Islamic societies for men to pay maintenance to ex-wives for very long periods. There are many hadiths suggesting that the Prophet ﷺ thought that in his society, at least, prolonged maintenance was not necessary for a divorced woman. It was intended that she would probably swiftly remarry, or go back to her father's household. For example, Fatimah the daughter of Qays was not granted maintenance so long as she was taken care of (Abu Dawud 2278). Ijtihad for a modern society would be based on the Islamic principle that as regards the woman, she should be supported somehow (perhaps by a welfare state?), and that as regards the man, any burden of payment by the husband should not be so severe as to place his future life in difficulties. A woman is entitled to be provided for by her husband if she is married, or by her father if she is not. After divorce, she might return to her parents' home and revert to her pre-marital status. If she has no parents, her closest male relatives should support her until she remarries, or she could possibly be supported by her adult children. If she has none of these, an Islamic government is obliged to give an allowance. In these circumstances there is no case for imposing on the ex-husband an obligation for life—which could lead to men trying to evade the law, or women seeking vengeance through heavy financial settlements. They could even be tempted to act immorally by living with a boy friend rather than marrying him, in order not to lose the maintenance! However, if it was genuinely the situation that a divorced wife could not find any other means of support, the divorcing husband should consider the prior ruling of one Muslim not being allowed to deliberately put another to hardship, and make provision.

In a recent case in India a divorced woman appealed to a non-Islamic court and was awarded maintenance for life. The husband's lawyers objected that this was an insult to womanhood—implying that her only means of survival was to depend on a man to whom she had once been married, and that she had taken what she had no right to take. Nevertheless, she won the case. In a different case, in Bangladesh, a judge recently concluded: 'Considering all the aspects, we hold that a person, after divorcing his wife, is bound to maintain her on a reasonable scale beyond the period of iddah for an indefinite period, until she loses the status of a divorcee by marrying another person.'

(Justice M. Ghulam Rabbani and Justice Syed Amirul Islam in an appeal filed by Hifzur Rahman vs. Shamsun Nahar Begum).

One should consider this hadith: 'Some of you may be more eloquent in putting their arguments than others. Let a person reflect that if I award him/her something to which he/she has no right, I am only awarding him/her a piece of fire. He/she may take it or leave it.'

CUSTODY OF CHILDREN

What generally happens after any divorce is that the children remain with one of the parents, and the other parent is allowed access to them, and visiting time. Sometimes they lose one of their parents completely, and never see them again. Often, after a visit, they are disturbed and unhappy, and it takes time to calm down again and accept the situation once more, and try to make the best of it.

Sometimes the parent who has custody remarries, and there is friction between an 'old' child and any 'new' children that come along, or existing children of the second spouse.

In the West, as in Islam, custody is nearly always granted to the mother, but in Islam, no matter which parent keeps the child, it is the responsibility of the father to pay for their upkeep. As regards small infants:

> 'The mothers shall give suck to their offspring for two whole years, if the father desires to complete the term. But he shall bear the cost of their food and clothing, on equitable terms. No soul shall have a burden laid on it greater than it can bear. No mother shall be treated unfairly on account of her child, nor father on account of his child. An heir shall be chargeable in the same way. If they both decide on weaning, by mutual consent, and after due consultation, there is no blame on them. If you decide on a foster-mother for your offspring, there is no blame on you provided you pay (the mother) what you offered on equitable terms. Fear God, and know that God sees well all that you do.' (2:233)

It is obviously far less of a financial burden for the mother if her divorced husband keeps the children. When the divorced husband takes the children, it also frees the woman from the burden of being a single parent, with all the stigma still attached. However, the hadiths are quite clear that the Prophet ﷺ considered custody of small children with the mother to be the normal thing, subject to certain conditions.

Amr b. Shuayb reported that a woman said: 'Apostle of Allah, my womb is a vessel for this son of mine, my breasts a water-skin for him, and my lap the protection for him, yet his father has divorced me and wants to take him away from me.' The Apostle ﷺ said: 'You have more right to him, so long as you do not marry.' (Abu Dawud 2269; Ahmad, Bayhaqi and Al-Hakim)

This view is held by the schools of Malik, Abu Hanifah and al-Shafi'i. Abu Hanifah also maintains that if the woman remarries a relative, she still retains the prior right to keep the child in her custody, but al-Shafi'i disagrees with this. ('Awn ak Mabud II, 251).

Re-marriage to a non-relative alters the parental right to the child involved in a divorce, since the mother's new husband is not a blood relative of her offspring, and might suffer in the new relationship. In such a case, although it may be decided to leave the child with the mother and step-father, the actual father of the child has a renewed right to take over the custody.

However, in most cases the father of the child will also remarry, and the relationship of the previous child with the new step-mother has to be considered too.

As regards other children, the Prophet ﷺ advised leaving the choice to the children concerned, and to keep the whole matter as amicable as possible.

A Persian woman who had heard of the Apostle's ﷺ judgements came to seek settlement of her case.

Hilal b. Usamah reported that the Prophet ﷺ said to the child: 'This is your father and this is your mother, so take whichever of them you wish by the hand. The child took his mother's hand, and she went away with him.' (Abu Dawud 2270, Tirmidhi, Nisai, Ibn Majah, al-Hakim)

A further hadith regarded the case of the Prophet's ﷺ close companion, Umar ibn al-Khattab, who divorced his Ansari wife, the mother of his son Asim. He later met her carrying the child, in a very impoverished state, and since the child was weaned by that time, he tried to take the child. The child was pulled between them until he cried out in pain! The father insisted that he was more entitled to the child than she was, but when they approached Abu Bakr (who was Caliph at the time) for judgement, he ordered that the mother should keep the boy because her 'fragrance and comforting warmth' were better for him than the father's presence, until he became old enough to choose for himself.

A further hadith of Abu Bakr reinforced this, saying that the mother was more entitled to her child, until she remarried. As soon as a child was old enough, the choice of parent should rest with him or her.

All settlements regarding children should be done amicably and without spite or rancour, and with the best interests of those children being the prime consideration. The heart-rending stories that hit the press occasionally reveal that people are far from perfect, and often act irrationally and spitefully—and this is never in keeping with the spirit of Islam.

REMARRIAGE

Western society should try to understand the logic behind Islamic action. It is not intended to be cruel or vindictive, but it is accepted as obvious that it will be much easier for a man to find another woman to mother his children than for a woman to find another man who agrees to take her on with an existing family, and care for them adequately. It can and does happen, but women in the West will admit that such men do not 'lie thick upon the ground', especially when the lady involved is past the first flush of youth. Many middle-aged women with children are simply left to get on with it, and cope single-handed for the rest of their lives.

It is a very grim business, and often the divorced woman has no idea when the marriage breaks up of what lies ahead of her. She can think only of the relief of being separated from a man she does not love or who has rejected her, and is probably longing for rest and peace of mind. Her mind may be full of hope, and plans for the future, on the grounds that there are obviously just as many divorced men as women, so she will not be left out if she wishes to remarry later. It is only when the cruel truth strikes home that most men remarry women younger than themselves, sometimes much younger, that the divorced woman is forced to accept unpleasant reality.

In fact, a divorced woman or a widow should stand a better chance of finding a husband in Islam, as all her family and friends will try to help her and will suggest suitable matches; nobody likes to see a woman on her own, particularly if she is in distress. All of the Blessed Prophet's wives except one were widows. Age does not present so much of a problem for the woman either, since Muslims have before them the excellent example of the Prophet Muhammad's ﷺ first love, a widow over 15 years his senior to whom he was faithful until she died at the age of 65, some twenty-five years after his marriage to her.

Alcohol, Drugs and Tobacco

Intoxicants are the key to many evils.

'A man was brought and asked either to rip up the Holy Qur'an, or murder a child, or bow in worship to an idol, or drink one cup of alcohol, or sleep with a woman. He thought the least sinful thing was to drink the cup, so he drank it. Then he slept with the woman, killed the child, tore the Holy Qur'an and bowed in worship to the idol.' (A story of Uthman ibn 'Affan).

Alcohol and drugs are strictly forbidden to the Muslim, not only wine—which existed in plenty at the time of Muhammad ﷺ—but any form of more modern alcoholic liquor or intoxicating substance. There is one major reason for this. They are all substances that take away the control of the mind, and render individuals no longer in authority over their own bodies.

The word for any intoxicant is *khamr*, and as the word 'intoxicant' implies, it is a kind of poison. The word 'khamara' means 'veiled, covered or concealed', and alcohol and drugs are khamr because they 'veil' the intellect.

Ibn Umar recorded from 'A'ishah: 'Every intoxicant is khamr, and every intoxicant is forbidden.' (Muslim 4964)

Al-Hakim ibn Hisham once said to one of his sons: 'O my son! Beware of wine, for it is vomit in your mouth, diarrhoea in your intestines, a hard punishment on your back, causes children to laugh at you and the Almighty to imprison you.' (Imam Bayhaqi—Seventy-seven Branches of Faith p. 31)

THE PROBLEM.

> 'O believers! Intoxicants, gambling, and trying to foretell the future are the lures of Satan; if you wish to prosper, you must keep away from these things. It is Satan's plan to stir up enmity and hatred in your midst with them, and lure you away from remembering Allah, and from prayer.' (5:93-94)

The drinking of alcohol has become a major problem in the modern world, and the behaviour in public of people affected by alcohol is becoming increasingly disturbing. Since alcohol remains in the bloodstream longer than most people realise, some people now spend virtually their entire lives under its influence, probably quite unaware of how it is affecting and altering them.

Most people are hardly aware of the extent of the problem. One can scarcely watch a programme on TV without the drinking of alcohol being taken for granted, and not shown as harmful in any way. In fact, the media programmes frequently present alcohol as a useful and pleasant social habit—the expression of hospitality.*

Some governments (e.g. the USA, India) have tried in the past to prohibit the consumption of alcohol—but have not succeeded. If one believes that Satan uses devious tricks to combat Allah, then alcohol must be one of his greatest

---

* Young people in the UK are forbidden by law to drink alcohol until they are 18 years of age. Any survey will show that most young people arriving at puberty actually drink it regularly, and many experiment with various drugs.

successes—and perhaps it is only when one sees it in that light that one can combat it successfully.

Like smoking, taking alcohol (or other drugs) is a powerful addiction, and even if a person knows perfectly well what the harmful results are likely to be, most still carry on taking it until disaster strikes.

DISASTROUS EFFECTS OF ALCOHOL

Muslims are against alcohol for many reasons. Firstly, of course, it was forbidden in the Qur'an. Apart from that, it damages the individual by harming a person's mind, it harms the general health, affects the ability to work, and can lead to mental breakdown, despair, suicide, and bankruptcy. It damages family life by causing neglect, cruelty and harmful behaviour and shame and dishonour for partner or parent. It damages other people by causing accidents and hurting innocent people, by encouraging immoral behaviour, and by filling hospital beds and thereby possibly depriving other invalids of treatment.

Husayn b. Ali reported his father Ali as telling him that a she-camel fell to his lot out of the spoils of war at Badr, and the Blessed Prophet also gave him another. 'When I made up my mind to consummate my marriage to Fatimah (the daughter of the Blessed Prophet ﷺ) I prevailed upon a goldsmith... to go along with me (to do some business), and thus I should be able to arrange my wedding feast. While I was arranging the equipment, my two she-camels were sitting down alongside the apartment of one of the Ansars. I collected (my things), and then found to my surprise that their humps had been hacked off and their haunches cut open and their livers had been ripped out. I burst into tears and said: 'Who has done this?' They said: 'Hamzah b. Abdal Muttalib (the Prophet's ﷺ uncle) has done it, and he is in this house dead drunk in the company of some of the Ansar, with a singing girl...She said in her song: O Hamzah, get up and attack these fatty she-camels...'

Ali told the Prophet, and when he came to the drunken Hamzah, the latter retorted rudely: 'Who are you but the slave of my father?' Allah's Messenger ﷺ realised he was intoxicated, and turned on his heels and came out. (Muslim 4881). (This incident occurred before alcohol had been declared unlawful.)

ISLAMIC PROHIBITION

At the time of the Prophet ﷺ, many people drank a great deal of alcohol; it was perhaps even more widespread than it is today! The teaching of Allah in the Qur'an took human weakness into account, and the prohibition of alcohol was given gently, in stages. (The surahs concerning khamr are not in chronological order in the Qur'an; the order of all the surahs was ordained by Allah before the death of Muhammad ﷺ, according to His will—that is why the surah numbers seem 'out of order').

Firstly, Allah pointed out that both nourishing and harmful products can actually come from the same plant— the date and vine.

> 'And from the fruit of the date-palm and the vine you can derive wholesome drink and food. Behold, there is a sign in this for the wise.' (16:67)

One should start to think about this. Many things in life can be used either for good or for evil. When humans are faced with decisions regarding the use of any provided thing, it is for them in their freewill to choose the path they will take, and what they will do. How they act will depend to a great extent on their understanding of the general will of Allah, and whether or not they wish to draw closer to Him.

The second verse regarding khamr pointed out that the harm caused far outweighed its pleasant effects. Even so, people were still left to form their own judgements as to whether they should continue to drink it or not. It was still not forbidden.

> 'When they ask you concerning wine and gambling, say:
> In them is great sin and some profit; but the sin is greater
> than the profit.' (2:219)

Thirdly came the first verse that was a command—the request that Muslims should not have their minds intoxicated when they came to prayer.

> 'O you who believe! Do not come to prayer with a
> befogged mind, but come when you can fully understand
> all that you are saying.' (4:43)

Since alcohol obviously befogs the mind, it was clearly intended that no Muslim should make their prayers under its influence. And since the salah-prayers were said five times during the day, and alcohol affects the body for many hours, this would mean that those who practised prayer were already virtually willing to give it up!

Finally came the complete prohibition in surah 5:93-94, already quoted at the start of this chapter.

As the news of the clear command spread among the Muslim people of Madinah, the effect was dramatic. Those who were drinking at the time poured away the drinks in their hands; they went through their houses and establishments and smashed the wine containers, pouring the liquid out on to the sand.

Anas b. Malik recorded: 'I was the cup-bearer of some people in the house of Abu Talhah (his father) on the day when liquor was forbidden. Their liquor had been prepared from dry and fresh dates when the announcer made the announcement...Behold, liquor has been made unlawful.' The liquor flowed in the lanes of Madinah. Abu Talhah said to me: 'Go and spill it.' And I spilt it.' (Muslim 4882)

This is not to say that there are no weaker Muslims who do drink. Everybody knows that there are. Any rule, whatever it is, is only necessary because it is trying to stop a certain kind of behaviour which is extremely difficult to curb, behaviour which brings pleasure. Rules are necessary because humans are weak and need certain support if they are to achieve success in a way of life that demands self-denial.

Many people regard the total prohibition of alcohol as too extreme and severe—they argue that one little drink does no-one any harm, it may relax the nerves and make a person more sociable, and so on. All these things are irrelevant to a Muslim. The point for a Muslim is not in the degree to which a pleasurable substance is harmful or not, but simply that Allah willed people not to touch this substance, and if they care about His will, that is the end of the story.

'Of that which intoxicates in a large amount, a small amount is haram.' (Ahmad, Abu Dawud, Tirmidhi)

'If a bucketful intoxicates, a sip of it is haram.' (Ahmad, Abu Dawud, Tirmidhi)

The Blessed Prophet 🕌 did not hesitate to order a flogging for people who drank alcohol and made themselves a public nuisance. There are numerous hadiths illustrating this.

Anas b. Malik reported that a person who had drunk wine was brought to the Apostle 🕌 who gave him 40 stripes with two lashes. Abu Bakr also did that, but when Umar assumed the caliphate he consulted people and Abd ur-

Rahman said: 'The mildest punishment is 80 stripes', and Umar prescribed that.' (Muslim 4226)

There is no actual penalty for drinking laid down in the Qur'an, but one can draw a comparison from the fact that a flogging is the mildest punishment mentioned in the Qur'an for slandering—and being intoxicated frequently causes the drunkard to become abusive and antagonistic towards others. The Prophet's ﷺ nephew Ali pointed out that 'when a man drinks he becomes intoxicated, and when he is intoxicated, he raves; and when he raves he makes up lies.' (Imam Malik).

However, crashing into people's homes to search for hidden alcohol, and administering punishments for things done in private are not part of Islamic Law.

In Islamic Law, people do not have the right to pry into private dwellings, or secretly spy on others to see if they can catch them out being guilty of some fault. 'Private sins' are a matter between each individual's conscience and God who sees everything.

Abu al-Haytham quoted Dukhayn the scribe of Uqbah b. Amr as saying: 'We had some neighbours who used to drink wine. I asked them to stop, but they refused. I said to Uqbah b. Amr... I am going to call the police for them.' He said: 'Leave them.' I came again to Uqbah b. Amr and told him that the neighbours had once more refused to stop drinking wine, and that I was going to call the police. He said: 'Woe to them! Leave them alone. I heard the Apostle of Allah ﷺ say (like this).' He then repeated the tradition: 'He who sees something which should be kept hidden and conceals it will be like one who has brought to life a girl buried alive.' (Abu Dawud 4894 and 4873.—In Abu Hashim's version, he said on the authority of Layth: 'Do not do it, but advise them and warn them.' (Abu Dawud 4874)

This does not mean that drunks can get away with abusing others behind closed doors, however. Any antisocial, threatening or dangerous behaviour which has been drawn to public notice, and has been witnessed or admitted four times, must always be dealt with.

A flogging is an immediate physical and psychological deterrent that makes any person think twice before becoming a nuisance or a danger to others. Therefore it is not regarded as excess cruelty, but as an example and warning to others. The guilty are punished but should not be wounded. They are not imprisoned, but may return immediately to their work, their household and their livings.

As it happens, the Holy Prophet 🕊 did not have a 'hard and fast' rule for every case of people taking alcohol, but gave different punishments in different circumstances.

Ibn Abbas recorded that a man who had drunk wine and become intoxicated was found staggering in the road, so he was taken to the Prophet 🕊. When he approached Abbas' house he escaped and fled inside where Abbas was, and grabbed hold of him. When this was mentioned to the Prophet 🕊 he laughed and said: 'Did he really do that?' And he gave no command regarding him.' (Abu Dawud 4461)

Abu Barda Ansari reported that the Prophet also said: 'None should be given more than 10 lashes' (Muslim 4234).

On other occasions the Prophet 🕊 ordered beatings, sometimes by hand, or with sandals, garments or palm branches (see Abu Dawud 4462-4465). Ali sad: 'The Apostle of Allah 🕊 and Abu Bakr gave 40 lashes for drinking wine, and Umar made it 80. All this is sunnah and standard practice.' (Abu Dawud 4466).

So what about a Muslim who is weak and drinks? Has he or she left Islam? Just as the Blessed Prophet ﷺ made it quite clear that just as you cannot continue to commit theft or other crimes and still regard yourself as a true believer, the same must apply to alcohol or drug-taking.

The drinker is certainly doing wrong—but let us remember that the prohibition of alcohol is hardly the only command for a Muslim. There are commands to govern every aspect of conscious life. Muslims are also commanded not to hate, or be spiteful, or use foul language, or he proud or mean, and so on. Unless you are a saint, you will probably commit all these sins at some time or other—what matters is your attitude of mind once you become conscious that you are committing these sins. Either you believe you cannot be forgiven your weakness, you have 'left Islam' and Allah will consign you to Hell for it; or you believe that He is truly the Compassionate, the Merciful, who will accept your repentance and forgive you. It applies to every form of disobedience to the will of Allah.

The important thing is to be conscious of what you are doing, and analyse the reasons why. Deliberate, conscious defiance of the will of Allah stemming from a hard and unreasoning heart is a very grievous matter; so is deliberately aggressive behaviour, flaunting your lack of concern in an abandoned and shameless manner. Any Muslim tempted to drink should think about this.

ALCOHOL USED IN MEDICINE.

Wayl al-Hadrami reported that Tariq b. Suwayd al-Jufi said: 'I prepare it as a medicine.' Whereupon the Prophet ﷺ said: 'Alcohol is not a medicine but a disease.' (Muslim 4892, Tirmidhi)

'Allah has sent down the disease and the cure, and for every disease there is a cure. So take medicine, but do not use anything haram as a medicine.' (Abu Dawud)

Unfortunately, many modern medicines use alcohol as a base and preservative for their substances. This presents a problem for the Muslim who wishes to keep the prohibition absolutely. A devout Muslim should inquire as to the content of the medicine, and if alcohol is present should check with the doctor or pharmacist whether a substitute is available.

Since the principle of Shari'ah is always to promote welfare, if there is no substitute and the medicine is necessary, in these circumstances it would be allowed—on the same principle that allows haram foods in cases of dire necessity.

'He has explained to you what He has made haram for you, except that to which you are compelled.' (6:119)

The spirit of Islam is always to bring peace and well-being and happiness to humanity, stemming from Allah's love for us.

If a pious person refuses to take medicine because it has alcohol in it, and consequently becomes worse and even dies, then that is their business and a matter between themselves and Allah. However, it is a misguided act of piety, and is unnecessary. The spirit of the faith is to see that person made well, and not to deny medical help.

'If one is compelled by necessity, neither craving it nor transgressing, there is no sin on him; indeed, Allah is forgiving.' (2:172-3)

It is the duty of Muslims in the medical profession to do speedy research into the problem and come up with alternatives to medicines containing alcohol, if possible, so that the question does not arise any longer.

KEEPING A BARRIER

True Muslims will keep a barrier between themselves and any contact with alcohol. It is not really enough to give up drinking. Even being in the presence of alcohol is a danger, because of its very nature.

'Allah has cursed khamr, those who produce it, those for whom it is produced, those who drink it, those who serve it, those who carry it, those it is carried to, those who sell it and those who buy it.' (Tirmidhi)

It erodes a person's standards, and lures into laxity. Muslims who live in societies where alcohol is freely available are now beginning to compromise by sitting in pubs, or mixing socially in houses where people are drinking, even though they themselves will not touch alcohol but will have a fruit juice.

One can see the reasons why they do so. It is not pleasant to be regarded as stand-offish, and unsociable, especially when one is trying to get on in that host community, and has made friends. However, this is dangerous if a Muslim wishes to keep the prohibition against alcohol. It is quite obvious how easy it is to weaken, and once one drink is taken, the habit seems to seize the person immediately.

Because of the seductive nature of alcohol, it is forbidden by Islamic Law based on the Shari'ah of the Blessed Prophet ﷺ to:

- trade in alcohol
- own or work in a place which sells it*

---

* In the UK, many Muslims run 'Corner-shops' that sell alcohol. It is a lucrative business, and can make all the difference to their income. However, it has caused accusations of hypocrisy to be laid at the door of Islam, as non-Muslims generally know they should not be selling alcohol.

- sell grapes to someone when it is known they will make wine with them
- give alcohol as a gift, even to a non-Muslim, on the principle that they should not give or receive anything that is not pure.

The Holy Prophet ﷺ did not even allow alcohol to be given to a non-Muslim as a gift.

'Some asked him: 'Why spill it? Why not give it away to the Jews?' Whereupon he said: 'He who has made it unlawful has also forbidden it to be offered as a gift to other people.' (Muslim 4882 n. 2400)

'If someone stockpiles grapes during harvest time in order to sell them to a Jew or Christian or anyone else who produces khamr, he will be leaping into the Fire with his eyes open.' (al-Tabarani)

A CAUTIONARY TALE

There is one story about a Caliph ordering the flogging of people who were not themselves drinking, but just sitting with drinkers. This group included a highly religious person who was actually fasting—going without any food or drink at all. The Caliph ordered this man to be flogged first— because he was the one who should have known better!

'If you sit with them, you will be like them.' (4:140)

DRUGS

The plant world abounds in substances which dramatically affect the human body, either as cures for sickness, antidotes to poison, or as poisons, soporifics or hallucinogens—things like dock leaves for the sting of nettles, aspirin prepared from willow-bark to dull pain, digitalis from foxgloves to stimulate the heart, and so on. Nowadays the medical profession manufactures artificial substances also, to give similar effects.

The use of substances to provide cures for illness is not forbidden in Islam, as we have seen:

'Allah has sent down the disease and the cure, and for every disease there is a cure—so take medicine, but do not use anything haram.' (Abu Dawud)

Many scientists are concerned that various plant species will die out on the planet before their use in medicine has become known.

However, many plant substances—such as marijuana, cocaine, opium, nicotine etc.—are powerful intoxicants which effect the human mind, and are therefore also khamr, and are frequently misused in a haram way.

'Sinful people smoke hashish because they find it produces rapture and delight, an effect similar to drunkenness... it produces dullness and lethargy... it disturbs the mind and temperament, excites sexual desire, and leads to shameless promiscuity.' (Shaykh Ibn Taymiyyah)

REASONS FOR DRUG USE

Drugs are often used by people either as a means to escape from the pains and distresses of their lives, or to indulge in an exciting world of fantasy experience which might prove dangerous, and to bring on a 'high', a feeling of artificially induced well-being and euphoria.

The problem is that 'fantasy' experiences may be dangerous, and any good feelings conjured up are only artificial, and not real. Any drug-user who starts off experimenting with substances because of their euphoric or illusory effects soon gets caught in a downward spiral as they become acclimatised to the drug and ever larger amounts are necessary to produce the same effects. Soon, the user is 'hooked', and if deprived of the drug will know all the desperation of withdrawal symptoms and violent cravings. 'Hooked' people will do anything to get hold of the drug to satisfy these cravings—and so what started off as a pleasurable experience becomes a deadly trap leading to crime and death.

As regards the users who take drugs in order to escape from the pains and trials of life, all they are doing is refusing to face up to reality and refusing to contemplate practical activity which will alleviate their problems. Instead of turning to Allah or to other people for help, they are simply creating bigger problems for themselves and gradually putting themselves in a condition where they will be beyond help.

All these things are totally against the spirit of Islam.

RESULTS OF USING DRUGS

Drugs impair the faculty of reasoning and decision-making, and lead to irresponsible behaviour—which can never be a good thing. Secondly, they cause physical decline and laziness, affect the nerves, and cause the decline of the user's general health, as the care and state of the body becomes less and less important to them. The drug user loses the sense of 'being in present time and reality.'

Thirdly, using drugs causes moral insensitivity, as the person becomes increasingly obsessed by the search to satisfy their cravings, and begins to care nothing for the feelings or well-being of others. The will to do anything constructive is damaged. Families are neglected as the drug user has less desire to please them or look after them, and eventually no regard for their feelings at all. Their only concern becomes their personal satisfaction.

Very often the path of the drug-taker leads straight into crime, especially theft, as money runs out and is desperately needed to pay for the drugs. In short, it is a downward spiral, often leading to the gutter, and death.

The Muslim general principle against drug use is the same as that for alcohol, based on the acceptance that Muslims are not the owners of their own bodies, but Allah is. Any substances which are harmful or injurious to the body, or might even cause death, are haram.

'Do not be cast into ruin by your own hands' (2:195)

'Do not harm yourselves or others' (Bukhari)

NOBODY ELSE'S BUSINESS

Some drug-takers argue that since they are not harming anyone else but themselves, what they do in private is their own business. This can never be acceptable in Islam. For a start, it is not true—everyone concerned with the drug-taker is harmed in someway. There is no suffering greater than that of parents or grandparents obliged to watch the physical and moral decline of their offspring and be unable to stop them or ultimately help them. Also, as previously stated, the Muslim does not regard the human body as one's own property to do with as one wishes with complete disregard—it is the property of Allah, and at the Judgement Day every person shall answer for their lives.

This is one good reason why Muslims regard it as vital that human beings are trained towards discipline and self-control from an early age.

SMOKING

Although there is no mention of smoking in the Qur'an (which was given before the discovery of tobacco), if Islamic principles are applied, it can be seen that the use of tobacco should be regarded as makruh—if not haram. It is one of the major causes of disease and death of the individuals who smoke, and it has also now been proved that people who are obliged to be in the company of smokers can be damaged (and even develop fatal cancers), even though they do not smoke themselves.

Anything which harms others or one's self is not recommended in Islam. Non-smokers have the right to breathe clean air, unpolluted by the smoking habits of others. If Muslims must smoke, they should observe certain rules of polite behaviour in order not to give offence to others, or risk harming the lungs of others.

Further, it cannot be considered polite for Muslims to smoke in the company of people who do not wish to suffer the unpleasant smell of stale smoke on their clothes, or in their houses. Smoking not only makes rooms and furniture smell, it also discolours the decorations and causes unnecessary expense. Needless to say, it is highly unlikely that the visiting smokers will offer to pay for the wallpaper and ceiling tiles they have damaged!

Smoking in any public place where there are young people should be discouraged, because it sets a very bad example. It might induce someone to think it was 'grown up', and copy the habit. Many Muslim people already feel it is impolite to smoke in front of their parents or grandparents; it should also be obvious that the reverse is perhaps more to the point, and that elders should not set a bad example. It is surely wrong for any Muslim to encourage any other person to start a harmful habit.

Similarly, it is wrong for a Muslim to tempt back to smoking any person who has given the habit up. Therefore special care should be taken not to smoke in the presence of a friend who is struggling with withdrawal symptoms.

THE REAL TRUTH

The tobacco industry needs to 'hook' around 300 new smokers every day in each country—to make up for the 300 or so customers who die every day from its harmful effects!

Justice, Crime and Punishment

JUSTICE

There is a long-standing argument between those who maintain that all people are of equal value, and those who regard this point of view as ridiculous. The Qur'an is very clear on one thing:

'Goodness and evil cannot be equal.' (41:34)

Equality is not a matter of wealth or poverty, but of worth; it is a matter of character. It is perfectly possible for all souls to be born of equal value, if that is the will of Allah, but as humans grow out of infancy and begin to make personal decisions, they do not stay equal.

People are given freewill, and often choose to do something contrary to the will of Allah—which makes them of less value. How the community deals with wrongdoers is the concept we call justice. The surah already quoted above gives us the starting point straightaway.

'Repay evil with what is better, then the person who was your enemy will become your intimate friend.' (41:34)

This is the justice of Allah—not to see wrongdoers relentlessly hunted down and made to suffer retribution, but the powerful desire to see peace, right and order restored, by the removal of the enmity or the failing that lay behind the wrong. The offending *person* should not be hated and despised, only the offending *behaviour*.

Jabir b. Abdullah recorded: 'A person should help his brother whether he is an oppressor or an oppressed. If he is the oppressor, he should prevent him from doing it, for that is his help, and if he is the oppressed he should be given assistance (against oppression).' (Muslim 6254)

In fact, Islam teaches strict justice, carried out according to the principles of honour tempered with mercy. If someone has been wronged, then it is the duty of all Muslims to unite to have the wrong put right. This should not just apply to wrongs done to fellow Muslims—*all* injustices should be addressed and none allowed to go unquestioned, even if the injustice was being done to one's worst enemy. In Islam, there should be no enemy at all except Satan, for only Allah has the knowledge of whether or not a person might not turn again and come to Him.

Once an injustice or tyranny is put right, the Muslim should cease hostility and forgive:

'Fight them until there is no more tumult or oppression, and justice and faith in God prevails; and if they cease, let there be no hostility except to those who continue to oppress.' (2:193)

To a Muslim, the effort to alter a situation is not regarded as interference in someone else's business. If Muslims ignore any wrongs done, then they are themselves in the wrong, and have in effect submitted themselves to the tyranny and abandoned the path of Allah. How can it ever be considered right to blink the eye, to let injustice go unchallenged, and ignore it? In Islam that is rightly seen as a weakness.

FORGIVENESS

Supposing you have done something wrong, but it was purely a private matter and affected only yourself and no-one else? Well, if it was completely private, then no-one else knows about it and it is something wholly between yourself and your Creator. Allah, of course, sees everything. He may choose to 'cover' your fault, or He may reveal it. Every person doing in private something of which they would be ashamed if it were made public knowledge, should think about this. Allah may punish or He may forgive, according to His will.

If you cannot see that what you did was wrong, then you are in the state of ignorance and cannot be blamed since consciousness has not entered the action. If you can see your fault and are sorry for the wrong thing, then it is certain that Allah the Compassionate will have mercy, for He is always kind. But the repentance must be genuine, and a real attempt made not to repeat the fault.

> 'If anyone does evil or wrongs his own soul, but afterwards seeks Allah's forgiveness, he will find Allah Oft-Forgiving, Most Merciful.' (4:110)

If the fault is repeated, Allah knows the weakness of humans, and again it is for Him to judge and not for other humans—but weak people must ask themselves whether or not they are simply using their knowledge of Allah's love as an excuse. We know Allah has extraordinary patience with us, more than any human; nevertheless we should not seek to deliberately provoke or anger Him.

> 'If Allah were to punish people according to what they deserve, He would not leave on the earth a single living being; but He gives them a chance for a certain length of time.' (35:45; 16:61)

It is accepted that Allah always forgives the truly penitent person; however, gaining forgiveness from another human is harder!

If a person has done something wrong in public, it is a different matter, because when any action can be seen by others (especially by young people) there is the question of setting an example. The upkeep of public morals is involved, and has to take precedence. So, if any Muslim admits to doing some wrong thing, even if it was done only to themselves, or perhaps boasts about it or regards it as a light matter, then punishment may follow.

Allah may forgive you if you are sorry, but if you have wronged another person, their demands of justice have to be satisfied before you can be forgiven by them. The wronged person could ask for compensation, or insist on punishment.

If some wrong has been done against you, then it is always considered better in Islam to forgive and be charitable, so long as refusal to take revenge is consistent with honour.

> 'The reward for an injury is an equal injury back; but if a person forgives instead, and is reconciled, that will earn reward from Allah.' (42:40)

However, if the refusal to take action over the wrong done is really because of weakness, or laziness, or fear, then the so-called 'forgiveness' is not genuine at all, but is only a cheap alternative to the action of seeking to put right. The resentment is still there, the wound is still festering, and remains unhealed.

When people have wronged you, they are not usually in a hurry to make amends; sometimes they feel angry, or embarrassed, or ashamed—and they do not wish to face the person they have hurt. The first move of a Muslim should be to seek out the wrongdoers, to reason with them and hold out the hand, in the hopes that they will stop their offensive actions and become friends.

> 'If the enemy starts leaning towards peace, then you also start leaning towards peace.' (8:61)

Allah the Compassionate One is the supreme example.

Abu Hurayrah recorded: 'I am near to the thought of My servant as he thinks about Me, and I am with him as he remembers Me. And if he remembers Me in his heart, I also remember him in My heart, and if he remembers me in assembly, I also remember him in assembly, better than him; and if he draws near to Me by the space of a palm, I draw near to him by the cubit... .and if he comes towards Me walking, I come at the run towards him.' (Bukhari, Muslim 6471)

It is not without good reason that all our surahs except one remind us with each recital that our dear Lord is the Compassionate, the Merciful. How easy it is to chant the words; how hard to understand them, and take His love as our example!

Abu Bakr recorded the beautiful prayer for forgiveness taught to him by the Blessed Prophet himself ﷺ: 'Recite, 'O Allah! I have done great wrong to myself... and there is none to forgive sins but You Alone; grant me your pardon, have mercy on me, for You are the Most Forgiving, the Most Compassionate.' (Muslim 6538)

JUSTICE AND HONOUR

What kinds of situations would require the positive action of a Muslim? Muslims should be slow to anger, slow to take offence. Nevertheless, they have a responsibility as human beings, as Allah's khalifahs on earth, not to blink the eye at injustice or suffering.

Firstly, all Muslims should find the courage to rise in defence of the cause of Allah. To refuse to do this would be a major weakness. Consider how we would behave if one of our friends was hurt. We would hurry to protect them and offer help and support. If we just ignored them and allowed them to be harassed and insulted, we would be very poor friends. And who is our chief Friend, the One who loves us most of all? Muslims do not need to be told that His honour is precious.

However, this does not mean that if we hear or see some ignorant person being abusive about Allah or Islam that we leap upon them and beat them up, or even kill them. The Prophet 鑗 set us the very clear example of *never* doing that, but of accepting insults and abuse patiently, and with dignity—showing by example how Islam was greater and more noble than the ravings and cruelties of its oppressors.

Allah does not need us to defend *Him*. It would be a very simple matter for Him to wipe out His 'enemies' with a mere breath. The fact that He does not do so is a sign to us, a very important sign. We should try to be like Him— and hate the wrongdoing and the offensive behaviour, but not the person doing it. That way, insha' Allah, the person in the wrong will become made right.

Defending the *cause* of Allah means rather defending justice, fair play, and all the other commands Allah has laid upon us. It does not mean attacks and vengeance on foolish atheists and hot heads, who should be looked on with

---

* For example, the cause of Allah was done little good service when certain Muslims in Pakistan sought the death penalty for a child who had daubed unpleasant slogans on a mosque wall; or when Ayatollah Khomeini issued his fatwah and placed a reward on the head of Salman Rushdie; or in any example where Muslims of one type abuse and persecute those of other types, or rant and rave against the 'kafirs' Allah would like to see converted!)

compassion rather than hatred, and are in need of saving from the terrible doom that may await them if they do not change their characters.★

What sort of matters require the action of the Muslim? There are many. They include any action in defence of a person's honour; the restoration of peace and freedom, and the deliverance from tyranny; acting in defence of individual honour, to protect home and family, and other loved ones, or any other wronged individual.

In every case it is always to be hoped that the outcome of justice will be forgiveness and a return to peace.

NO-ONE ABOVE THE LAW, OR UNPROTECTED BY IT

The only true law for the Muslim is the Shari'ah, the Law of God. Nevertheless, it is the duty of Muslims to be peaceful and law-abiding citizens in whichever country of the world they happen to live. It is not the place of Muslims to incite lawlessness, except under the condition of tyranny as suggested earlier. In normal circumstances, each country is doing its best to establish a right code of conduct, and all Muslims should respect that.

No citizen should ever be above the law, no matter how powerful, rich or influential. If any person can buy his or her way out of a rightly-deserved punishment, then that society is corrupt and should be challenged. True Law requires that officials should be above bribery and preferential treatment.

Similarly, no citizen should be beneath the protection of the law, no matter how humble. Every citizen should have equal rights, including an adequate right of defence if accused of something.

Judges should be people of adequate good character and knowledge, or those they try to judge will suffer.

Buraydah recorded: 'Judges are of three types, one of whom will go to Paradise and two to Hell. The one who will go to Paradise knows what is right and gives judgement accordingly; but the one who knows what is right and acts tyrannically in judgement will go to Hell, and also the one who passes judgement on people while ignorant.' (Abu Dawud 3566)

As regards religious matters, no-one should ever be forced to act against the dictates of their own consciences.

No human being should ever be sentenced to prison unless they have been properly convicted of a crime by an unbiased court of law. No person should ever be threatened or punished or imprisoned because of the fault of others, or in order to intimidate others.

No punishment should be carried out on people who are not fully responsible for their actions. The Blessed Prophet 鷺 particularly spoke against penalising children, or people the who are mentally ill or disturbed though stress.

'A'ishah recorded: 'There are three persons whose actions are not recorded—a sleeper until he wakes, a lunatic until restored to reason, and a child till it reaches puberty.' (Abu Dawud)

A woman who committed a sexual offence while the balance of her mind was disturbed was instantly acquitted. (Abu Dawud 4385-89)

The Blessed Prophet 鷺 was sometimes obliged to sentence people to severe penalties, and even allowed the death penalty on a few occasions, but this was something he hated doing (see p. 216). He never hesitated from ordering the penalties for flagrant and witnessed wrongdoing, but on several occasions he stated that he would have preferred it if an unwitnessed guilty person had not insisted on admitting his or her offence, knowing he would be forced to give the necessary punishment in order to purify them. The Blessed Prophet ﷺ took the point of view that if Allah had chosen to conceal their offence, and there were no witnesses, the guilty person was being very hard on himself or herself if they gave themselves up and insisted on forcing his hand. This is why the hadiths record that people who did this were actually of very strong faith and wished to completely purge themselves of their offence; and their repentance was certainly accepted by Allah.

Nevertheless, having said this, the Blessed Prophet ﷺ did not shrink from ordering and having administered capital punishment when it was considered right. One should remember that the death penalty was prescribed for all manner of offences in pre-Islamic times, and was common-place until curtailed by the Prophet ﷺ.

Abu Hurayrah recorded one man who refused every opportunity to be pardoned for his adultery until he had been stoned. The Prophet ﷺ said: 'Look at this man whose fault was concealed by Allah but who would not leave the matter alone, so that he was stoned like a dog.' He came to the corpse of an ass with its legs in the air. He said: 'Go and eat this ass's corpse.' They replied: 'Apostle of Allah! Who can eat of this?' He said: 'The dishonour done to your brother is more serious than eating some of this. By Him in Whose hand is my soul, he is now among the rivers of Paradise, plunging into them.' (Abu Dawud 4414—another case was recorded in Abu Dawud 4366)

Yazid b. Nuaym recorded: 'Mayz came to the Prophet (on the advice of Huzzal) and admitted (having committed adultery) four times in his presence, so he ordered him to be stoned to death. But he said to Huzzal: 'If you had covered him with your garment (i.e. not given him the advice to insist on this punishment) it would have been better for you.' (Abu Dawud 4364)

PUBLIC JUSTICE

Muslim justice should always be carried out publicly. This is not done for the sake of barbarity, or to please a blood-thirsty audience, but because it is vitally important that justice is seen to be done, and that judges should not have the opportunity for corruption and brutality behind the scenes.

Muslims cannot approve of trials and punishments being carried out in secret, with the possibility of inhumane treatment and torture. It would be naive to assume that corruption in the name of the law did not take place all over the world—so the more public the affair the better the safeguard.

Iyad b. Himar recorded: 'The inhabitants of Paradise are three; one who wields authority and is just and fair, one who is truthful and has been empowered to do good deeds, and the person who is merciful and kind-hearted to his relatives and to every Muslim.' (Muslim 6853)

PUNISHMENT

Three things are regarded as being particularly dishonourable in Islam—theft, sexual permissiveness, and crimes associated with drunkenness or drug-addiction. Of course, it should go without saying that in any truly Islamic society there would not need to be punishments for any of these things, for they would simply not exist. The Messenger of Allah ﷺ observed:

'The fornicator who fornicates is not a believer so long as he goes on doing it; and no thief who steals is a believer so long as he goes on committing theft; and no drunkard who drinks wine is a believer as long as he keeps on drinking.' (Muslim 104—recorded by Abu Hurayrah)

There are strict limits for penalties laid down in Islamic law, and these are not intended to be barbaric cruelty as many non-Muslims imagine, but on the contrary reasonable deterrents to safeguard society. Islamic law bears in mind the harm done to victims and establishes strong deterrents, rather than encouraging a soft tolerance for criminality and cruelty. Unfortunately, in some countries which are supposed to be Muslim some savage punishments are carried out that are the culture of the particular country and are not in accordance with Islam. If that country claims to be Islamic, there is need of reform. Whereas it is true that a deliberate criminal offender would have good reason to think twice before committing the offence, a person forced into offending behaviour through genuine need or through pressure of circumstances should expect sympathy and help from a truly Islamic state.

FLOGGING

An example of a punishment laid down by the Blessed Prophet ﷺ which often raises eyebrows in countries that have abandoned corporal punishment is flogging This was prescribed for several offences committed by Muslims, including drunkenness and adultery.

However, it was not intended to be a savage beating inflicted capriciously according to the whims of brutal guards. If a flogging had to be administered by a Muslim, it should be done with control, in accord with justice, and in the kindest possible way in the circumstances. It is un-Islamic to add any extra torments to the prescribed punishment. When one studies the list below, one can see immediately the difference between a flogging according to Islamic principles and the cruel beatings of societies not governed by these principles: (a) It was not thought proper to flog a sick person until he or she was well again (see Muslim 4224). (b) The flog should not be so heavy that it would wound the body beneath the skin, nor so light as it would not be taken seriously. (c) The beating should not touch face, private parts or head. (d) It should not be done with full force, but also not so lightly as to not be taken seriously. (e) Men should be flogged standing and women sitting. (f) Women should be properly clothed and not have their bodies exposed by stripping. (g) Flogging should not be done at times of extreme heat or extreme cold. (h) Men should not be tied to posts and flogged on the bare back. (i) Flogging can be split over several days if the condemned person's condition demands it, but it is preferable to get it over within in one session. (j) Flogging should never be done by a cruel administrator but someone who understands the spirit of Islamic Law. (k) A woman who has had a baby may not be flogged until the child is weaned. (Muslim 4225 n. 2180).

Abu Umamah b. Sayf-Hunayf recorded that a certain man suffered from illness so much that he wasted away until there remained on him only skin and bones. Someone's slavegirl went in to him and cheered him up so much that he had unlawful intercourse with her... (He admitted it because he felt ashamed and wished to be purified, but his friends pleaded for him on account of his terrible condition). The Apostle of Allah ﷺ commanded to take a hundred twigs and hit him once. (Abu Dawud 4457)

THEFT

'As to the thief, male or female, cut off their hands: a punishment by way of an example.' (5:41)

The Qur'an lays down a severe punishment for theft, but it is not true that Muslim countries are full of one-handed people! On the contrary, any true Muslim would not even consider committing theft, because of the belief that Allah sees everything, and only a fool would sacrifice nearness to Allah in the afterlife for the sake of a temporary temptation.

In Islam, where a theft has been detected, the guilty person is not supposed to be instantly dragged off for the amputation of limbs. The circumstances leading up to the theft should be examined very carefully. If it can be proved that the thief stole out of dire need, because the family or individual was starving, and the State had not been able to fulfil its obligation as regards providing for them, then there should be no question of losing a hand. Hands should only amputated when it can be proved that the person is a persistent thief, and there is no chance of reforming their character. Then and only then should it done in Islam, to act as a deterrent.

In these cases, no impartiality was to be shown to people because of their rank or social standing or sex:

'A'ishah recorded: 'A woman of a high and noble family was brought to the Prophet accused of theft, and they begged that she be spared the punishment. He said: 'I swear by Him who holds my life in His hands, that even if my daughter Fatima had committed this crime, I would have amputated her hand myself.' (Bukhari, Muslim 4188, Abu Dawud 4360)

In a primitive and savage society the laws of Islam should come as a tremendous relief, a genuine attempt to bring about justice. Unfortunately, there is a danger of brutality and lack of true Islamic justice in societies where ignorant or cruel people are in authority, or where mobs stirred up in anger or outrage assume they have the right to dole out summary punishment. However, it is strange that in its desire to be 'kind' to its citizens, many societies that have abandoned capital or corporal punishment seem to condone almost any outrage perpetrated against their helpless citizens rather than deal with the miscreants!

Incidentally, the best way to 'cut off the hand of a thief' is to create such excellent social conditions that no-one steals though need.

FINAL JUDGEMENT BEFORE ALLAH

'No bearer of burdens shall be made to bear the burden of another.' (6:164)

'Let them bear, on the Day of Judgement, their own burden in full—and also something of the burdens of those without knowledge whom they misled!' (16:25)

Every Muslim believes that human judgements can be wrong, or influenced by bias or ignorance of circumstances—but Allah sees and hears everything, and no person can escape His true judgement on their life. On that Day, no-one will be able to make excuses for another—we will all stand alone, as individuals.

If anyone has accepted judgement against someone else wrongfully, knowing it to be wrong, God sees all and the final judgement will be fair.

'Eat not your property among yourselves in vanity, nor seek by it to gain the hearing of the judges, that you may knowingly devour a portion of the property of others wrongfully.' (2:188)

The Blessed Prophet ﷺ knew that he was only human, and it was quite possible for him to make mistakes or to be swayed by a clever lawyer. He gave this warning to the criminal who might feel smug in his or her escape from justice:

The Prophet ﷺ said: 'When you bring your case to me, some of you may be more eloquent in expressing their side than others. I will judge based upon what I hear, and if I happen to give someone something belonging (rightfully) to his fellow citizen, he should not take it, for I would be giving him a piece of the Fire.' (Bukhari, Malik, Ahmad)

Green Islam

'O Lord!

I beseech Thee for guidance, righteousness, chastity, and self-sufficiency.' (Prayer of Muhammad)

After many centuries of neglect and mistreatment of the planet by people who simply saw its resources as a free gift to be exploited so that they could get rich quick, it has become fashionable to be 'green.' This means that the

wealthy industrial nations of the world are at last admitting the terrible damage their activities have caused to our environment, and are so concerned that they are belatedly considering what to do about it.

Muslims, who have always regarded the earth as Allah's gift to humanity, should be in the forefront of this movement, and not lagging behind.

> 'Do you not see that it is Allah whose praises all beings in the heavens and on earth celebrate, and the birds of the air with wings outspread? Each one has its own mode of prayer and praise. Allah knows well all that they do.' (24:41)

> Allah has created every living thing from water; those that creep on their bellies, or have two legs or four; Allah creates what He wills, and has power over all things. (24:45)

Muslims believe that human beings have an enormous responsibility, for Allah has handed the planet over to them to look after and cherish and protect. Humans are to be Allah's vicegerents, guardians of His creation and responsible for every part of it. They are certainly not to damage or pollute or destroy it. On the Day of Judgement, Muslims expect to be asked concerning their responsibility towards Allah's earth and the creatures on it. They will be examined as to whether they used or abused the natural resources (animal, vegetable and mineral) which Allah entrusted to them.

> 'It is He who has made you custodians (khalifahs), inheritors of the Earth.' (6:165)

> 'It is Allah who has subjected the sea to you... and He has subjected to you all that is in the Heavens and the Earth.' (45:12-13)

An example of the Prophet ﷺ being concerned about even basic details was recorded by the uncle of Abu Rafi. b. Amr al-Ghifari: 'When I was a boy, I used to throw stones at the palm-trees of the Ansar. So I was brought to the

Prophet ﷺ who said: 'O boy, why do you throw stones at the palm trees?' I said: 'I want to eat the dates.' He said: 'Do not throw stones, but eat what falls beneath them!' (Abu Dawud 2616).

THE BALANCE

'Allah has lifted the heavens up high, and has set up the Balance.' (55:7)

That balance is very important. Muslims believe it is the very key to our survival. It used to be quite common for mathematically-minded astronomers to point out that we could not possibly be unique in space. By statistical probability, there must be literally millions of planets in other solar systems with life on them, perhaps similar to our own. However, despite all the advances in science, there is still no evidence whatsoever of any other rock in space with a living ecology like our own. It is quite possible that we *are*, in fact, all alone in space.

The Muslim keeps an open mind as to whether or not there are other planets with life on them. What is vital is that our planet *does*, and that we must cherish it.

RESPONSIBILITY

Muslims believe that Allah has given us freewill, and that it is our duty to stop the present suicidal trend of selfish destruction of the Earth's resources. It is not good enough just to 'read about it' and 'tut-tut' over the things we know are wrong practice and abuse of our resources. Muslims should be actively and keenly involved in the battle against those selfish individuals who pollute our world for economic gain.

Scientists have observed that human activity now affects the atmosphere and climate in a drastic manner. Notable examples are the increase of the 'greenhouse effect' caused by CFC gases which warm up the planet and deplete its protective ozone-layer, and 'seeding' clouds by dropping chemicals into them to produce rain. They consider that uncontrolled industrialisation has been very wasteful with the earth's resources, and that industry run by people who do not believe that they are Allah's guardians, has adopted a couldn't care-less attitude to what is taken out of the earth, how thoughtlessly it is used, and how waste products are disposed of or dumped. Money-making companies have behaved blindly in regard to the effect of their actions. We are already suffering the results of the massive applications of herbicides and pesticides to plants, the overdose of artificial fertilisers to our soil, and the polluting of the seas with poisons and chemical wastes.

HARMONY IN NATURE

Muslims—especially in such places as those liable to flood, hurricane, volcano, earthquake or desert—are aware that there is violence in nature, but it is part of an underlying harmony, a deep balance which maintains all life. Many so-called natural disasters have been created by humans—for example, the famine in the Sudan (a formerly food-exporting country) was caused by neglecting the ecology and growing too much cotton as a cash-crop to pay back interest on loans; the flooding in Bangladesh was made worse by uprooting the forests.

We have yet to understand fully the damage done by cutting down the earth's rain-forests (whose trees supply so much of the planet's oxygen), but ecologists are alarmed.

The terrible pollution caused by lead petrol and the release into our atmosphere of CFC gases are two disasters that governments are desperately trying to put right, with variable success.

As regards living species, many are rapidly becoming extinct that have survived all these centuries, and the cause for much of this lies in either pollution of their natural habitat, damage or destruction of their food supply, or over-fishing or over-farming.

If net-mesh is too small, or if pregnant animals and fish are taken; or animals are hunted to extinction for their fur or skin or tusks or body oils; or rare creatures are gunned down for sport; or hedgerows are obliterated and all wild land put under artificial cultivation—maybe on the Day of Judgement we will have to answer about these things.

THE CONSEQUENCES

If deliberate disruption is caused to the earth's natural systems, the consequences and casualties are all too clear—species of living things become extinct, deserts spread, our atmosphere is reduced, and millions are impoverished and suffer starvation.

Muslims regard their planet as a place created out of love, and therefore it should be sustained through love. The Muslim desires to live at peace with Nature, and to bring about its wholeness.

HOW MUSLIMS CAN BE GREEN

There are many small things that can be carried out in every household. The important thing is to be aware of what we are doing, and the principle is to avoid waste, damage and pollution.

For example, plastic bags, cartons and containers can be re-used, and whenever possible people could buy recycled products, especially paper. Bottle banks can be used for the return of glass products. Nobody should throw away as rubbish anything that can be used again or returned to a manufacturer for recycling. Foil and bottle tops can be collected for charities—such as guide-dogs for the blind. Many other things are worth money if recycled, and it is up to local corporations to make sure this 'rubbish' is sifted and sorted.

To preserve our precious wood, Muslims should consider buying pine furniture in preference to rarer woods, and try to find out if the furniture was made by a responsible company that plants replacement saplings. They should discourage the waste of paper and packaging. All extra paper and plastic uses up trees and fuel quite needlessly.

Muslims can cut down their use of energy in numerous ways—by turning lights off, or washing up by hand instead of by machine. They could ride a bike instead of automatically going everywhere by car.

They should not buy products obtained from the killing of rare or endangered species of animals, such as fur or ivory, or rhinocerus horn, or parts of tigers. They should not buy products that have been cruelly tested on animals captured or bred for this purpose.

They should try not to use aerosols containing the ozone-destroying CFC gasses, or use any products which are not biodegradable, that is, will not break down and rot naturally.

They should not use detergents that pollute the water supplies, and preferably not use petrol with lead in it.

It is no excuse to think that our own little contribution won't make any difference to the big companies—we have to take the lead. Manufacturers won't go on producing things that people refuse to buy.

'My heart is tuned
to the quietness
that the stillness of Nature inspires.'

Hazrat Inayat Khan.

SOME GREEN HADITHS OF PROPHET MUHAMMAD

Abu Hurayrah recorded: 'The whole Earth has been created a place of worship, pure and clean.' (Muslim)

Hakim ibn Hizan recorded: 'O Hakim, these riches are green and sweet for whoever takes them without greed; they are a source of blessing. But they are not blessed for him who seeks them out of greed. He is like the one who eats but is not filled.' (Bukhari)

'Whoever plants a tree and diligently looks after it until it matures and bears fruit, Allah the Most Glorious will count as charity for him anything for which its fruits are used.' (Ahmad)

Anas b. Malik recorded: 'If a Muslim plants a tree or sows a field and humans and beasts and birds eat from it, all of it is love on his part.' (Bukhari)

Animals

Allah loves every one of the creatures He has made, and therefore the principles of mercy and compassion are to be extended to every living creature.

Anas and Abdullah report: 'All creatures are Allah's children, and those dearest to Allah are those who treat his children kindly.' (Bayhaqi)

Cruelty to animals is totally forbidden in Islam. This ruling applies in any country and in every circumstance—

particularly where animals are used to work for humans, or
to provide dairy produce or their flesh to eat. It applies
particularly to the methods of killing animals where their
flesh is required for our tables.

Muslims are required by Allah to:

> 'Feed, for the love of Allah, the indigent, the orphan and
> the captive, (saying): 'We feed you for the sake of Allah
> alone; no reward do we desire from you, nor thanks.'
> (76:8-9)

In this passage, many scholars include the dumb animals
that are under subjection to humanity in the category of
'captive'; these animals must be properly fed, housed and
looked after, and the righteous person does not forget them.

Beasts of burden should never carry or pull loads too
heavy, and it is totally against the spirit of Islam to allow
horses, donkeys, bullocks or any other animal used to drag
carriages or carts too heavy for them, to labour until they are
exhausted, or until their flesh has raw patches and sores—a
common enough sight in many so-called Islamic countries.

Kindness also requires that the manes and tails of horses
are left in their natural condition:

Utbah b. Abd al-Sulami said that he heard the Apostle
of Allah ﷺ say: 'Do not cut the forelock, manes or tails of
horses, for their tails are their means of driving flies away,
their manes provide them with warmth, and blessing is tied
to their forelock.' (Abu Dawud 2536)

Animals should be kept in as natural state as possible,
and therefore the castration of male animals is regarded as a
cruel and unnatural practice, and forbidden.

HUNTING

Islam teaches that a person should never hunt just for

sport, but may only take the life of animals for food or other useful purpose.

'If someone kills a sparrow for sport, the sparrow will cry out on the Day of Judgement, 'O Lord! That person killed me for nothing! He did not kill me for any useful purpose!' (al-Nisai, Ibn Hibban in Sahih)

Abdullah ibn Amr ibn al-'As recorded: 'Whoever kills anything bigger than a sparrow without a just cause, Allah will hold him accountable for it. The listeners asked, 'O Messenger of Allah, what is a just cause?' He replied, 'that he kill it to eat, not to simply chop off its head and then throw it away.' (Ahmad, al-Nisai, al-Hakim)

If a creature can be tamed or controlled by humans so that it may be properly slaughtered in due course, it is forbidden to hunt it.

Where an animal or bird (such as a hawk or a dog) is a natural predator, it cannot be blamed for doing what comes naturally to it, since Allah has created the instinct in the creature—but deliberate cruelty is never to be encouraged. All hunting should only be for food, and any animal used for hunting should be very well trained, always under control, and not clumsy or savage.

> Say: 'Whatever is good is lawful to you. And eat of what is caught for you by those you have trained among hunting animals, teaching them as Allah has taught you, and mention the name of Allah over it.' (5:5)

The criteria for a trained animal are that when it is called, it responds, when commanded it hunts, and when restrained it stops immediately. The dog or hawk must not eat the hunted creature itself.

Ahmad recorded: 'If you send your dog after the game, and it eats part of it, you should not eat it, for the dog has hunted the game for itself and not for you; but if it kills the game without eating it, you can eat it as it has caught it for its master.' (Bukhari and Muslim)

If possible, one should reach the hunted beast while there is still life in it, and slaughter it in the halal way.

'When you set your dog (for the chase), mention the name of Allah. If he catches the game, and you reach it while it is still alive, cut its throat.' (Bukhari and Muslim)

If the animal is hunted with a weapon, the weapon should not be cruel (like a club for bludgeoning), but efficient—such as would pierce the animal (i.e. a spear, sword or bullet) and not such as would club it or throttle it. Throwing stones at or clubbing a wounded animal is totally forbidden.

> 'Forbidden to you are the flesh of that which has died a natural death, and...that which has been killed by strangling or beating or by falling or by being gored, and that which has been (partially) eaten by a wild beast except that which you make lawful by slaughtering (before its death)...'
> (5:4)

This prohibition reveals Allah's kindness to animals in several ways—it shows concern for human beings, that they do not harm themselves by eating meat from an animal that maybe died from eating something poisonous itself, or that was diseased; it shows concern for other wild animals and birds that are flesh eaters, since the carcasses of animals left lying are a source of food for them and are devoured by them; and it encourages humans to look after animals and see to it that they do not die of disease and malnutrition—and if an animal in their charge becomes diseased, either a cure will be sought for it, or it will be humanely slaughtered.

BLOOD-SPORTS

The Blessed Prophet Muhammad forbade any so-called 'sport' which involved goading animals into fighting each other—a common enough practice in his time. By the same principle, all modern existing blood-sports such as fox-hunting, big game hunting, badger, bear or dog-baiting, or fights to the death between cockerels, are also condemned.

THE LUXURY TRADE

The idea of humans clubbing baby seals in order to get their fur for luxury garments is abhorrent to a Muslim.

Any destruction of animal life simply to satisfy the desires of wealthy ladies cannot be approved of.

However, the Blessed Prophet ﷺ did not approve of deliberate waste. If an animal died, the prohibition was only against eating its flesh—use should be made of its skin, horns, bones and hair.

Ibn Abbas recorded: The freed maid-servant of the Prophet's wife Maymunah was given a sheep and it died. The Prophet ﷺ passed by its carcass and said: 'Why did you not take its skin to be tanned and use it?' They replied: 'But it is dead.' The Prophet ﷺ said: 'What is prohibited is eating it.' (All hadith collections except Ibn Majah)

Tanning an animal's skin purified it, no matter what the animal.

Sawdah (the wife of the Prophet ﷺ) said: 'One of our sheep died, so we tanned its skin and used it as a waterskin, putting dates in it to sweeten the water. We used it until it wore out.' (Bukhari)

FACTORY FARMING

Farming in itself is perfectly allowable, and a good way of caring for animals. But sadly, some modern methods of farming have become extremely unnatural and cruel, and deprive the animals of all enjoyment of life. Keeping livestock in cramped and dark conditions, and force-feeding them unnatural food-stuffs in order to interfere with their natural flavour or fat-content, or to make them grow so quickly that their natural life is unreasonably shortened, are forbidden. Millions of 'battery-farmed' chickens have a life of no more than 45 days from egg to the table, and can hardly stand because their body weight has been artificially increased—and yet anyone who has kept chickens can tell you that each hen is an 'individual' and should live several years!

Raising larger livestock in closely confined spaces, is also forbidden. This applies to the 'battery' methods of growing calves (and pigs) for the table, and any other kinds of animal that are hardly given room to turn round in.

Any slaughter of farm animals should be done with sensitivity, and not in conditions that cause panic and distress to the animals.

ANIMALS IN CONFINEMENT

Some animals are kept in appalling conditions—either for factory-farming purposes, or in zoos. It is against the spirit of Islam to keep any animal tied up, in dirty conditions, or confined in a small space, just for human convenience.

The Prophet ﷺ once made his companions free two little captive birds:

Abdullah b. Masud recorded: 'We saw a bird with her two young ones and we captured the young. The bird came and began to spread the wings. The Apostle of Allah ﷺ said: 'Who grieved this bird for its young ones? Return its young ones to it.' (Abu Dawud 2669 and 5248)

Muslims believe that humans who treat animals and birds in a cruel manner will be answerable for their actions on the Day of Judgement.

ANIMAL EXPERIMENTS AND VIVISECTION

It has become commonplace in our modern world for various experiments to be tried out on animals for all sorts of reasons. Some of these are genuinely beneficial to humanity, and involve progress in medicine and medical welfare. Others are for cosmetic purposes, or involve testing reactions to various substances, even to cigarettes.

Following the principle of compassion and kindness towards all Allah's creations, any experimentation simply for reasons of luxury goods or vanity, are totally forbidden. Muslims should inquire carefully if the products they buy have been produced by halal methods, in other words, without inflicting any cruelty on any other living thing.

In the matter of medical progress, if there was no possible alternative to an experiment on an animal, then a Muslim might accept the argument of necessity for the experiment; but it would be far preferable to look for some other method of investigation. Experiments should never be attempted lightly, or without very good reason.

BRANDING

When domestic animals have to be branded to show ownership it obviously causes pain; the Blessed Prophet Muhammad ﷺ forbade the branding of any part of their body except the hind-quarters.

'Do not brand any animal except on the part of its body furthest from its face.' (Hadith)

Jabir recorded: 'Did it not reach you that I cursed him who branded the animals on their faces and struck them on their faces?' (Muslim 5281, Abu Dawud 2558)

THE PROPHET'S KINDNESS TO CATS

There are numerous stories recounting the Prophet's kindness to animals, especially cats. A famous one involves a cat that had given birth to kittens on his cloak. Rather than disturb them, Muhammad ﷺ took a knife and cut round them, leaving them a generous part of his cloak as their blanket.

The Prophet's ﷺ friend Abu Hurayrah was given this nickname (Father of the little she-cat) because he was frequently seen in the Prophet's ﷺ house with a small cat in his arms.

Nafi and Ibn Umar recorded that: 'A woman was punished because she had kept a cat tied up until it died, and she was thrown into Hell. She had not provided it with food or drink, and had not freed her so that she could eat the insects of earth.' (Muslim 5570 and 6346)

The Blessed Prophet ﷺ regarded the cats that lived alongside humans in their swellings as 'part of the family.' He even used the water they had been sipping for his ablutions, without regarding it as unclean.

Kabshah bint Kab b. Malik, the wife of Ibn Abu Qatadah recorded: 'Abu Qatadah came to me and I poured out water for him for ablution. A cat came and drank some of it; he tilted the vessel for it, and it drank some more. He saw me looking at him and asked me: 'Are you surprised, my niece?' I said: 'Yes.' He then reported the Messenger of Allah as saying: 'It is not unclean, it is one of those who live with us.' (Abu Dawud 75)

Dawud b. Salih quoted his mother's story that her mistress sent her with some pudding to 'Ai'shah who was offering prayer. 'She made a sign to me to place it down. A cat came and ate some of it, and when 'Ai'shah had finished her prayer she ate from the place where the cat had eaten. She stated that the Messenger said: 'It is not unclean, it is one of those who live amongst you.' She added: 'I saw the Messenger performing ablution from water left over by the cat.' (Abu Dawud 76)

DOGS

Muslims regard the dog as an animal whose saliva breaks wudu for prayer. There are certain hadiths which suggest that the black dog was particularly associated with evil and Satan, and that dogs should not be kept in the house.

Abu Talhah reported: 'Angels do not enter a house in which there is a dog or a statue.' (Muslim 5230)

The Prophet at one time did sanction the killing of dogs, but this was not an indiscriminate destroying of dogs as a species, but the pruning of stray dogs and those which were infected by rabies and other dangerous diseases.

Many Muslims keep dogs for herding and protection, and respect them as hard-working and devoted loyal animals, and there are mentions of the permissibility of hunting with the dog in the Qur'an, as we have seen.

People at the time of the Blessed Prophet seem to have taken very literally a particular command of his to cull the wild dogs, which the Prophet had to abrogate in order to save their wholesale destruction. The following hadith suggests the Prophet's true attitude to dogs, and also that he obviously knew of and did not condemn situations where the dogs were kept domestically and were able to lick platters clean.

Ibn Mughaffal recorded: The Messenger of Allah ﷺ ordered the killing of dogs, and then afterwards said: 'Why are the people killing them?' He granted permission to keep the dog for hunting and for (the security) of the herd, and said: 'If your dog licks a utensil wash it seven times and rub it with earth the eighth's time.' (Abu Dawud 74)

The following two stories are representative of the attitude of the Blessed Prophet ﷺ towards an animal regarded as despised by some people.

'Once, during a severe famine, a student of religion saw a dog lying on the ground so weak it could not even move. The student was moved to pity, and immediately sold his books and bought food to give to the dog. That very might, he had a striking dream. 'You need not work so hard to acquire religious knowledge, my son. We have bestowed knowledge upon you.' (Muslim story—The Muslim Voice, January 1990)

Abu Hurayrah recorded: 'Once, while a man was going on his way, he became severely thirsty. He found a well and went down in it, drank water, and came out. Suddenly he saw a dog panting and eating soil dying of thirst. He said to himself: 'This dog has reached the same condition of thirst that I reached.' So he went down again into the well, filled his (leather) sock with water and came up and supplied water to the dog. Allah appreciated this action of his and forgave him.' (Abu Dawud 2544)

MISCELLANEOUS

There is a hadith recording the Prophet's ﷺ anger

when someone who got stung by an ant took vengeance by wiping out the whole colony:

Abu Hurayrah recorded: 'An ant bit (one of the earlier) prophets, and he ordered that the whole colony of ants should be burnt. And Allah revealed to him: 'Because of one ant's bite you have burnt a whole community from amongst the communities which sing My glory.' (Muslim 5567, Abu Dawud 5246)

He once became very angry when he was visiting the house of Hakam b. Ayyub with Anas b. Malik, when he saw some people who had tied up a hen and were shooting arrows at it for fun. Anas' grandson Hisham recorded that the Prophet ﷺ promptly forbade tying up of animals and making targets of them. (Muslim 4812, 4813, Abu Dawud 2810).

The Blessed Prophet ﷺ once even rebuked his beloved 'A'ishah, who had mounted a wild camel and was making it spin round and round. She recorded that he ordered her to show kindness. (Muslim 6275)

Like most Arabs, the Blessed Prophet ﷺ had a particular tenderness for camels. Abu Hurayrah recorded that when they were on the move the Prophet ﷺ said that they should be driven quickly through arid land, and driven slowly (i.e. allowed a chance to graze) on fertile land. (Muslim 4723, 4724)

HALAL SLAUGHTER

Muslims may not eat any sort of meat, unless it has been killed in the quickest and most painless manner, and with prayer in the name of Allah.

> 'O believers! Eat of the good things that We have provided for you, and be grateful to Allah, if it is Him you worship. He has only forbidden you carrion meat and blood and the

flesh of pigs, and that on which any name other than the
name of Allah has been invoked.' (2:173; 5:3)

Shaddad b. Aus recorded: 'Truly Allah has commanded
goodness in everything; so when you kill, kill in a good way,
and when you slaughter, slaughter in a good way. Every one
of you should make his knife sharp, and let the slaughtered
animal die comfortably.' (Muslim 4810)

There is a growing trend towards vegetarianism for
Muslims, but this is purely a matter of individual conscience.

Muslims do not agree with the methods of slaughter
common in the West, in which animals are supposed to be
stunned electrically before slaughter. The 'stunning' often
kills them. They maintain that to cut the throat with a very
sharp knife is the least painful method and not electrocution.
If no knife is available, a sharp rock, piece of wood or reed
can be used. The slaughtering is done by either cutting the
throat or by piercing the hollow of the throat. The best way
is to cut the windpipe, the gullet, and the two jugular veins.

Adi b. Hatim recorded: 'O Messenger of Allah, we go
hunting and sometimes we do not have a knife with us. We
may find a sharp rock or a piece of wood or a reed.' The
Prophet ﷺ said: 'The object is to make it bleed with
whatever you have, and mention the name of Allah over it.'
(Ahmad, Abu Dawud, al-Nisai, Ibn Majah). This does not
mean clumsily causing the animal suffering by attacking it
with any thing that came to hand—only with what is as sharp
as a knife, i.e. a flint.

Every Muslim male has the responsibility of knowing
how to kill an animal, and should be prepared to take this
responsibility upon himself if he is prepared to eat meat.
Muslims regard those who simply buy meat from unknown
sources, and who do not know how or where it was killed,
as being irresponsible.

When Muslims kill an animal, they have to observe certain rules. The knife that will kill the beast is never to be sharpened in front of it. The creature is to go to its death in a kind atmosphere, well fed and watered, not suspecting what is about to happen—and certainly not in the slaughterhouse atmosphere of torture and terror.

Ibn Abbas once reported that the Prophet ﷺ saw a man who was sharpening his knife after laying down a sheep to be slaughtered. He rebuked him saying, 'Do you intend to make it die two deaths? Why did you not sharpen your knife before laying it down?' (al-Hakim)

It is forbidden to deny food or drink to an animal on the grounds that it is just about to be killed.

Islam also prohibits the slaughter of one animal in front of another, for the same reason. Animals should be killed quickly, while a prayer is being said.

Some Muslims refuse to eat any meat unless they know for certain that it is halal, but it would seem from the Prophet's ﷺ recommendation that this is an extremist attitude:

'A'ishah recorded: The Prophet ﷺ was told that 'People bring us meat and we do not know whether they have mentioned the name of Allah over it or not. Shall we eat of it or not?' The Prophet ﷺ replied: 'Mention the name of Allah, and eat.' (Bukhari)

The Maliki school of jurists diverges from the other schools of thought by recommending that Muslims also accept some of the modern methods of slaughter as makruh and not haram. They interpret the Quranic statement that 'The food of the People of the Book is permitted to you' (5:6) to mean that chickens killed by beheading, or animals slaughtered by electrocution in proper humane conditions are permissible, providing it is done humanely and with the intention of eating (i.e. strangling or clubbing) (Ibn al-Arabi; see 'The Lawful and Prohibited in Islam' Yusuf Qaradawi, American Trust Publications, p. 62).

THE STATE OF IHRAM

When Muslims are in a state of ihram (or purity) for religious reasons, for example when on Hajj, they are in a state of total peace and serenity, and all living things are in sanctuary in their presence. If a chicken appeared right in front of such Muslims, they would be totally forbidden to touch it in a harmful way.

> 'O you who believe! Do not kill game while you are in the state of ihram.' (5:2, 5:98)
>
> 'Hunting is haram for you while you are in the state of ihram.' (5:2)

Jihad

'O Lord! I seek Thy protection against creeping sloth and cowardice and miserliness, and I seek Thy protection from oppressive debt and the tyranny of people.' (Prayer of Muhammad)

Jihad is the principle of Islam which is active rather than passive. The word comes from 'juhd' which means 'effort', and the verb 'jahida' means to be tired as a result of making an effort. Jihad, or 'striving', applies to any sort of activity made by any person because of love of Allah.

For most Muslims, the concept is purely a personal one, and refers to the deliberate effort made by each individual to serve Allah to the best of their ability, by a life of devotion, self-sacrifice, and love and compassion for others.

Abu Sa'id reported: The Prophet ﷺ was asked: 'Which believers are most perfect in respect of faith?' He replied: 'Those who strive in the path of Allah with their life and property.' (Abu Dawud 2479)

In fact, true jihad means the genuine and active application of the striving to be charitable and just in worship of Allah and in the routines of everyday life. It covers every aspect of Muslim life:

Abu Dharr recorded: 'All glorification of Allah is charity, all praise of Allah is charity, all affirmation of the greatness of Allah is charity, all affirmation of the unity of Allah is charity, sexual relations with your spouse is charity.' (Muslim 2198)

MILITARY JIHAD

The word jihad is often used in speaking about a military situation, when Muslims are called upon to fight for the honour or preservation of their faith. Harb al-Muqadis, or 'Holy War', is the logical extension of 'fighting for one's rights.'

The Blessed Prophet 變 was asked about the rightness of people fighting. Was warfare justified when people were fighting in defence of honour, or a particular cause which could be justified as fighting for the cause of Allah?

Abu Musa recorded: A Bedouin came to the Apostle of Allah 變 and said: 'One man fights for reputation, one fights for praise, one fights for booty and one fights to be seen (and admired). (Which of them is in Allah's path?) The Apostle replied: 'The person who struggles so that Allah's word is carried out is the first on Allah's path.' (Abu Dawud 2511, Bukhari)

Islam is often accused of having forced defeated peoples to accept the faith 'at the point of the sword.' In fact, such a situation would be totally contrary to true Islam, for the Qur'an teaches quite clearly that no person can be forced in the matter of religion. When Muslim warriors gained their historical conquests, the 'formula' was usually to offer the defeated people the chance to become Muslim if they wished, and if not, to pay a tax in order to finance the Muslim military and civil force that now undertook to protect them. Many conquered peoples, especially Monophysite Christians who had been persecuted by Byzantine Christians, welcomed the Muslims as liberators, and were only too pleased to accept. Others did not object to paying for the benefits the Islamic rulers brought with them (see Abu Dawud 2606).

Jihad does not mean forcing other people to accept Islamic beliefs, but striving to bring about a society in which Muslims are free to obey Allah's laws, leaving others free to worship or not as they wish.

Usually, when people feel suppressed, or are aware that tyranny is spoiling the life of a community, they hope that it will be enough to point out the injustices, and the consciences of the rulers will be enough to have them put right.

Sometimes, however, this is not the case, and it becomes necessary to make a decision about what to do next. If a conquering force is poised to over-run a community, what should that community do? Sit back and accept it? Or resist in every way possible?

Democracy is government or rule acceptable to the wishes of the majority. This is a basic principle of Islam, and whenever a country is ruled fairly by democratic principles, everything usually goes peacefully and well. Once an individual, or group of individuals, begins to have unaccept-able authority over the rest, or once the government tries to impose rules that are unacceptable to the will of Allah, they should be resisted—at first by reason, and in the end by force if necessary. A Muslim who strives in such a way is called a Mujahid (plural Mujahideen).

JUSTIFIABLE WAR

Can war ever be justified? Muslims believe that it can, in certain circumstances—in self-defence; in defence of one's family, tribe, or country; in order to fight oppression, and to put right injustice.

Any loss of life is to be regretted, but if it is done in the true spirit of justice, then it has to be accepted. Islamic principles demand that oppression be tackled, and if that means actual physical fighting, then so be it.

Aus b. Shrajil reported: 'If anyone walks with an oppressor to strengthen him, knowing that he is an oppressor—he has gone forth from Islam.' (Bayhaqi)

Abu Sayd reported: 'The most excellent jihad is to speak the truth in the face of a tyrannical ruler.' (Tirmidhi, Abu Dawud, Ibn Majah, Nesai)

Salim Abu al-Nadr reported: 'Do not go looking for an encounter with an enemy; ask Allah for health and security. But when you meet an enemy, be steadfast and enduring; your should know that Paradise is under the shade of swords!' (Muslim 2625)

NATIONALISM

Nationalism, however, is definitely not regarded as a justifiable reason for war in Islam. Some Muslim countries have been as guilty of nationalism as any other countries of the world, but this has been wickedly divisive and has done Islam a great deal of harm. Many Muslims have previously taken up the cause of 'pan-Arabism', whereas it should have been 'pan-Islam.'

Nationalism is completely contrary to the spirit of Islam, which teaches that devotion to Allah is the only true and acceptable loyalty, and that this should cut across all boundaries of race and colour and class.

The Prophet's 🕮 words on the subject could not have been more clear.

'Whoever proclaims the cause of Nationalism is not one of us; and whoever fights the cause of partisanship is not one of us; and whoever dies in the cause of nationalism is not one of us.' (Abu Dawud)

Wathilah bin al-Asqa asked: 'O Messenger of Allah, what is nationalism?' He replied: 'Nationalism means helping your people in unjust causes.' (Abu Dawud)

It is nationalism that has caused all the major disastrous wars of this century—the First and Second World Wars, (Hitler's so-called socialist philosophy was nationalism carried to the ultimate extreme!); the Zionist/Israeli versus Arab conflict; the India/Pakistan split; the wars in Vietnam, Korea, Africa, Afghanistan, Kashmir, and the recent Falklands War, Gulf War, and Serbian/Croatian/Bosnian War.

It is not often that ambitious leaders consider invasion of a neighbouring country simply out of a desire for aggrandisement—although the world has known plenty of Alexanders, Julius Caesars and Ghenghis Khans! In most cases of invasion, the aggressors justify what they are doing in the eyes of their people by playing upon the feeling of nationalistic outrage—that some other country has seized or taken away part of what was rightly theirs, and all they are doing is taking it back.

PEACE

One of the basic aims of Islam is to bring about peace.

'If the enemy incline towards peace, do you also incline towards peace, and trust in God; for He is One Who sees and hears everything.' (8:61)

However, in order for peace to be genuine, there must be absence of oppression and injustice. The kind of 'peace' where the weak are simply putting up with things because they are afraid or unable to tackle the strong is not recognised as peace in Islam.

The Muslim warrior is honoured as the protector of the faith and the community's rights, who has to suffer pain and discomfort and self-sacrifice in order to protect what he loves. This sacrifice is appreciated and respected.

> 'Against them make ready your strength to the utmost of your power, including steeds of war, to strike terror into the enemies of God and your enemies, and others besides, whom you may not know, but whom God knows. Whatever you spend in the cause of Allah shall be repaid to you, and you shall not be treated unjustly.' (8:60)

WEAPONS AS DETERRENTS

Although indiscriminate killing can never be justified, neither can allowing a community to become so unprotected that it becomes a helpless target for thugs and invaders.

Muslims believe that they have a duty to protect loved ones, and the faith. In an ideal world, there would be no cruel and wicked people who attack and overpower the weak, steal the land and the crops, and rape the women! Until that time comes, Muslims believe they need to have the weapons necessary for their defence. 'Steeds of war' now includes all sorts of technical weaponry.

RULES OF JIHAD

There are very strict rules for fighting a jihad. It is not an 'ordinary' war. Firstly, the jihad must be started and organised by a religious leader, not just by any politician. It must be for a recognisably just cause, in the name of Allah, and according to the will of Allah.

Anas b. Malik recorded the Prophet's ﷺ prayer: 'O Allah, You are my Aider and Helper; by You I move, by You I attack and by You I fight.' (Abu Dawud 2626)

The object of the war must be to bring about good and not evil. It must always be as a last resort, after every other means for settling the problem has been tried and has failed. It should never be fought out of aggression, or desire to gain territory.

The killing of people in jihad should never be indiscriminate, therefore weapons that do not distinguish between actual warriors and the innocent population should not be used. Innocent people should not be made to suffer, and trees, crops and animals should be protected.

Apart from any other consideration, when Saddam Hussein of Iraq tried to present his invasion of Kuwait as a jihad, the simple fact that he released oil into the Gulf Waters and deliberately destroyed the earth's natural resources as part of his tactics instantly proved otherwise.

Obviously, under jihad conditions, mass destructions such as would take place in nuclear war would never be called jihad, and are totally forbidden in Islam.

HUMANE TREATMENT OF ENEMIES

Fighting in a jihad is to be prolonged only so long as the tyrant continues to oppose. Once the enemy is defeated, the principle of mercy is to be applied instantly, and all hostilities should cease. The enemy should never be executed vindictively after their capitulation.

Wounded enemy soldiers are to be given exactly the same treatment as wounded members of one's own forces.

The women and children of the enemy should never be molested or harmed. It would be a gross sin for a Muslim soldier to rape the women of the defeated enemy.

'Fight them until there is no more tumult or oppression, and there prevail justice and faith in Allah; and if they cease, let there be no hostility except to those who practise oppression.' (2:193; 8:39)

'Hate your enemy mildly; he may become your friend one day' (Tirmidhi). Bayhaqi reported it from Abu Hurayrah.

TRUE AND FALSE MARTYRDOM

Any person who is literally martyred in the cause of serving Allah is called shahid. Martyrdom for Allah is not the same thing as Nationalism. Someone can lay down their life for their country without being religious at all—and this is not jihad. Sometimes it is very difficult to distinguish between the two forms of sacrifice—it depends on the principles involved.

For the true martyr for Allah, Muslims believe that the sacrifice of their life will earn them forgiveness for any wrongs they may have committed during their lifetimes, and they will go to Paradise.

When Allah calls to jihad, it is a sign of a Muslim's sacrifice of his or her own life to God that they would not hang back. The offering of one's very life to Allah proves one's faith in the Hereafter.

> 'O believers! What is the matter with you, that when you are called to go forth in the cause of God you cling heavily to the earth? Do you prefer the life of this world to the Hereafter? The comfort of this life is but little when compared with the Hereafter.' (9:38)

Muslims, when faced with the duty to overthrow tyranny, are actually held at fault by Allah if their fears for their own lives, or reluctance to put aside their own everyday matters get in their way. It means they are putting those things before Allah.

> 'Unless you go forth, He will punish you with a grievous penalty and put others in your place.' (9:39)

The true warrior for God goes forth, no matter what the odds, determined to show faith and do the right thing, come what may, even if it means his or her death. God knows and understands all a person's sacrifice.

'Go forth, lightly or heavily, and strive and struggle with your goods and your persons, in the Cause of God... .If there had been immediate gain, and the journey easy, they would (all) without doubt have followed you; but the distance was long... They would swear by God, 'If only we could (have done), we should certainly have come out with you.' They would destroy their own souls; for God knows that they are certainly lying... .Those who believe in God and the Last Day ask you for no exemption from fighting with their goods and persons; and God knows well those that do their duty.' (9:41, 42, 44)

The true Muslim faith, when dedicated to Allah's service, is that:

'Nothing will happen to us except what Allah has decreed for us; He is our Protector.' In God let the believers put their trust.' (9:51)

However, just as in a family or street or village dispute, it is not always a wise or good thing to go rushing out intent on destruction and revenge, but to seek peaceful and lasting ways to heal the hurts, so Muslims should be careful in the ways they defend their Lord.

In the heat of passion and hurt, it is easy to throw all caution and good sense to the winds, and deliberately seek to become a shahid or martyr for the sake of pride or glory; but any mother will tell you that although she would be happy to see her son defend her honour, she would take no pleasure in his unnecessary death, and gain no satisfaction if his zeal also destroyed many others.

The true Muslim should try to learn all the techniques

of tact and diplomacy, and keep the worthy sacrifice, the ultimate gesture, for the last resort—remembering that Allah seeks the putting-right of the wrong thing.

Incidentally, the Prophet ﷺ did not approve of young men using jihad in the military sense as an excuse for neglecting their religious jihad in other directions, for example, their duty to their parents.

Abdullah b. Amr recorded: A man came to the Apostle ﷺ and said: 'Apostle of Allah, may I take part in jihad?' He asked: 'Do you have parents?' He replied: 'Yes.' He said: 'Then strive for them!' (Abu Dawud 2523)

Abu Sayd al-Khudri said that when a man from the Yemen asked to join jihad, he was told to go and get his parents' permission first. If they agreed, well and good, otherwise he was to devote himself to them. (Abu Dawud 2524)

If true martyrdom is to be the fate of a person, it should be because it is Allah's will, the only possible outcome of events in the circumstances, and something beyond the control of the shahid. Otherwise, there is the temptation of glory-seeking, for it is unfortunately a tragic fact that the faith of some people in their zeal for the Hereafter is quite sufficient for them to accept the temporary discomforts of a dramatic death for quite the wrong reasons! It is far too simplistic to assume that every Muslim soldier who dies in battle will go straight to Paradise; some are fighting in wrong causes—human nature always assumes that one's own particular campaign is perfectly justified and right—but it is all too easy to be misled by emotion and the clever talk of those skilled in rhetoric.

We must remind ourselves that Allah does not straight-away rush forth and condemn our enemies to destruction:

'Hold fast, all of you, to the Rope which Allah has stretched out to rescue you; don't be divided amongst yourselves! Remember with gratitude the blessings Allah has given you. For you were enemies, and He joined your hearts together with love, so that by His grace you became friends.' (3:103)

THE GREAT JIHAD

The Prophet ﷺ pointed out that to be Muslim meant taking part in the one 'great jihad.' This was the ceaseless campaign against one's own personal desires, which so often are selfish and conflict with the wishes of Allah. It involves, in fact, all the topics considered and discussed in this book.

'The most excellent jihad is that for the conquest of self.' (Bukhari)

It is jihad whenever a Muslim is called upon to make an extra effort, to place the body under discipline and make it do something it would probably be reluctant to do on behalf of Allah—for example to get up before dawn in order to pray, and to go without food, drink or sexual pleasure during all the hours of daylight in the month of Ramadan.

It is jihad when someone examines their income and wealth and because Allah wishes it, gives a set and regular amount away as zakah. It is jihad when they do not cling to personal possessions, even if they treasure them, but can find the generosity to give them up in the service of others, simply because they love Allah. The more valuable a possession to yourself, the more valuable it is to Allah when you give it away for love of Him; but it applies to all manner of simple acts of kindness.

Abu Dharr reported: 'When you make broth, add more water—remembering your neighbours!' (Muslim 6358)

Abu Hurayrah recorded: 'O Muslim women, none of you should consider even a sheep's trotter too insignificant to give to her neighbour.' (Muslim 2247)

'When a person with affection puts a piece of food in the mouth of his wife in order to strengthen the bonds of love, he is rewarded for it!' (Hadith)

It is jihad when Muslims try to love and forgive someone who has hurt them or insulted them, and do not cling on to feuds and grudges. It is jihad every time a mean or spiteful remark leaps to the lips, and is not spoken; and every time an unworthy or suspicious thought creeps into the mind, and is dismissed.

Abu Hurayrah recorded: 'Beware of suspicion, for suspicion is a great falsehood! Do not search for faults in each other, nor yearn after that which others possess, nor envy, nor entertain malice or indifference; be the servants of Allah!' (Muslim 6214, Malik)

Ibn Masud recorded: 'No companion of mine should convey to me anything unpleasant concerning another, for I desire that when I meet a person my mind should be clear with regard to everyone.' (Abu Dawud, Tirmidhi)

It is jihad when a western woman, proud of her hairstyle, or her figure or her shapely legs, 'gives them up' for Allah and dresses modestly, and no longer seeks to draw attention to herself in this way.

'The world and all things in it are valuable, but the most valuable thing in the world is a virtuous woman.' (Abu Dawud)

It is jihad when Muslims take care of their own bodies, which are all part of the earth Allah has given to humanity as their trust.

'A'ishah recorded: 'There are ten demands of nature: cutting close the hair on the lips, letting the beard grow, brushing the teeth, cleaning out the nose, paring the nails, washing out the base of the fingers, removal of the hair on the armpits and pubic areas, washing the affected parts after a call of nature, and rinsing of the mouth.' (Muslim)

It is jihad to be gentle and generous with those who have fallen on hard times, or who may be indebted to you. Muslims should not attempt to take advantage of their misfortunes, but should help them as best they can, for love of Allah.

Abdul Yasar recorded: 'He who gives a breathing-space to a person who is in difficult circumstanes, or who remits his debt, will be saved by Allah from the anxieties of the Day of Resurrection.' (Muslim)

It is jihad every time a person helps another, and goes out of their way to be a friend, and carries a burden for another (whether literal or the burden of sorrow or distress); it is especially jihad when a person goes on helping another even when they are tired, or uncomfortable, or being made to suffer for it. It is jihad when you are loyal; when you do not betray someone in need of your confidence, when you stand by a person who needs your support.

Another word for the 'great jihad' could well be 'love'! In this sense, we could take the famous hadith of the Prophet ﷺ on the subject of charity, and substitute the word 'jihad.'

Hammam b. Munabbih recorded: 'To bring about a just reconciliation between two enemies is jihad (charity); helping a person to mount his animal or to load his baggage on to it is jihad; a good word is jihad. Every step towards a mosque is jihad, to remove obstacles in the street is jihad, smiling upon the face of your brother is jihad.' (Muslim 2204)

Khuraym b. Fatih reported: 'If anyone makes a contribution towards Allah's path, seven hundred times as much will be recorded to his (or her) credit.' (Tirmidhi, Nasai)

Therefore, brothers and sisters, if you have the awareness of Allah in your hearts and minds, let your whole lives be dedicated to His service, that His gracious will may be done on this earth, and that you may truly be His vicegerents and faithful servants and stewards until you receive the call to return to Him, Who is the Source of all our being. Amen.